I Wouldn't Change
A Minute

I Wouldn't Change A Minute

ALVIN J. FUTTERMAN

To order additional copies of this book, contact:
Xlibris Corporation
1-888-795-4274
www.Xlibris.com
Orders@Xlibris.com
74376

CONTENTS

This memoir is dedicated to the two women who have made my life possible and wonderful. My mother, Millie, who fed me; taught me to read and write, add, and subtract; and convinced me that I could do anything. She inspired me to reach for greater heights and was a good friend at all times.

My beautiful wife, Muriel, who has been next to me for all these years (sixty and still counting), has been my rock and best friend. Everything I have accomplished has been together with her, and she has convinced me that I could do everything. What a wonderful partner to have!

Life Begins

When he was asked about the meaning and purpose of life, the Dalai Lama replied that the big secret was to be happy. He said that warm heartedness and compassion were the two main ingredients. I would agree with him but would like to add family, love, and honesty as three equally important parts.

I have been very fortunate to have had the enjoyment of all these ingredients that have contributed to making my life a wonderful one.

At different times in your life, things happen, which seemed to have occurred before, but your feelings at the time are very different. Receiving a second-hand bicycle, for my tenth birthday, was an even happier occasion than buying my Corvette, in 1979, although at the time, nothing could have been better than that Corvette. My father buying a used car, when I was eleven years old, that allowed us to make trips out of the neighborhood, and even long ones as far away as Canada, was a happier occasion than the day I bought my Mercedes convertible, although at the time, nothing could have been better than that convertible.

The things that happened to me as an adult are very important and appreciated, but they were extensions, improvements, to what I was doing. The used bicycle and the used car were momentous occasions that opened up whole new avenues of enjoyment and adventure. They enabled us to do things we were not able to do before.

Life has been very good to me, and it is hard to measure, one great thing against another, so I'll just say that *everything* has been wonderful. Thank you, everyone.

The big bonus of life is having grandchildren, and I am writing these memoirs especially for my three grandchildren. I want them to know even more about me than they know now so that they, in turn, can talk about me to their children and tell them the stories that I have told to my grandchildren, many of which I am probably repeating here, although I am sure we will find new ones as well. Evan is the son of our daughter Donna and her partner, Virginia Casper, who have been together more than thirty years. Matthew and Lauren are the children of our son, Richard, and his wife, Ellen (nee) Adin, who were married on July 9, 1989.

Evan was born on November 10, 1985, and graduated on May 27, 2007, from Vassar College, with very special honors. He was first in his major, geography, and made Phi Beta Kappa, although I am certain that he will be majoring in the welfare of others as he goes on in life.

Matthew was born on March 31, 1992, and he is now, in September 2009, in his senior year at Roslyn High School. Lauren, his sister, was born on May 3, 1995, and is in her freshman year at Roslyn High School.

My mother, Millie Friedman, was born in Braddock, Pennsylvania; and my father, Louis Futterman, was born in Russia in a town called Kishinev, which is now a city in Moldavia, and was brought to this country, by his mother, when he was about one year old, as his father had preceded them in immigrating here to get a job and set things for his family's arrival.

Although we did not have much financially, we had an abundance of love, concern, and pride, as well as inspiration. My mother gave me all this throughout her entire life. She took care of me, she studied with me, she helped me with everything, and she gave me the confidence that every person needs to go out and do in this world. She assured me that I could do anything and everything and made sure that I did. My mother was my friend her entire life. She was proud of all my accomplishments and always spoke of me in only the most loving way. She made and kept me happy. My mother was a secretary and worked almost up to the week that she passed away of a heart attack at the age of sixty-five, while my father, reluctantly, was a bricklayer and later owned his own grocery store. I thank them for teaching me how to be a good human being and how to treat other human beings.

We lived with my grandmother until I was about eleven years old, and it was my grandmother, Nettie Friedman (nee Offner), who took care of me during the day while my parents were working.

When my sister, Arlene, was born three and one half years after me, she took care of her as well while they were away at work.

My mother worked mainly for New York City agencies and often brought home some of her coworkers. Our living arrangements were not great, but in those days (in the middle of the Depression), not too many working families had many luxuries. Many of my mother's friends from work were black, and I am sure this played a great role in my later liberal thinking and feelings. She brought us up without prejudice and showed us by example. My father, after graduating from high school, was brought to work by his father, who was also a bricklayer. From comments that my dad had made to me, I don't believe he was very happy doing this, but that's what his father told him to do, and he did it. I think he was embarrassed and ashamed of this laborious work and must have been very happy and relieved when he joined the *American dream* and entered into his own business. Because bricklaying was essentially an outdoor job, he did not work most of the winter or in the rain. It must have been a helpless feeling, not being able to go to work for your family, but there were a whole lot of other people in worse situations than us in those days. We were healthy and had a roof over our heads and food to eat and lots of love—always.

At a very young age, before I even went to school, my mother taught us children a prayer. I could not fall asleep if I did not recite this simple prayer every night. The prayer was the very holy She-ma, in the Hebrew language, which she really did not know or could even read in that language, but she made sure that I said it before going to sleep. I continued saying this prayer until I was about fifty years old, every night; and I don't know why I stopped, but for some reason, I did. In English the prayer would be translated into the following:

> Hear, O Israel, the Lord our God, the Lord is One. Praised be His name, whose glorious kingdom is forever and ever.

It is a simple prayer, and I never missed a day.

I have only a snapshot in my mind of the luncheon that was served in my grandmother's house for my Uncle Albee's bar mitzvah. I was two years old, and I do not remember anything else of that day except for them setting up tables in the parlor and dining room of her house. We were already living there with my grandmother at that time.

My grandmother, Nettie, and my grandfather, Alexander Joseph, owned a brownstone at 706 Lexington Avenue in the Bedford-Stuyvesant section of Brooklyn. My grandmother had come to the United States from Hungary when she was about fifteen years old and had come to be a servant in the home of her older brother who, she later told me, did not treat her nicely. My grandfather, who had emigrated about the same time, was very enterprising and did all sorts of mechanical work and repairs for other people. He was also a locksmith. The house consisted of two stories plus a full basement. My grandfather had passed away a few years earlier, before I was born; and I was named after him, or at least the initials and the Hebrew name were the same. After he died, my aunts and uncles, as well as my mother, all worked and helped support the house, my grandmother, and themselves. The house was narrow, as most brownstones were, but very deep and had a front parlor, a dining room, two small bedrooms, a kitchen, bathroom, and a small back porch, all on the main floor. There was an icebox in the back of the house, and an iceman would deliver a big block of ice twice a week. I do not know if there were electric refrigerators in the early 1930s, but we didn't have one. The icebox, however, kept the milk, butter, and whatever else was necessary to keep cool adequately. My grandmother and Uncle Albee occupied the two bedrooms downstairs, and my other uncles and aunts, with the exception of Uncle Murray who slept in the parlor (living room), were married and lived elsewhere. Upstairs there was a full two-bedroom apartment in the back, and in the front was a large bedroom (ours) and a small room adjoining it with a table and four chairs. My mother, father, sister, and I all slept in that large bedroom. My parents had a double bed, and my sister and I each had our own single beds on each side of my parents.

We were quite poor, we were in the throes of the Depression, but we did not know it (or at least my sister and I did not know it); so there was no reason for us not to be happy, at least not for the lack of money. And we were, as I remember, very happy. As I mentioned, due to the weather conditions of the day, my father sometimes could not work, but my mother's work as a secretary kept her busy every day. We did not expect too much, but it did seem like we had whatever we wanted. I am sure, now, that my parents did not think so but never complained to us. They were hard times, but love and family seemed to take care of everything. There was only one bathroom downstairs for our family, my grandmother, and uncle; but I honestly cannot remember ever being unhappy over our living conditions. Maybe I just didn't know that there was anything different, but everyone in the neighborhood was poor, and there was no television to show you how other people could live. The Doyles lived on our right. Two of their sons were priests, and a daughter was a nun. On our left were the Fagins and my only friend, Billy. His father was a subway motorman.

The basement of the house was mostly taken up by the fabulous workshop of my grandfather, and I remember being totally awed by the tremendous selection of tools and vises that was neatly kept there. My Uncle Harry was a plumber, and he eventually took over those tools and used the workshop whenever he needed it.

An elevated train ran down the middle of Lexington Avenue. It was part of the Broadway-Brooklyn line, and though very noisy, you learned to live with its inconvenience. I am sure that there are many people today who are poorer and with many more inconveniences than we had, but since they can make the comparisons with others, I am also sure it is more difficult and more frustrating. It was a very old-fashioned train that ran on the tracks. This was the early and mid-1930s, and it seemed as if you could almost touch it from the window in our bedroom. You could see very clearly the passengers on the train, as it passed, as well as the motorman and the conductor; and they, in turn, could see very clearly into our bedroom, if the shades were not drawn down. The station was right on our corner, one minute away, and I used that elevated train to go to junior high school before we moved to Manhattan in 1937-38. The noise was quite loud as the train rattled past our house. But like everything else, you get used to it and almost tell yourself that you like it.

Although I do not have many memories of living there, I can only remember being happy there and seeing all my aunts, uncles, and cousins every week as they visited my grandmother almost without fail. My uncles and my father usually played pinochle, an interesting card game, which I later learned and enjoyed playing with my friends. My aunts and my mother would be talking in the kitchen, and weather permitting, my cousins and I would be outside playing. I don't remember that anybody owned a car, although my uncles Louie and Harry sometimes had small trucks for their businesses. In our last year of living there, my parents bought a secondhand Chevrolet; and that summer we took a trip to Tupper Lake, New York (near Canada), in the Adirondacks where my father's brother, Fred, and his wife, Esther, lived. Tupper Lake was between Lake Placid and Saranac Lake, two great vacation spots in a most beautiful area. It was a leisurely trip up there, my father never drove too fast, and our first stop was Lake George. I slept in a room with my grandmother, and my sister slept with our parents. I remember our room was actually extended over the shore of the lake, but what I remember most of that trip was arriving in the town of Saratoga, very thirsty from a long ride. We didn't have bottles of water in the car at that time, and I remember rushing out of the car to get a drink from the fountain in the park that we were passing. Saratoga is very well-known for its water, which has a very high content of minerals, excellent for a mineral bath, but simply awful for a thirsty young boy. Everyone had a good laugh as I was shocked by the bad taste.

I do not remember much else about the trip, but I know that my parents gave me everything they could, and I cannot remember ever being sad. Times were simpler then, and it seems as if it was easier to do without. You did not know too much of what was going on in the rest of the world. I do remember, however, very vividly on my tenth birthday getting the gift I dreamed of: a blue two-wheel Columbia bicycle. It was not a Schwinn, and it was not new, but it was *mine*.

I was born on June 16, 1927, and I was beautiful. I was three and a half years old when my sister Arlene was born on November 13, 1930. We all immediately called her "Honey," and that is still her name today, to all of us. I do not think I have ever called her Arlene. My brother Stanley came into this world ten years later, on September 12, 1940. My sister Janie was born five years after that, on August 18, 1945. But my life really started when I met Muriel Adelberg, just before the Memorial Day weekend in 1948. It was just about sixty years ago, as I speak today. We were married on February 12, 1950, and it has been a wonderful and fantastic life together. I fell in love the moment I saw her. Muriel has been loving and understanding and has been a wonderful wife and mother. My life, before meeting Muriel, is just a series of snapshots—quick, instantaneous moments—whereas afterward the memories are longer and flow.

Muriel's mother was Evelyn (nee Brass), and her father was named David Adelberg. Muriel has one brother, Arnold, who married Harriet Diamond, and they have two daughters. Danielle is married to Stephen Hamil, who was born and raised in England, and they have one daughter, Emma. Danielle is a microbiologist and a professor at Midwestern University. Erica, the younger of the two daughters, recently married Russ Bogin, and they live in Manhattan. Erica is a financial consultant and has an important investing position with a foreign bank. Russ is an attorney.

Arnold and Harriet live in Grinnell Iowa, where Arnold, recently retired, was a professor and head of the mathematics department. Harriet is a librarian.

My brother Stanley and his wife Linda (nee Roth) have three boys, actually men now. David married Marnie Stetson. He is a lawyer for the Bank of America, and they have two children, Cole and Catherine. Marnie is teaching in Upper Montclair, New Jersey, where they live. Danny is married to Anya Epstein, and they have two daughters, Sylvie and Eve. Danny is a successful actor and screenwriter. Anya is also a successful screenwriter. They currently live in Los Angeles. Matthew is married to Amy Einhorn, and they have three daughters, Ashley, Tess, and Jolie. Matthew is a sports columnist with the *Wall Street Journal*, and Amy has an important position in the publishing world under her own name for Putnam. They live on the Upper West Side of Manhattan.

My sister Honey married Henry Greenwood, and they also have three children. Jack, the eldest, is a doctor and is married to Karen. They live in eastern Long Island. They have two sons, Stephen and Adam. Ken is now retired with a generous pension from Actors Equity for whom he worked for many years, after graduating from law school, and his life partner is John Kelly, an executive in the entertainment world and a great guy! They live in Manhattan. Robin, their daughter, is not married and is a school psychologist, living in upstate New York.

Janie, my baby sister, whom I named, married the terrific Martin Alvin Schmidt; and they have two children, both of whom are successful lawyers. Michael, a partner in a large New York/Long

Island law firm, married Jen Sholemson; and they have two beautiful girls, Jordy and Alyssa. They live here on Long Island; and Stacy, who is not yet married, lives in Boston, where she works for Fidelity, and travels throughout the country working on labor relations for the company, often giving lectures and presentations.

My mother was one of seven children; and in the order of their births, there was Bella, who married Nich Contos, and they had a son, Milton. My Uncle Lou married Henrietta, one of my mother's closest friends; and they had two sons, Albert and Walter. My mother was the third one born and then my Aunt Molly. Actually my mother was going to be named Molly, but she was very small at birth, and they were not sure she would live; therefore, they did not want to use such a wonderful name as Molly and called her Millie instead. My Aunt Molly married David Green, and they had one son, Karl. My Uncle Harry married Mildred Ellenbogen, and they had one daughter, Leona. My Uncle Murray married Irene, and their son was named Alexander. My Uncle Albie, the youngest, married Rose Wiener who is the only living uncle or aunt I have today; and they had two daughters, Anita and Barbara. As I have said before, all these uncles and aunts came to visit their mother, my grandmother, every Sunday. Many times my Uncle Harry and Aunt Mildred would visit on a Saturday, and usually she would take me to the movies on Gates Avenue. My sister Honey was too young to go at the time. They lived in New Jersey, where they had moved so that they could take care of the children, two of them, of my Aunt Mildred's brother, whose wife died very early in life. I remember being sent out of the living room one Sunday when I proudly announced that my father had three aces while a game of pinochle was going on. I had just learned what an ace was.

My father's parents were Ida Crystal and Shimmin (Samuel) Futterman. My father also came from a family of seven children, six brothers and one sister. Dan, the eldest, married Bessie; and they had two children, Edna and Fred. Edna married Sidney Jarkow, her high school sweetheart, whom my uncle, a bit of a successful snob, did not think was rich enough for his daughter. Sydney became extremely successful and was a large contributor to the Anti-Defamation League, whose Latin American division is named after Sydney Jarkow. Edna was lovely and vivacious, and the two of them became very close friends of Muriel and me.

Sydney was movie-star handsome, a great athlete, an animal hunter in Africa, as well as a Nazi hunter in South America. My Uncle Joe married Sally, and their two children were Burt and Rita. Then came my father, followed by my Uncle Fred, who married Esther; and they had three daughters, Anne, Dorothy, and Susan. Uncle Jack, the most personable and generous of my uncles, married Doris; and they had two daughters, Susan and Anita. The youngest brother, Al, married Lee; and they had three daughters—Iris, Gail, and Jackie—and one son, Steven. I am not sure where my Aunt Rhoda fit in the order of children, but I believe she was the second eldest. She had an unhappy life, never marrying until late in middle age, and that was unsuccessful also. I have wonderful memories of all my uncles and aunts, all of whom I knew well, and remember the kindnesses of all of them toward me. I used to baby-sit for my Uncle Jack and Aunt Doris's daughters and was very well rewarded for my time. My Uncle Al was a great athlete in high school, and due to the closeness of our names, I was able to claim and show some of the medals he had won as mine. My Uncle Fred bought me my first tricycle.

My Aunt Rhoda always had sweets and some small gift when she visited. My Uncle Joe and Aunt Sally lived in the Bronx, so our visits were not that regular.

My father's family was also very close, and they kind of adopted my mother's mother as their own since theirs had died years before and Grandma Nettie was an altogether fabulous person, so I had the opportunity of seeing them regularly as well. A lot of people fussed over me and made sure that I was a happy little boy, and I felt loved at all times.

The dates that I will quote in these memoirs will be close, if not exact. The names of the people and the time that everything took place will also be very close, if not exact. All the years that have passed, sometimes blur, the actual dates and names, and a lot of years have passed!

The first part of my life that I can remember was very full of my grandma Nettie. I vaguely remember my father's parents, who were alive when I was born but died before I was five years old. I have a snapshot in my mind of being propped up in the corner and being fed a combination of spinach and mashed potatoes by my mother. I probably was less than two years old, but it was a good camera. The first thing that I can truly remember is going into the kitchen at my grandmother's house in Bed-Stuy, as it is more familiarly known today, asking for my mother. My grandma explained that my mother had gone to the hospital to get me a new sister. My grandmother, who could not read or write English, only spoke to me in that language—she could read and speak Yiddish but never did to me. I was three and a half years old, and of course, that didn't mean anything to me; but very soon after that, my mother came home and brought my new sister with her.

I also remember my mother teaching me the alphabet and putting the letters together to form words and then to read. She taught me numbers and then to add them, multiply, divide, and subtract them. These are all brief snapshots deep in my mind. But by the time I reached the first grade (I started kindergarten at age four and a half), I was so far ahead that it seemed that I was pushed forward, skipping grades. I was fifteen and a half when I graduated high school. My mother just kept teaching me, and I was so eager to learn. It was a winning combination! Throughout my life, I have tried to accumulate knowledge, and I was fortunate enough to have had many opportunities to do so.

Until my sister Honey got married at the age of seventeen, we were practically inseparable. We shared a room from the moment she came home; and when she was old enough, every Saturday my mother would drop the two of us off at the local movie theater, which had a children's section and a matron supervising, who made sure that we all behaved. It is amazing to think that you could have a section for young children without parents and all behaving by themselves, but we did. Honey was quite young when we first started going to the movies, and she had to sit up on the armrest so that she could see the screen. I didn't see the screen too well either, but that was because I needed glasses and my eyes had never been tested. I had spent about a year looking at a screen that was really not clear. At the age of nine, I got my first pair of glasses, and it was a total revelation as to how clear everything was up there on that big screen. Before that, everything was a blur in the distance and in everyday life. I remember being embarrassed on my first day in school with my glasses and having to put them on by putting my head under my desk so no one would see. I went to PS 11 on Reid Avenue and loved school. I remember walking home with Betty Smith, pretty face and long black curls, and carrying her books. I think she was pretty, and Adele Klauber, her best friend, wasn't bad either. We had a lot of fun in school, learning, and we had many parties while we were still quite young.

I also remember playing box ball and stoopball as well as stickball. In box ball there was a square court, and the ball was pitched to you on a bounce, and you hit it with your hand and ran the bases. Stoopball was played by throwing the ball against the stoop, which were the steps in front of a house, and trying to bounce it over the head of the fielders. Stickball was played like baseball except you would pitch the ball, a small rubber ball, on a bounce, and you hit it with the stick of a broom. All three games were played in the street, and there were always plenty of kids around. But I wasn't very good athletically and was usually one of the last kids picked to play.

I do not remember too much else of those days in public school except for my teacher in fourth grade. Mrs. Hartsfield, who was African-American, took a liking to me, and the feeling was mutual. She was a wonderful teacher who was always very supportive and protective. She is the only teacher that I can remember at that time, so she must have been very special. Most of my best and clearest memories were when we moved to Manhattan because my father had purchased a small luncheonette in an office building on Nineteenth Street and Seventh Avenue; he did not have to be a bricklayer anymore, and I'm sure he felt liberated.

And so at the age of eleven, we moved to our new apartment; and I attended a junior high school in Greenwich Village, Hudson Park Junior High School, while my sister went to a public school, located right on the corner of the street where we lived. We lived on Twentieth Street and Ninth Avenue at 365 West Twentieth Street, and my sister's school was on Twentieth Street and Eighth Avenue. It was quite a revelation coming from Bedford Stuyvesant in Brooklyn, not the best of neighborhoods even then, to a fourteen-story building with a doorman. The change was quite extreme but quite easy to make and, being in Manhattan, was such a new and great experience for all of us. We were able to do so many new things, and my mother had given up her job as secretary to help my father in his new business. About 10:00 a.m., he would wheel his trolley, containing a coffee urn and other coffee-time goodies, throughout the building.

At lunchtime there were sandwiches, cakes, soft drinks, tea, and coffee, all served in the small space that they had in the lobby of the building for his business. At 3:00 p.m. he repeated the 10:00 a.m. service, and business was good. I do not think it would have survived today, but as the Depression was ending, it was good.

Since there wasn't television in those days, we had great radio programs, and you were able to attend and be in the audience at these radio programs, all of which were live. I remember being at many drama performances and quiz shows. When I graduated from junior high school, I was accepted to a very special high school called Townsend Harris High School. It was located in the sixteen-story building that also housed the business school of the College of the City of New York on Twenty-third Street and

Lexington Avenue. The high school occupied the ninth through the twelfth floors, and the rest of the building was occupied by the college. The special high school had its own accelerated program where it did the usual four-year course that every other high school did in three years. It required special curriculum, and it was a great honor to be there. It was probably among the top three high schools in the country.

I graduated from high school at the age of fifteen and a half, in 1943; and because I had been a student at Townsend Harris, I was automatically accepted to City College (CCNY), which was one of the top ten academic schools in the country. Townsend Harris was a very expensive school for the city to run for what was a relatively small number of students. We were the smallest high school in the city, and when budget matters got tough in 1941, the mayor Fiorello La Guardia decided that they would have to close the school and the last graduating class would be in June 1942. At that time I had only six months left to finish high school, but I had to enroll in my neighborhood high school. Since we were back living in Brooklyn by then, I went to Boys High School for my senior year and actually graduated from there.

Of all the teachers through my entire school life, I can only remember two who left lasting impressions on me. The first one was Mrs. Hartsfield, and even now I can see very clearly the cheerfulness and encouragement that she always gave to me. The second important teacher that I can remember was Mr. Diamond, also an African-American, who was my English teacher and adviser at Townsend Harris. He stressed the positive thinking that I have always found comfortable and rewarding.

Hudson Park Junior High School, in Greenwich Village, was one of the most unruly schools in New York City. A movie was made a few years after I attended this school, and it certainly had this one in mind as it was called *Blackboard Jungle*. That title described the school very well, and unfortunately, many of the students wound up in great trouble, and several were sent to prisons in New York State.

I was a short chubby studious boy who wore glasses and was very lucky that the other students never bullied me. I cannot say the same for all the teachers since they had to have someone to blame, and the other boys were older and a lot more threatening. On one occasion I remember everyone "marching" into the classroom with a large piece of white paper, which we all proceeded to rip into small bits and drop the pieces on the floor as we went to our seats. By the time everyone was seated, the floor was completely covered, almost like snow. Naturally, the teacher blamed me (!) and called me the ringleader. I was just happy that the guys had included me in their plot.

I did very well at the school where there was very little competition, and that graduation I received a math medal, as well as other awards. I had only two friends in that junior high school, one of whom was Harold Berkowitz and the other was Philip Cohen. I do not know why these names stick with me so clearly, but it was such a great two years that we spent together. We spent a lot of time at a gym in a synagogue on Twenty-eighth Street, near Eighth Avenue. I remember on one occasion we were paid a visit by Sid Luckman who was the starting quarterback for the Chicago Bears, after having played at Columbia University, and was a native of New York City, and his family had been members of this particular synagogue. He came to the gym with two other teammates, one of whom was an all-star end Ken McAfee, and threw around a football with us for a very thrilling experience.

Sid was the first quarterback to successfully execute a winning season with what was called the T formation, where the quarterback starts every play standing right over the center, which is what most every high school, college, and professional team uses today. Previously, the ball was centered back to any of the players in the backfield, who then either ran or threw the ball downfield to an eligible player. What we see played today was used for the first time by Sid Luckman and the Chicago Bears, who beat the Washington Redskins 73-0 in the championship game of that year. I really regret having lost contact with Harold and Philip since those two years were so great.

I was bar mitzvahed in a small synagogue, where I studied Hebrew for two years, and became very proficient in my reading. The luncheon, after my bar mitzvah, was held at a restaurant called the Café Royale on Fifth Avenue and Forty-third Street. The synagogue was located on Twenty-third Street between Seventh and Eighth Avenues, and as of a couple of years ago, it was still there. I became very observant for the year after my bar mitzvah. I put on tefillin, a religious ritual, every morning; said the morning prayers; and wore *titzehs*, the shawl that looks like loose hanging threads under my shirt! I was too young to grow a beard.

Not too long ago, one evening, Muriel and I decided to go to the movies to see a film starring our nephew Danny, and the only theater it was playing in was on Twenty-third Street, in Manhattan, just a few doors down from my little synagogue. Since we were fairly early for the film, we decided to visit the synagogue, which Muriel had never seen before. There was a rather old man looking after the synagogue, and I explained to him that I had been bar mitzvahed there sixty-five years earlier, and I would like to show my wife the interior. After being kind enough to doubt that I was that old, he gave us a tour. I remember commenting that there used to be a balcony, for the women, as this was an Orthodox synagogue. "Yes," he said there was. But the congregants had gotten so old that the women, who sat in the balcony apart from the men, no longer could climb the steps to go upstairs, so they separated the downstairs part with a curtain so that the women could now sit on one of the sides. We thanked him for the tour, I left a donation, and we enjoyed the movie.

Townsend Harris was a lifetime experience. All the students had, in their previous schools, some of the best grades in the city, but yet it did not seem highly competitive since we were all taught at this high level to begin with, and everyone was capable of keeping up. I had started in January 1940; but soon after my bar mitzvah, in July 1940, we moved back to Brooklyn, since my mother was pregnant with my brother, to an apartment at Sixty-four Church Avenue, near Dahill Road, in Flatbush; but I continued to travel to Townsend Harris until it closed, by which time we had moved again to 365 Pulaski Street, Brooklyn, which was near to Boys High School and also to my father's new business that was an Italian-American grocery store in partnership with an uncle of my mother at Thirty-one Sumner Avenue, Brooklyn.

I traveled to Townsend Harris by taking a bus to the subway and the subway to Lexington Avenue and Twenty-third Street in Manhattan. Since Townsend Harris was in a tall sixteen-story building, in the middle of New York City, we did not have any high school athletic teams, just intramural; and since it was an all-boys school, there weren't many social events either. However, I only have very fine memories of the school and its program, and I do love all sports, as well as all girls, so nothing was lost.

We lived on Church Avenue for two years, and my brother Stanley was born soon after we moved in, on August 18, 1940, and that made life very different.

After not having a baby in the house for ten years, it felt great having a little brother, and it still does. As soon as we moved back to Brooklyn, I had two jobs that summer. The first one was getting up about six o'clock in the morning to deliver milk and rolls in the neighborhood from a small grocery store next to our building.

By 8:00 a.m., I was finished with that work and went back upstairs, usually to sleep a little while again. In the afternoon I had a job at a nearby kosher butcher shop, delivering orders of meat, again in the neighborhood, on my bicycle. Yes, the same two-wheeler I had gotten for my tenth birthday. That job also was only for about two hours a day; and, after finishing there, I often rode on my bike to Coney Island, about 30 minutes away, to meet up with my new friends, if they had already left. Every day was great, and the friends I made while living on Church Avenue was my first introduction to boys and girls being together—and knowing it.

If I did not go by bike, I could take the trolley, which was also about thirty minutes, and we would hang out on the beach for the rest of the afternoon. On those days when there was no work, or I was able to finish early, I went by trolley with them. The girls would get baby-sitting jobs on the weekend, and we would go over to keep them company. We played music, talked, tried to dance, and just got to know one another much better. Those friendships were so rewarding that even after we moved to other locations, I continued to go back to Church Avenue and all my friends there. I had two separate sets of friends on Church Avenue; one of them was based on being close to my age, and the other group I was friendly with was based on school.

When I was a senior in high school, at the age of fifteen, the girls my age were only freshmen and sophomores. The group I knew in high school was all at least two years older than I. It eventually worked out, with me becoming friendlier with the people of my own age, and socially it was the right thing. I remained friendly for a long time with Stan Spielman, Lenny Fisher, and Shelly Farber, all of whom lived in the same building, six stories high, as we did. A group of girls happened to live in the next building, and among them was a set of twins, Lucille and Leona. These sisters often baby-sat for other neighbors, and they were the ones who taught me how to dance, especially the jitterbug or Lindy hop. I became quite good at it, good enough to actually enter a contest with my sister Honey, which we actually won! We danced well together, and I was able to throw her over my shoulder and land still dancing, which, of course, impressed everyone, including me and the judges. I lost touch with most of these friends when I went on to college, although we did meet every now and then to talk about the great times we had.

On December 7, 1941, my uncles Murray and Albie took me to a football game at the Polo Grounds in Upper Manhattan. It was known mainly as the home of the baseball team the New York Giants. But it also played host to the football teams of that time.

The New York Giants were playing against the Brooklyn Dodgers (yes, there was a Brooklyn Dodger football team), and during the course of the game, announcements were made regularly over the public address system asking all servicemen, both army and navy, to return to duty immediately. Nothing else was said or explained, but it was obvious that something serious had happened. It was only after the game, when we left the stadium, that we learned from big black-and-white headlines on "extra" newspapers that Japan had bombed Pearl Harbor. No one that I knew had any idea of the location of Pearl Harbor. But we soon learned that it was the home port for the entire Pacific Fleet in Hawaii.

The attack had destroyed almost half of our ships there, and we were now at war. World War II had started in 1939 when the Nazi army of Germany attacked its neighbors. Our sympathies were with the Allies (such as France, England, Holland, Denmark, Norway, Sweden, and the others) and against the Axis of Germany and Italy. Adolf Hitler, the leader of Germany, had expressed the desire to exterminate the Jewish people—all the Jewish people. He succeeded in eventually killing six million Jews in Europe, out of a total of twelve million in the world, and several million others of different religions. While the United States helped the Allies, they did not officially enter the war until the attack on Pearl Harbor, where we declared war not only against Japan but also against Germany and Italy, which by this time had captured all of Europe, except those that remained "neutral" like Switzerland and Ireland, and was threatening to invade England. Ireland eventually helped the Allies, but Switzerland remained "neutral," acting as Hitler's bank and keeping, forever, most of the deposits of those who were victims of the madman Adolf Hitler.

The day after the football game, an assembly was called at the high school; and as we sat in the gymnasium, which had balconies, we heard our president Franklin D. Roosevelt on the radio tell us of the attack, which he said "will live in infamy" and officially told the nation that we were now at war. World War II lasted another three and a half years with the terrible loss of life by every country involved. We fought on two fronts, one in Europe and the other in the Pacific Ocean. Japan had conquered most of Asia, including the Philippines (a possession of the United States), Hong Kong and Singapore, and all of Southeast Asia. Except for Russia, Germany and Italy had taken over all of Europe.

After the first two years of high school at Townsend Harris, I had become a fairly active member of the French club and the math club. I was also taking part in the student council, although I had to curtail some of these activities as my father needed me to help him at the luncheonette. I was a member of the staff of the school newspaper, which I enjoyed very much and which would have probably been the last activity for me to give up, if I had to.

There were only six months left to the life of Townsend Harris high school, as the year 1942 started. The school was closed in June 1942. I understand that a Townsend Harris has opened in Queens, but this one is nothing like the original one I attended, which had a unique three-year curriculum and the automatic admission to CCNY. Arthur Bauman was the editor of the newspaper, and I was like a roving reporter. We decided one day early in 1942 to go see the phenomenon of Frank Sinatra, who was then performing at the Paramount Theater in Times Square. You would first see a first-run movie, and then the stage show would start, and this program would continue three or four times a day.

Frank Sinatra was the idol of all teenage girls, and the lines of them outside the theater stretched around the block. You could sit in your seat for the entire day, for the single price of admission; and many of the girls did exactly that, bringing food and candy to keep from starving. It was almost impossible to get into the performance unless you got there very early or were prepared to wait until probably the last show.

Arthur and I worked out a scheme where we presented ourselves as reporters for the school newspaper and requested an interview with Frank Sinatra. We did not get the interview, but we did get two seats up front, and we stayed for two shows. Frank Sinatra had left the Tommy Dorsey orchestra and was on his own as a singer, and the mobs of young girls had increased substantially, with many fainting and all others screaming as Frankie crooned his love songs in his inimitable fashion. We had cut school to go to the Paramount, but it was well worth it, and we were surely heroes to many of our friends.

I traveled to Townsend Harris until June 1942, and then in September I attended Boys High School until January 1943 when I graduated. After Townsend Harris, the last semester at Boys High was very easy. When I graduated high school, I was fifteen and a half years old, and I immediately started at the College of the City of New York (CCNY). It was located all the way uptown in Manhattan, at 137th Street and Convent Avenue. It increased my traveling time to about one and a half hours each way, as it involved taking a bus to the subway and then a long walk to the school.

But all this was fine with me as I was now in college, and I enjoyed going to school and was interested to learn everything. The traveling was not a total loss, as I was usually able to do my homework, including reading, on the subway. I majored in romance languages, studying Spanish and French, and had to take courses totaling five years in Latin.

It was there that I met Joe Heit, who lived in Manhattan, in Washington Heights, which was not very far from the school. Since our names were very close in the alphabet, and at that time you would generally be seated alphabetically, we usually sat next to each other in every class that we both attended. Joe was my age, inexperienced in life, and we had much to talk about, especially on Monday mornings after active weekends, as we learned about people on our own, especially if those people were other young girls. Since we lived relatively very far apart, we did not see each other on the weekends and, of course, had different experiences to talk about.

Most of the young men of college age, which was usually eighteen, had been drafted into the army or navy or had enlisted in one of them. There were not too many young men in school, and it was great having a friend like Joe throughout all the time there—or at least most of it. We were both in the class of 1947, and in June 1945 we became eligible for the draft, even though the war had ended. We both decided that we would join the navy, which was offering great programs for college students; but unfortunately, for me, my eyesight required glasses, and the navy was not accepting enlistees who wore glasses. Joe was accepted for the program but was not taken until the end of the year, and I was drafted instead into the army in January 1946.

My sister Janie was born on September 18, 1945, the same year that my parents had bought their first and only home at 1761 Troy Avenue in Flatbush, Brooklyn. The army insisted upon drafting me, even though I only had a year left at school, the war was over, and despite my mother's suggestion that they draft my father instead! My grandmother had sold her house as we moved to East Ninety-sixth Street in Brooklyn and was still living with us, always enriching me with her memories.

It was not very long before I met up with Joe again. We met while we were both in basic training in Mississippi. I was stationed in Biloxi, and he was in Gulfport. Since he had gone into service earlier than me, he was able to get a weekend pass several times and visited me while I was restricted to my base. I remember on one occasion, there was some disturbance in the barracks, and the military police were called in. Everyone had to stand up at attention, in their underwear. Joe was sleeping over, as there were some extra beds available. There we all were, forty-nine of us, in khaki underwear (both top and bottom), and Joe Heit, in his white U.S. Navy underwear.

When I was first drafted, I was sent to a camp in New Jersey, Fort Hancock; and after two weeks of exams, both physical and written, and an awful lot of wasted time, I was ready for a trip home. However, things do not happen so quickly or easily in the army. But luckily they had planned on closing Fort Hancock in the very near future, and many of the services that were available had already been closed.

One of those was the optometrist, and so, when I was "lucky" enough to break my glasses (on purpose), they had to issue me a pass to return home and get them fixed.

After two weeks in the army, I returned home in full uniform and was welcomed by my mother as a hero. I even had time to take Shirley Benjamin to the movies, where I got a special rate as a "man in service." After stopping off for some ice cream, I walked Shirley home. We paused in the entrance hall of her house. It was freezing cold, and we were dressed accordingly. We started to kiss; and although she was wearing a heavy blouse, a heavy sweater over that, and a heavy winter coat, I put my hand on the area where the left breast would be. She asked, "What are you doing?" and I answered quickly, somewhat embarrassed, "I am in the army now!" My glasses got fixed the next day, returned to camp at Fort Hancock, and shortly afterward was shipped out for basic training at Keesler Field, Mississippi.

The decade between 1940 and 1950 was a very eventful and meaningful time for me. I went from being a bar mitzvah boy to a married man. I graduated from high school and from college, and in between, I had several jobs. I went into the army and was discharged as a veteran, returned to school, met my dream girl, and married her on February 12, 1950. It seems that I had just been bar mitzvahed, and actually it was, in June 1940.

The United States had been attacked, went to war in many parts of the world, and was successful and victorious; and through it all, I became a man. My only regret about this era was that I did not attend either my graduation from high school or college. Both graduations took place in June, and I had finished all my studies in January of the same year. In both cases I did not graduate with my schoolmates as I had to change schools during my senior year in high school, and my college education had been interrupted by a year in the U.S. Army. So the significance and joys of both graduations had been diminished, and the other graduates had not been friends of mine throughout school. Despite these reasons, I still regret not being there in a graduating gown and smiling for pictures with my parents.

During the summer of 1943, I worked at a drugstore that had a soda fountain counter and also served lunches at Twenty-five Broadway in downtown New York City. My job consisted of dusting off all the shelves and the bottles on them every morning and then making deliveries of lunches in the area. I was also asked to fill in as a dishwasher since that person had to report to the army, and it took two weeks to get a replacement.

I was already in college, so in September I returned to CCNY. The next summer I got a job at the main post office in New York City, sorting mail and sending it on its way to every little town and city in the United States. At the job I remember sitting next to Patrick Ryan, a good-looking young man of twenty, who would regale me with stories of his romantic conquests, at least every other day. I was very impressed, but by the end of the summer, I was anxious to get back to school. But I did promise myself I would polish up my dancing, especially since he would meet all these girls at dances. Before the next summer, 1945, just before turning eighteen, I received a telephone call from a friend that I had met from my Church Avenue days who had a job as a bellhop at a hotel in the

Catskill Mountains. His name was Shelly Farber, and he told me that if I would like to come up to the Catskill Mountains for the summer, there was a job at the hotel as an assistant bartender. I, of course, jumped at the opportunity; and in late May after school finished, I traveled by Short Line bus to White Roe Lake Hotel in Livingston Manor, New York.

The hotel was located high on a hill on the shores of a beautiful freshwater lake, and catered to a young, unmarried crowd. There were about 450 guests, and they generally stayed in rooms of three or four in the room for about $65 per week. That included three full meals every day and activities all day long, including dancing in the afternoon and entertainment and dancing at night. Weekends usually saw well-known comedians doing their acts, as well as professional performances by singers and dancers.

Every night there was something else happening, and the Catskills was really the place to be. Neither Las Vegas nor Puerto Rico, which later replaced the Catskills, was fashionable then or easy to get to. The Catskills was merely a bus ride away, only about seventy miles from New York City. The staff consisted mainly of young college men working for the summer to pay for their school expenses when they got back to college in the fall. The majority of the guests were young ladies who had jobs in the city and spent their two weeks' vacation "in the mountains" being romanced and entertained for a reasonable price. Actually, it was cheap!

Even then, every well-known entertainer worked in the Catskills, which was the showplace of the country. Names such as Bob Hope, Danny Kaye, Dean Martin and Jerry Lewis, Henny Youngman,

Red Buttons, and a host of other well-known people in show business. I believe there were more than 150 hotels in the area, all providing the same type of accommodation and food, plenty of it, and entertainment and romance. The entertainers often did shows at two or three different hotels in one evening. At our hotel, the rooms were located in a large main building, which also housed the dining room, and we also had about a dozen cottages, very old-fashioned; but the room wasn't the reason to go to White Roe or any of the other hotels. Actually, there were no new buildings at that time. The entertainment center and the bar at which I worked were in a separate building called the Casino and was the center of all-night activities.

Wednesday nights at White Roe were usually basketball nights, and most of the college basketball players in the country honed their considerable skills during the summer at Catskill hotels. During the day, they worked as waiters, busboys, and bellhops. You could earn as much as $2,500 per summer strictly on tips, which went a long way to paying expenses at college during the following semester, especially if you were going to a city or state college, where there were not any, or very little, charges for the education.

Despite the fact that I was in college and had worked the previous two summers, I was quite naive and inexperienced regarding intimate associations with women. At the bar that summer, my eyes were opened very wide as I watched and especially listened to all that was said and done. It was exciting. I was earning real money while truly enjoying myself. The tips were always generous. The male guests, who were usually thirty years and older, were always trying to impress everyone else, and they all impressed me. I knew I was growing up and loving every minute of it. Unfortunately, my fellow workers at the hotel expected free drinks at the bar, but I could not accommodate them as my bosses were always around the busy bar, a very important money earner for the hotel. In fact, "Pop" Weiner, the father, and the original founder, told my friend Shelly that "Alvin is a very good worker, but he should put all the money for the drinks in the cash register, not the 'tip dish.'" Instead of replying "Alvin wouldn't do that," he replied, "I will tell him to stop." I was not too happy with that.

The war ended that summer, and the celebration at the bar that night, I can still hear ringing in my ears when the news was reported. It was momentous. I could feel my personality developing at the bar that summer, and I was very happy with my life, even without a girlfriend. At the end of the season, the Wiener family, including "Pop," was so pleased with my work that I received a bonus, which was the first one that had ever been given at the hotel. The family consisted of "Mom," "Pop," and their three sons. Jules, the eldest, was married to the most beautiful and elegant wife, whose name escapes me. Mac was married to Jean, and they had two small children. John, the youngest, was still in the army. In later years we became very friendly with John and his wife, Lynn, and still remain close to them today, sixty years later. John and his then-girlfriend, Lynn, hosted an engagement party for Muriel and me at the hotel in 1949.

That first year at White Roe was very exciting and took me to a different level in every aspect. I went back to school at CCNY, and boy did I have stories to tell to Joe.

The next year I went back to White Roe but this time as a bellhop, along with my friend Shelly and two other young men. We shared one room, two bunk beds, and a bathroom at the end of the hall. As a bellhop, you got the chance to meet all the new girls first, every week or every other week, as they were checking in. There were no luggage carts or elevators. There were three floors in the main building, and we would carry everyone's luggage to their rooms.

In the Catskills, the hotels were known for the different age groups to whom they catered. There were "family hotels," "young married hotels," and our "singles" hotel. White Roe had a great reputation for having a wonderful young "fast" crowd, and it was well deserved. The summer of 1946 was just as exciting as that of 1945. But now I was able to have most nights off to enjoy all the facilities and even visit other hotels. On Tuesdays our basketball team would visit an opponent's hotel to play.

Atlantic City did not have gambling as yet, so as I mentioned previously, the Catskills was the place for fun in the summer. The staff was allowed to use all the facilities and was encouraged to do so, especially with the female guests. We swam most every day in the lake, in a large wooden pool anchored to the shore, and mixed with the guests. There was Latin dancing on a wooden floor setup on the lawn during the day and a full menu of sports for all. It truly is a shame that this has all disappeared with the advent of cheap airplane fares and venues such as the Caribbean, Vegas, Atlantic City, and all the other attractive vacation spots that exist today. It might just be nostalgia, or a faulty memory, but I think that the Catskills of that time was superior to anything that we have today for pure fun.

After the summer of 1946, I went back to CCNY for six months at which time I was drafted into the army. I spent about two months in Mississippi for my basic training, which consisted of drills, extensive exercises, and lessons on how to take apart and put together a rifle, even though as I have mentioned, the war was over by now. The United States still maintained bases overseas and continued to send soldiers to replace those who had already served their time.

While in Mississippi, I met a basketball player who was quite famous in New York, having played center for St. John's University. His name was Ivy Summers. Ivy was six feet six inches, which was reasonably tall in those days; and Keesler Field, knowing of his reputation, immediately put him on the basketball team, which played against other bases. Ivy would tell me that he was treated like royalty since he was one of the important reasons for the success of the team.

I remember him telling me that the officers would do anything within reason to make him happy, even if he asked them to send *me* to a specific army base after basic training. He was quite sure they would accommodate him and asked me to think of where I might like to go. I was in the air force, and I thought of places that I would've been very happy to be sent to next. My first choice was Stewart Field in Newburgh, New York, which was actually the airport for West Point. It was sixty miles away from New York City and actually in the Catskill Mountains.

My mother was spending that summer in the Catskills, along with my sister Honey, my brother Stanley, and my baby sister, Janie. They rented a bungalow for the summer in a "colony," which was also a feature of the Catskill Mountains; besides, families who could not afford to pay the price of a hotel could rent a small house for the wife and children, and the husband would come up on the weekends. There were no services, and the wife did all the cooking and cleaning, but the family escaped the oppressive heat of New York City without air-conditioning. That is exactly what my parents did on several occasions.

My second choice was Mitchell Field, which was located in Long Island, next to East Meadow, where Muriel and I eventually bought our first house. Mitchell Field would also have been a lovely spot to spend my time in the army. Just as he promised, Ivy was granted his request for me to be sent to Stewart Field, which is where I spent the rest of my year in service. Ivy was out of town for a basketball tournament when I received my orders and shipped out immediately, and I never saw him again for about thirty years. Talking one day with my close friend and attorney Murray Goldberg, he mentioned that one of his golfing partners at his club was the former basketball player from St. John's Ivy Summers. You can just imagine my shock at hearing that name in the early 1970s.

Murray arranged to invite us to his club for dinner along with Ivy and his girlfriend, and it was a very joyous occasion for me. Life brings us many pleasant surprises, and meeting up with Ivy in Mississippi was certainly one of the most pleasant in my life. I could not believe it, but he did not remember me! He simply did not remember me, my name, or the incident in Mississippi. I had known him for about six weeks thirty years ago! And I had simply disappeared from his memory. The same week I met Ivy at Murray's club, a stranger walked up to me and said, "Townsend Harris, 1942!" He looked vaguely familiar, but in this case, *he* had remembered me! We had a good time that evening, Ivy and I, and our friendship was renewed and continued for the next twenty-five years, ending only with his untimely passing away.

Just one quick memory from Mississippi. While still in Biloxi, four of us (all from the New York area) obtained a weekend pass and spent the Saturday and Sunday in New Orleans. Usually, if hotels had rooms past 7:00 p.m., they would give them free of charge to a serviceman. That particular weekend was a very crowded one in New Orleans, and there were no free rooms available. We did, however, get four beds in the trauma area of Tulane University's hospital.

At Stewart Field, I was assigned to work in the administration office at the hospital. It was not a very large hospital, but it was there for the air force base, on which it was located, and for the West Point cadets, who were required to take their air training at the base. We ate very well there, along with the cadets who were in training. However, their strenuous exercises and programs took care of all the calories, whereas I was sitting at a desk all day and not using up many calories. I gained about twenty-five pounds during my year in the army.

Life was good, and I almost considered staying in the air force, which was at that time a part of the army, not separate as it is today. At the request of the officer in charge, I took several intelligence tests at West Point and accomplished some of the highest marks ever recorded there, I was told. I guess they asked all the right questions on those tests. However, I realized that an army career was not for me. In addition to my clerical duties, I was also allowed to watch surgical operations and other procedures, which provoked a great interest in me, and that tempted me even more. Unfortunately, I did not have the ability to foresee the possibility of a medical career, and it seemed beyond our reach financially.

I had been studying to be a teacher of foreign languages, but that too was fading in my mind, as I felt I needed something more challenging. But I had no idea what that was. Most weekends during the summer of 1946, I would hitchhike from the base to my mother's bungalow, a little more than an hour away, in the Catskills, on Friday afternoons and returned early Monday morning ready to work. It was an interesting summer but seemed to be a waste of my time since nothing extra was accomplished. But it was all a part of my maturation, and the experience would always be useful. The lieutenant colonel at Stewart Field, Colonel Hoffman, reminded me again in the fall that based on my past grades I had a possibility of going to West Point, and he would follow up for me, if I were so inclined.

But by then I knew I wanted to go back to CCNY and get on with my life, whatever that might be. After the summer, and until I was discharged the following January, I would spend weekends at my parents' house in Brooklyn and mostly go back to my friends and Church Avenue. I had two girlfriends that I would see, but they were "movies and an ice cream soda" dates; and within a year of leaving the air force, I gradually lost touch with them.

I was discharged from the army in January 1947 and went back to school to finish up my senior year. I met a freshman named Bettye Loel and several of her friends, who, unfortunately, all lived in the Bronx. She had a boyfriend named Morty Friedman, who had been in the navy and who I was to meet that summer of

1947 while working again at White Roe Lake Hotel, where I was to return as a bellhop. Bettye was a freshman, and I was a senior, but we took the same economics course and just happened to sit next to each other. We became very friendly, and she and Morty became our closest friends throughout our lives.

Bettye and Morty had a great friend from their neighborhood on Mosholu Parkway who was known by the nickname "Hipster," whose real name was (and is) Bernie Robinson. Morty, Bettye, Bernie, and his wife, Judy, remained our friends until the unfortunate death of Morty in 2008 and Bettye in 2009. My last semester was spent taking all the courses that I hadn't taken, which were required for my BA degree. One of my elective courses was Portuguese, which Bettye also took. It was fun having a female friend in school, and Bettye was a good friend.

The summer of 1947, as I mentioned before, I came back as a bellhop to the Catskills. Most of the work was concentrated on the Sundays when about 350 young single people, mostly female, arrived to check in, and the same amount checked out. The hotel's new chauffer that year was Morty Friedman to whom my friend Bettye was practically engaged to. Morty and Bettye were a couple, it seems, forever. They moved to Florida in 1970, so we only got to see them infrequently, from 1970 to 2000, although the last nine years we have spent the winter's coldest months down in Florida and have regularly been together. Before that, much too much time would pass between seeing them.

After that summer, I went back to school to finish and graduated in January 1948; Israel was founded later that summer. CCNY—with its all-local New York City students, mostly Jewish and Afro American—won both the NCAA and the NIT (National Invitational Tournament) basketball tournaments for the entire country, the first and only time in history. Now, both tournaments are played at the same time, and it is therefore no longer possible. What an accomplishment that was! At the time, the NIT was the more important, but today the NCAA definitely is of greater significance.

Toward the end of May 1948, I once again went back to White Roe to work for the summer, as I had not been able to find a job; and it was there that the most important part of my life occurred: I met my wife, Muriel, during the Memorial Day weekend, and while I am embarrassed to say that I do not remember the exact date, it was May 25 or May 26. I had just arrived, and my first view of her was this lovely young lady's back as she was walking up a staircase. I was with Morty, who had been there a few days earlier than me, and I asked him "Who is that?" He said that she was working at the hotel as a bookkeeper but was very independent.

Muriel had come up there to spend the summer because she thought it would be an interesting one, having heard about the hotel and having met the youngest son of the owner, John, now back from the army. Muriel was so pretty. As I stated earlier, we all became great friends. That summer was surely the best one yet. I had become very close to the Wiener family, and they allowed me great liberties that were not extended to other employees. They knew I was honest and dependable. In fact, a few years later, they even asked me to come up for the Memorial Day weekend to work, as they were shorthanded. During the afternoons, I sometimes was in charge of the public address system, which played music continuously.

That summer I often dedicated some of the songs to "our beautiful bookkeeper Muriel." I totally fell in love with her, and I'm not sure that she even noticed me, particularly at the beginning of the season. By the middle of July, everyone knew that Muriel belonged to Alvin, although Muriel did not know that.

Some of the weeks, the proportion of girls to men was so high that the management requested the female staff members to stay away from the casino and the nighttime activities to give the female guests a chance with the rather-scarce males and male staff. On some of those evenings when I had to work at the front desk and others were going to visit other hotels and the female staff left with some of the guys, it was understood that Muriel's expenses had to be paid by me. Perhaps by that time she also realized that this young bellhop might be something special for her.

Early in July the hotel needed a waiter for the bar area, and Morty called his friend Bernie, who came up and spent the rest of the summer with us. We all slept in the same room again, with two double bunk beds, along with another of the bellhops, a local fellow from Calicoon, New York. In August, Morty's girlfriend Bettye came up to spend two weeks at the hotel, and that was the beginning of a great friendship for the four of us.

By the middle of August 1948, Muriel and I were beginning to feel some very strong mutual attraction and good feelings. My sister Honey, who had been engaged to Henry Greenwood, was getting married on August 28. I had to go to New York to arrange for a tuxedo to rent for the wedding and to have it tailored. I discussed the situation with John Weiner, who was thrilled with the idea that

I have Muriel fly into New York and spend the evening in the city with me.

I do not think we had even kissed as yet, so it took quite a bit of selling on my part to convince her that she should come to New York City for a night. Robbie Newman was a local young man who had a pilot's license and owned a small single-engine plane. You have to understand that both Muriel and I were quite innocent about a lot of things, but she agreed to have Robbie fly her into Floyd Bennett airfield in Brooklyn. Lynn, who was Johnny's fiancée and worked in the entertainment field, was as excited as we were. Lynn's father, a psychiatrist, had been analyzed by Sigmund Freud and was a good friend of his. Lynn has produced a film on them and also published a book on their relationship.

I went in a day early on the bus, did my tuxedo fitting, and Muriel followed by plane the next afternoon. She stayed at the Waldorf-Astoria, as my guest, and never even told her mother or friends that she would be in New York that night, as it would have been a shocking thing to do. This was 1948, and the customs were very different, or at least we thought so, and the prices were considerably cheaper than you could imagine to enable us to do this. Lynn had arranged to get us house seats for the number one hit play on Broadway that season, *Mister Roberts*. I am not sure of the total cost; but the plane, the hotel, the dinner, and the nightclub were obviously doable.

I picked her up at the hotel, but to give you an idea of what was going on between us, she did not allow me to come into the room or stand too close to her in the elevator going down to the lobby.

The seats at the theater were great, and we thoroughly enjoyed the show. Afterward we went to a supper club for dinner, and the main act was the singer Billy Eckstine, one of Muriel's favorites. I did get a kiss at the door, but I never saw the room. The next day she took a taxi to the airport and was flown back to Livingstone Manor by Robbie Newman again. I followed a day later by bus. The Wieners all felt they had put this romance together.

Since we had gotten on so very well on this first date, I immediately invited Muriel to my sister's wedding to Hank, and she reluctantly accepted the invitation. I had to promise not to introduce her as my girlfriend to anyone. She was going to meet my family for the first time, and that in itself was a lot of pressure. The wedding took place at a catering hall called the Casa Del Rey on the hottest night of the year. There was no air-conditioning at the hall, and Muriel and I spent most of the night baby-sitting for my sister Janie, who was two years old at the time. It is almost impossible to imagine all this happening, but Muriel took it all in, as a good sport; and I was sure I had made a good choice, and everyone else was very impressed with "my girl," though Muriel refused to accept the title. The wedding was on August 28, and this time she stayed at the St. George Hotel in Brooklyn, and we did the same kind of a deal with Robbie and the plane, and I did not get to see that room either!

I was thrilled with the entire evening despite all the discomfort, but I am not sure that my date was as pleased as me. It is difficult to believe that I really thought we could pull this whole thing off—planes, hotels, theater, and dinners—with someone that I knew only three months, given the extent of the relationship. But we did, and we have been doing it for the last sixty-two years, so far. This time she did tell her parents that she was coming to New York—to the wedding of Alvin's sister—and had to return quickly to Livingston Manor the next day. What a wonderful life!

At the end of the summer, we all went home to pursue our regular lives. I called Muriel, and we went out on our third date: a baseball game at Ebbets Field to see the Brooklyn Dodgers. I brought along my then-seven-year-old brother, Stanley, probably because I would have been nervous being with this girl of my dreams alone. I had graduated college, but I didn't yet have a job. After looking very diligently, I finally found one in October. The best job I could get, with my college education and a BA degree, was as a messenger for a freight forwarding company in downtown New York.

During her lunch hour, Muriel would sometimes accompany me as I made deliveries of documents to steamship companies, banks, and foreign consulates. After two months, I received a promotion to work in the office and make telephone calls to find out when the documents would be ready to be picked up, now by some other messenger. As we didn't have much money but wanted to see each other as often as possible, we took some college courses at night together, studying textiles, not knowing that would be my entire future. I also studied typing and export procedure. That way, we managed to see each other regularly.

Once a week we were able to treat ourselves to a dinner at Smith's, a restaurant on Thirty-seventh Street between Fifth and Sixth Avenues. We would have preferred going to Keens Chophouse, one block farther south on West Thirty-sixth Street, but the hamburgers at Smith's were very good and half the price. The job I had did not make it too easy to think seriously about a wife and a family.

My father's brother Fred (his real name was Irving, which he did not like and, therefore, at a young age started calling himself Fred) lived in a small town in upstate New York called Tupper Lake. Although Tupper Lake was more than 90 percent Catholic, my uncle was the mayor, at the same time that Dublin, Ireland, had a Jewish mayor! Uncle Fred had two furniture stores in this small town that sold appliances such as stoves, refrigerators, etc., in addition to the furniture.

That part of the Adirondacks was absolutely beautiful, and some of the properties were owned by some of the richest people in the country. The next spring, 1949, my uncle offered me a job to work for him, with the idea that I would eventually manage one of the stores, if Muriel and I liked living in Tupper Lake. I spent that summer living with my Uncle Fred and Aunt Esther in their house, whose property went right down the lake. There wasn't very much to do there in the evenings, and by the time Muriel came up (after Labor Day) to spend the week, we had pretty much decided that our future was not going to be in Tupper Lake.

It was somewhat difficult telling my uncle that I would not be staying on. He was the one who had bought for me my first three-wheeled bicycle when I was a little boy. My uncle and aunt were very kind to me that summer, and it was a good experience being there. I learned to drive a car, although actually it was a small pickup truck, which I used to make deliveries, as well as weekly collections of payments from people who had made purchases. The truck was also my transportation during Muriel's visit. My uncle and aunt had three daughters, and though I was away from home, I was still with the family. However, I missed Muriel very much, and we did write to each other every day. We still have all those letters. After the difficult conversation with my uncle, I left three weeks later in October and came home to Brooklyn.

We became engaged, and I bought Muriel a gold watch since I couldn't afford a diamond ring, and we decided that we would marry on February 12, 1950.

After what I imagine was a great deal of coaxing from his wife, Muriel's Aunt Etta, Uncle Joe offered me a job in his textile export business, typing documents for the shipments that they made. My salary would be $45 per week. I gladly accepted, as it would be a start for our new life. The firm's name was Gulfstar Fabrics, and Uncle Joe had two other partners. Willie Sachs was the elder of the partners, and he had a brother, Jack, who worked in the warehouse. The other partner was Lou Fisher, much younger, who had been in the navy and brought much life and spark to this business and his older partners. Lou was married to Esther and had two young children, and his brother-in-law, George Babich, also worked in the warehouse. It was only fair that Joe should have someone from his family in the business, and since I was marrying his niece shortly, and his son was only thirteen, I became that person.

It was a wonderful year as I saw Muriel constantly, often sleeping over on the couch in the living room on Saturday nights, as she lived in Coney Island; and it was quite a trip, using public transportation, from her house to mine. It took a bus ride, a subway ride, and then

53

a trolley ride from our home on Troy Avenue to West Thirty-fifth Street, near Seagate, a gated community, at the end of Coney Island. It was a rather small apartment, but Muriel's mother, Evelyn, was exceptionally kind to this poor boyfriend of a glamorous daughter.

I am sure they would have preferred someone, or even me, with a little bit more money or status; but Muriel always said I had more potential than any of the guys she had met, and I hope that I have lived up to her predictions and her parents' expectations.

On Lincoln's birthday, February 12, 1950, we had a small wedding of just family at the Granada Hotel in downtown Brooklyn. It was unfortunate that we could not invite friends, but we simply could not afford it. We had a finger sandwich and dessert reception, but it was wonderful, and we were married. It was probably the wrong type of reception for our families and would have been much better suited for our friends. However, at that time weddings were more for the family and the parents' friends. We were so happy and so much in love it wouldn't have mattered if no one was there. We truly had each other.

For our honeymoon we decided to go to Puerto Rico and the new hotel that was just opening called the Caribe Hilton. We had taken all our $1,100 in wedding gifts to pay for the trip on Pan American Airways, six hours in those days; and we left at midnight, arriving, of course, at 6:00 a.m. in San Juan. The $1,100 also paid for the room, which was $15 per night. The room number was 712, and I have tried ever since, in over a hundred hotels, to get a room with the number 12 on the floor. We were the first to sleep in this room in this new hotel, the first built in the Caribbean after World War II, on its own beach!

We had a great time, although we did spend every night in the casino playing blackjack, trying to count the cards. The next day we would be very tired and usually slept quite late. When we got home, without the usual suntan from Puerto Rico, everyone mentioned that they knew how we spent our honeymoon—in bed all the time. The truth was that the bright lights in the casino did not have the same power as the sun, but I felt the assumptions were a great compliment and let it go at that.

Even though it was our honeymoon, the firm decided to give me samples to take along so that I could visit customers while I was there and also offered to pay the $60 airplane fare for the two of us to go to the U.S. Virgin Islands to visit customers there, with whom they had been in contact via mail. I was very successful on this, my first business trip ever, and sold much more than they had expected. My bosses were very pleased. However, after I returned, I went back to typing documents such as invoices, customs declarations, dock receipts, and bills of lading as well as bank drafts and letters of instructions to the bank regarding collection for the shipments that we made.

Jack and George, the brother and brother-in-law of the other two partners, were being sent out on small trips to Central America and some of the islands of the Caribbean. When they returned from these trips, they also went back to their jobs of packing in the warehouse.

As Muriel and I were planning our wedding, we also had to make plans as to where we would live. Housing was not readily available and especially at the prices we could pay. All the hundreds of thousands, probably millions, of young men who had served in the armed forces had returned home, starting in 1945, and this was only five years later, so new buildings had not had the chance to catch up with all the new apartments in demand.

We knew we would go almost anywhere that we could afford and was decent and not too far by subway from Manhattan where we both worked. That did not make it any easier to find anything. We got very lucky when I wrote a letter, obviously a good one, to a company that managed several apartment buildings in Jackson Heights, Queens. They came through and offered us an apartment at 8914 Thirty-fourth Avenue in Jackson Heights. It was a one-bedroom apartment on the sixth floor, which was the top, so actually, our first apartment was a penthouse! The rooms were a reasonable size, and we were thrilled. It was a five-minute walk to the subway at Roosevelt Avenue (Thirty-eighth Avenue) and Ninetieth Street. Our building was on Thirty-fourth Avenue, between Eighty-ninth and Ninety-ninth Streets, and only about twenty minutes' ride into midtown. I think our monthly rent was $52. We didn't have any furniture except the bed and dresser, a television set, and a folding card table, which was used as our dining table along with four folding chairs. We were so happy! We were on our way with our lives and somehow could almost feel that everything was going to be wonderful, as it all turned out to be.

In April of 1951 our firm received a cable from an agent in Ireland, advising that the country had received an allotment of dollars to buy luxury goods for the first time since World War II, and that included textiles. It is amazing that although the war was over for almost five years, textiles were still considered a luxury. The cable requested samples to be sent by mail by Mr. Sullivan, who was our agent there. However, Lou Fisher believed very strongly on actually visiting a market and suggested to the agent in Dublin that we send somebody along with the samples; that person could answer any questions on the spot and be in contact with the New York office immediately if needed. As both Jack Sachs and George Babich were away on their usual trips, I was that person.

Lou Fisher felt comfortable with me after my honeymoon trip, and this was a year later, and I had learned a good deal about textiles. He was confident that I could handle such an important trip and expressed that confidence to me. We were very happy at this opportunity as Muriel and I both realized that this was a very good opportunity to further my career. The firm made all the preparations and prepared all samples for me.

Airplane and hotel reservations were made in Dublin, and on Saturday, May 5, 1951, I took off on Pan American Flight One (which was their around-the-world flight) for London, England. I was flying to London to make a connection to take a flight back to Dublin, as there were no direct flights from New York to Dublin. Of course, there were no jet planes at that time, and we had to make a stop in Newfoundland, Canada, to refuel for a flight across the Atlantic and land in London in the morning. The plane itself was extremely comfortable, about forty passengers all in first-class; and you were able to practically put your seat all the way back, almost flat. Since the flight was going to be about fourteen hours, I fell asleep while flying over the Atlantic. I was awakened by a lot of commotion of people running back and forth down the aisle. The people were, of course, the cabin crew, and when I stopped one to ask what was happening, they told me that we had lost an engine and would have to land at the first available and nearest airfield that we came to. We had not physically lost an engine, but one of them had stopped functioning. It was a four-engine plane, and you usually can fly even on two engines, so there was no real danger, but we still had to land as soon as we could.

That was going to be on the west coast of Ireland, Shannon Airport, which was built as a possible first stop on the way to Europe, if needed, or as the last stop before heading back to the United States, depending on the winds and weather conditions. We were going to be stuck in Shannon for at least two days while they either repaired the engine or replaced the plane. This was a brand-new beautiful airport with great duty-free shops and accommodations, a completely new concept for airports.

Since my destination was Ireland, and I was already on that land, I asked the airline to remove my luggage, which they graciously did. I was then able to hire a car and driver to take me to Dublin. Dublin is on the east coast, and Shannon is on the west coast, so it was about an eight-hour drive. I arrived in Dublin almost on schedule, since I would have had to go through London and taken a flight back to Dublin. Except for the excitement and my good thinking, I was just where I was supposed to be, and I was ready to start my first real business trip.

I was just twenty-three years old, and this was my first trip traveling alone overseas. I wasn't nervous, but I certainly was anxious. The war in Europe, as I said, was over, but the entire continent was still in their rebuilding stage. Although every country had suffered greatly, Russia, Germany, and England seem to have borne the brunt of destruction. With its neutrality, Ireland remained untouched and simply beautiful. When they speak about the Emerald Isle, they really mean *green*. It was simply breathtaking. The grass, the trees, the bushes, the forests—green, green, green.

The trip from the airport in Shannon to Dublin was quite eventful. There were still very few tires available for cars, and we experienced six flat tires on the way to Dublin. We were held up in "traffic" several times by donkeys pulling carts, which contained fresh milk or vegetables. As I looked out the windows, with my mouth wide open, I was startled by everything I saw—both its beauty and simplicity. It seemed like the entire route had a low (about three feet high) stone wall. The towns that we drove through were probably the same as they had been for several hundred years, and the quaintness and peaceful feeling of it all defies description.

We stopped at a little pub for lunch, and the local people were overjoyed at meeting and talking to a "Yank." Every one of the dozen people there had relatives in New York, and they were thrilled to ask questions. I was probably the first American that they had met in their own country. There were very few tourists in Europe and the British Isles at that time, and certainly not too many businessmen, prior to this trip of mine. There were no dollars available to spend except for the construction of new buildings, which had not taken place in many years, and the necessary foods and medicines. However, everything was available in Ireland for the people, as it was all grown there, or, in the case of cows and sheep, raised there.

I particularly remember the butter in Ireland, which seemed the creamiest than any I had ever tasted. The eggs and the milk were so fresh, as they had likely come from the chicken or the cow that morning. I had arrived on Sunday, and my agent, Mr. Sullivan, was there at the hotel early Monday morning. He had totally fallen in love with the American singer and entertainer Bing Crosby, who was probably the most popular person in the United States as well. Mr. Sullivan had adopted his name and wanted to be called "Bing" by everyone.

I certainly was agreeable to accommodating him, and so Bing Sullivan and I spent the next two weeks together, seeing every available textile customer in Dublin, as well as traveling throughout the country to the different towns and cities located there. We went south to Limerick and Cork, and north to Sligo and Dundalk.

Not only did Mr. Sullivan want to be called "Bing," but he also felt that he could sing like him, which, unfortunately, was not the case. But everything was so wonderful that I was also agreeable to hearing him sing—a lot. We called upon department stores and other retail places as well. There wasn't much manufacturing in Ireland at that time, especially of imported fabrics, but there were many stores that sold textiles to be sewed at home. One of those customers was a rather exclusive store called Donnaleys, which was owned by two brothers, Sean and Ian. I became very friendly with Ian, a bachelor at that time, and for many years our friendship flourished. He was the younger of the two and was about thirty years old. He had a strong stutter in his speech, but he was so charming that after the first meeting I did not take note of it. His girlfriend Joan, who was the same age, was the first woman in Dublin to have her own business.

It was a coffeehouse, and it was the first such enterprise that would stay open past 9:00 p.m.! We spent many evenings together and the entire weekend that I was in Ireland.

It was a total coincidence, and a very pleasant one, that many years later their son represented a company from Wales in Florida, which was also represented by me in the Northeast, here in the United States. It sold a machine that counted money by its weight, even allowing for the dust and dirt that bills and coins pick up in normal usage. That Welsh company was called Tellermate, as the inventor hoped and expected it to be used by every bank teller in the world.

Joan's younger brother was a Catholic priest and spent a lot of evenings with us, as well as the weekends. He was closer to my age, and I remember sitting on the floor at Ian's apartment, discussing everything, all our differences, including religion. They were, of course, very much interested to hear about America and New York, and I wanted to hear all about Ireland and their lives in Dublin.

I knew that we would be friends for a long time, and that is exactly what happened. Sean was married and had five children, which kept him busy at home. Our agent, Bing, was also married with several children, and so he too was kept busy with domestic chores. My stay in Ireland was fantastic. I was put up in an old beautiful restored hotel called the Royal Hibernian. I remember eating in the restaurant of the hotel, which was called the Buttery on several occasions, and marveled at the freshness of the food and how well it was prepared and presented. I especially remember the young boys who were serving as apprentices, who were only fourteen and fifteen years old, learning their trade. I went back to Ireland many times, on business and pleasure, several of them together with Muriel. But that first trip was very special.

We made many friends in Ireland and did business there throughout the years. I later was the American agent, and buyer, for the largest retail organization in Ireland called Penny's. It had no connection to the large group here called JCPenney, but it was equally important in Ireland; and under the guidance today of Arthur Ryan, it has grown to become one of the largest groups in all of Europe. Arthur, the chairman of that company today, became one of my closest friends anywhere and entertained Muriel and me quite royally on our visits. On one trip he gave us a car and driver and sent us to an old castle that had been restored. It was spellbinding staying there in the 1980s. On my first trip to Dublin, aside from it being successful beyond what anyone had thought possible, I visited the racecourse, Trinity Church, Trinity College, the Blarney Stone, and every other place that have now become great tourist attractions but which at that time (almost sixty years ago) was simply part of a lovely country. We have been to the famous Abbey Theater to see great drama and have enjoyed wonderful meals in some of the great restaurants in Dublin.

My trip to Ireland was extremely successful as I sold about $250,000 worth of textiles! Never having sold before, except earlier on my honeymoon, I was just bursting with pride; and the office was very much impressed, with Lou Fisher being the loudest cheerleader.

I had been scheduled to spend two weeks in Ireland, but after finishing the first week, there was no more money left from the allotment that had been given for textiles, and so I called New York to tell them that I would be coming home. I spoke to Lou Fisher, who had by this time, during my first year in the business, taken over the supervision of the salesmen who were traveling; and he was so totally surprised at my success and good luck and could not believe that it happened so quickly. He asked me to stay the extra week that we had originally planned, just in case someone had a question. I think he was more nervous and excited than I was. The company had never done that amount of business in one week, and now they just did not know what to do with me. I stayed the extra week, but it really wasn't necessary. The orders were real, the customers were real, and their money was real! I had traveled to every city in Ireland, and it seemed as if every small town and village also. I would be twenty-four in just a month's time, and this was the adventure that started off all my other great adventures in life. I returned home on Friday, May 18, the date stamped in my passport.

I came home thinking I would be going right back to my job of typing up shipping documents. However, my bosses apparently thought they had found a real star and were already planning another trip to an area where they had done very little business: South America. I am sure that it was Mr. Fisher's confidence that convinced his other two partners, including my Uncle Joe. In two weeks' time, which was how long it took me to get the required visas and new samples made up for me, I left for the Southern Hemisphere in early June. At the time I was earning $45 a week, and Muriel was earning $55 a week as a bookkeeper at a firm that manufactured ladies' blouses. If anyone had offered me $100 a week, which is the total of what we made together, I think I would've signed up for life and been very happy. But no one offered the $100 a week.

I had majored in romance languages, particularly Spanish, throughout college; and everyone felt that I would be able to handle a month in South America speaking nothing but Spanish, which is what I had to do. I was not that confident, as I had never really spoken the language over an extended period of time, but I got through that month a lot easier than I thought I would.

Before I had started out on my trip to South America, we had made arrangements by mail and cables for me to meet up with an agent in every city who would help me to meet clients to show my samples, for which he would receive a commission. It was quite a collection of agents that we found.

Starting at Idlewild Airport, which is now known as JFK, the plane flew to Port-of-Spain, Trinidad, where it refueled; and then we went on to Rio de Janeiro, Brazil. Unfortunately, Brazil does not speak Spanish as it had been a colony of Portugal, unlike all the other countries in South America that had been colonized by Spain, and my one semester of Portuguese was not too much help in having a conversation. Brazil is, of course, an independent nation and is one of the largest countries in the world as well as being one of the richest in natural resources.

Rio is one of the most beautiful cities in the world and was (and is) a playground for the very rich from overseas, as well as for the poor from its own country. Flying into Rio is very dramatic, as you can see the large statue of Jesus Christ on top of one of its mountains, and the mountains just cascaded into the ocean. Lou Fisher made sure than wherever I visited, I stayed at the best hotel available there. He felt that we were a class organization and had to show the customers that we lived accordingly. Copacabana Beach, probably the main attraction in Rio (although there are many other ones), is so beautiful with those mountains dramatically coming down to the sea to a very broad white sandy beach with some of the most beautiful women in the world, showing off why they are thought of as some of the most beautiful women in the world.

High up the sides of the mountains existed some of the poorest slums in the world, and the contrast was startling.

In Brazil, the agent turned out to be a young man in his twenties, who thought I was there strictly on vacation and was quite willing to spend his time taking me sightseeing during the day and into the clubs at night. It was not surprising that he thought all this since, unfortunately, there was not any business to be had in Brazil as they have a large textile industry, and the dollars for textiles were simply not available for the fabrics to be imported.

It would have been wonderful to play the role of a tourist, but I was there on business; and while I did enjoy the unbelievable beauty and beauties of Rio, I departed after only two days there.

From Rio I flew to Buenos Aires, but Argentina, like Brazil, had no money available for textiles. But I do remember having an unbelievable steak in a famous Argentinean restaurant. Argentina was known for its baby beef, and the one I ordered was exceptional—and huge. Two of the waiters wanted to bet that I would not finish it. I was twenty-four. It was easy. Argentina was a huge exporter of beef around the world, and its quality was renowned. The dollar was very strong, so the prices were relatively cheap for someone who had the money to spend in Argentina. However, the weakness of their peso meant that everything they wanted to buy from outside the country would simply be too expensive. I did not waste too much time in this market either, and I moved on to nearby Montevideo, Uruguay.

The agent in Montevideo was a young Jewish man, about forty years old, who was very ambitious, worked very hard with me, as the customers were not used to salesmen visiting them. My samples were large and very attractive. He had been at the airport to meet me after the short flight from Buenos Aires.

We immediately started working and were successful in obtaining orders. We established some very good contacts and customers for the future as well. No American textile salesman had ever visited these countries, so the novelty of me being there, and the newness of the designs of my fabrics, appealed to anyone who had dollars to purchase the merchandise after being reluctant at first. Dollars in all these countries were allotted by the government, through the banks, where the customers had to make application for the exchange of money. We always got paid in dollars while the customer only had his own currency to pay to the bank. In later years it became automatic to exchange your money, but at that time it was a complicated and difficult process, probably on purpose, as no country had enough dollars to spend.

Montevideo was also a very beautiful city, with some extremely rich sections; but since June was their wintertime, the beach areas where tourists from Europe would come during their summer months were practically deserted. Since business had started to be good again, I was happy and pleased with the results.

My next flight was to Asuncion, Paraguay, a poor, undeveloped, and backward country that stayed that way under a ruthless dictator (they are always ruthless) general Stroessner for many years. The agents were German—a father-and-son team. The father was about sixty and the son probably about thirty. Their last name was Reuter, and the company's name was Representaciones Reuter. We had already done some very small business in Paraguay, so the Reuters were at least a little bit familiar with our company, which made my visit there easier and successful. They were very pleasant and gracious.

I also established an additional little business on my own, with the knowledge, of course, of Mr. Lou Fisher, who was not interested in anything but textiles. At that time it was difficult to do business if your business was small and you wanted to import directly, so I was often asked to get different products by some customers and agents. Lou Fisher did not mind, as long as it did not interfere with the work that I was doing for him. I made sure that if I ever started doing these favors as a business, I would only do it during my own personal time. And so when I was requested by the young Mr. Reuter to supply them with children's dresses and phonograph records, mainly of operas that were not readily available in Paraguay, I decided to give it a try. I did it together with an extremely close friend, whom I had met only two years before, a couple of months before Muriel and I were married. His name was Harold Yasskey, and Muriel and I had become very friendly with him and his wife, Delores. Unfortunately, Harold died at a relatively early age, while in his fifties, of cancer, despite visiting specialists all over the world seeking some cure.

Harold's father had owned the Hotel 14 in which the nightclub Copacabana was located, at Fourteen East Sixtieth Street; and for several subsequent New Year's Eve parties, about six or seven couples would rent a suite of rooms, at a very reduced rate thanks to Harold, at which we would drink, talk, and have hors d'oeuvres. The show at the Copa started just before midnight, at which time we would all descend directly to one of the best tables at the club where we had dinner and truly enjoyed some of the best entertainment that existed in New York and the country at that time. I do not remember why that business ended, but I can only think that we were both (Harold and I) too occupied with our main jobs and could not give the time necessary to develop a real business. Harold's father also owned a huge commercial laundry, and that occupied most of his time.

I helped the Reuters with their requests, but it never became a business. It was quite a revelation to spend time in Paraguay. The first three cities were all magnificent playgrounds for the rich of the world. Asuncion was like the backyard for the poor. It was dusty, dirty, and not very pleasant at that time. There wasn't even running water in my room at the hotel, which was the best hotel available, but somehow you learned to do whatever had to be done. I was able to wash myself from a bowl in my room and shave the old-fashioned way, using that same bowl, and then take a shower outside with a garden hose—very primitive but it did the job. But the business was good, and that was the main reason that I came to Paraguay, and I was only twenty-four years old!

I next flew on to La Paz, Bolivia, which is fifteen thousand feet high, with the airport, Los Altos, actually being one thousand feet higher. I had gotten so excited in the plane, as we flew over the Andes

Mountains, totally covered in snow. The plane was not very large and was not pressurized as other larger planes to the main cities were and as all planes are today.

To compensate for the very high altitude, we had to wear oxygen masks when going over the mountains. Seeing the exciting range of mountains, I foolishly took off my oxygen mask so that I could take better movie pictures to show my wife and family when I returned home. Unfortunately, without the oxygen mask on, I almost fainted, but luckily the flight attendants saw this and rushed to me to restore the mask. However, this little experience unnerved me and also affected the way I felt. I was met at the airport by an ambulance that took me to my hotel in La Paz. Apparently I was not the first visitor to arrive with such a ceremony.

A doctor was there waiting for me, and he quickly assured me that my dizziness would soon disappear and I would quickly be okay. It did not feel that way to me, and I was very nervous about it all and disappointed that I had been so foolish. However, after a day's rest, I was feeling normal again or as normal as you could feel at fifteen thousand feet. I started to do business in La Paz, with the help of the agent who had emigrated there from Czechoslovakia with his wife and daughter. They were good-looking people and made my stay in Bolivia very comfortable.

Business in La Paz was surprisingly good, and I think the confidence that I showed and felt put customers at ease with me. From La Paz I also flew to Santa Cruz, Sucre, and Cochabamba, other cities in Bolivia, which were all extremely interesting and different. I had good sales in all these other cities, helped no doubt by my personal visit. Cochabamba, in particular, was very memorable because the weather was like springtime all the year, at an altitude of five thousand feet and not that far from the equator. At least 90 percent of the people in Bolivia were South American Indians, and all the women in Cochabamba wore very interesting black or white derbies as their hats. Bolivia was very different from the rest of South America, with its Indian population and the incredible Andes Mountains. For me, speaking only Spanish for an entire month (except for a few words of English to my short fat friend in Lima, Peru) was an exciting experience. It also helped the picture of an American speaking their language and coming to visit them. I was always very warmly received and welcomed as a friend. The people were actually happy to give me orders from the samples that I was carrying. My twenty-fourth birthday took place during my time in Bolivia. Once I got back to La Paz, I finished up some of the loose ends that I had left and was soon off to Peru.

There aren't too many things that frighten me, but one of the worst ever was the ride to and from the airport at Los Altos down to La Paz and then back up again. The first time down I was in the ambulance and lying prone, so I wasn't able to see anything outside. However, when I flew out to Cochabamba and then Santa Cruz and Sucre, I had to be driven both to the airport and return to La Paz before having to take the trip again, when I left Bolivia. You have to ride around the side of a mountain for more than forty-five minutes. From the top, you can see La Paz in its entirety, and it is a tremendous thing to see. It is a rather narrow road, up against the mountain, and on your other side is just a sheer drop down. We have similar roads today, all over the world, but in 1951 that road was not very wide or in such great shape regarding being paved. It is very interesting to see how completely surrounded by mountains is the city of La Paz, even though it is fifteen thousand feet high. Every street in the city ends at the bottom of a tremendous cliff or mountain, and from my hotel window, I was able to see all of those snowcapped peaks. For all the days that I was in La Paz, I was not able to take a bath as it was simply freezing; and while you can dress warmly, even when you are in the room, it is a difficult thing to do when you take a bath. And there were no showers either at that time. I thought it would be a great business to sell deodorant there, as I used up most of mine during the days that I spent in La Paz. I was there in June, which was winter in South America. On to Peru!

The first city that I arrived at in Peru was Arequipa; it was an old port city but very picturesque. The comfort level was not much better than Paraguay. Our agent in Arequipa was a middle-aged Spaniard with a long handlebar mustache. We got on very well, did some business, and after two days, I left. My next stop was Lima, which was a modern city, and once again was going to be an enjoyable challenge for me. In Lima, as in Montevideo, we had a young Jewish agent, Carlos Franco, representing us, which was good as most of the customers in Lima were Jewish as well; and it seemed as if our agent Carlos was related to almost all of them. Peru remained a steady business country for us.

My trip to South America was glorious, with some very curious and interesting occurrences, probably due more to my inexperience and naiveté than anything else. The one story that I have probably told more than any other in my life occurred in Lima, Peru, which was now near the end of my trip.

I was staying at a hotel in downtown Lima called the Crillon. It was a rather new hotel and excellently located right near the center of everything. I decided to go to the movies on Wednesday night, as I was spending the entire week in Lima, and this was one of the few nights that I was not taken out to dinner either by a customer or our agent. I turned left after leaving the hotel and started walking toward the main square where the movie *Red River* was playing at the Metro Theater (The movie starred John Wayne, Montgomery Cliff, and Joanne Dru.) Because of the uniqueness of that night, I remember everything very clearly, and it all happened as I am writing it here.

As I reached the corner, there was a short stocky man standing there. He spoke to me in English, and throughout the conversation, I spoke to him in Spanish, as I wanted always to practice my use of the language, which was really getting good after almost a month. He told me his name was "Gordo," which in Spanish meant "Fatso," which described him quite adequately. In any event, as I approached near to him, he started talking to me, after introducing himself, and asked if I was looking for a girl to spend some time with. I told him that I already had a girl, and his answer to that, again in English, was that "your girl is not here; mine is in Lima." My answer, again in Spanish, was "that it was quite right my girl is in New York, and that is close enough for me."

Again he asked me if I was sure of that; and I, of course, said yes, and I was off to the movies. For some reason, he told me he would take care of everything, and again I thanked him and reminded him that I already had a girl and perhaps *he* could use the one he had in Lima. He smiled and thanked me. I walked for two blocks to the

Plaza San Martin, saw the movie (which was great), and walked back to the hotel. Gordo was still standing on the corner and gave me a "thumbs up" sign. I returned the "thumbs up," entered the lobby of my hotel, got my key, and went up to my room—and there, to my total surprise, was a pretty young lady inside the room, very scantily dressed.

I have to say it again, but I was very young inexperienced and totally taken aback. Again, practicing my Spanish, I asked her what she was doing there; and the reply was a simple, in Spanish, "You do not like me" in a very disappointed, pouting way. I tried to explain that I thought she was a very lovely young lady (she was probably about seventeen years old) but that I was there on business and had to go to sleep because I had an early-morning appointment. She insisted that the real reason was that I didn't like her and she would therefore leave. She proceeded to put on the rest of her clothes, which she had already removed. I gave her $10 for her troubles, she left, and I went to sleep. I was very amused by what had happened to me and realized how lucky I was that it all ended so easily, without any further problems.

The next evening I looked for my friend Gordo to apologize for any misunderstanding caused by my speaking in Spanish and him talking in English, but I could never find him and never saw either one of them again. On Saturday, as I was checking out of the hotel, I looked over my bill and noticed that they had charged me for *una persona mas* for Wednesday night. I called it to the attention of the cashier and told him that there was a mistake as no one else had stayed in my room (and as a matter of fact, I was upset that somebody in the hotel had allowed someone to come into the room) and the young lady had left as soon as I had returned from the movies. The cashier explained that they could not know what time anyone leaves, but they knew that someone was there; and according to government rules, they had to charge me. I told him that there was no way that I was going to pay for this; and if they wanted, they could call the police and we would straighten everything out, including their allowing someone into my room when I was not there.

I couldn't imagine going home with *una persona mas* (one more person) on the bill and showing it to my boss when I handed in all my expenses. He repeated that that was the law, and once again I asked him to call the police. He went into an office and apparently spoke to the manager, and then both came out to tell me that it was really the law of the country. However, since this was my first visit to Peru, and they did believe what I had said, and they did apologize for anyone else being in a room, they would not charge me for the extra person.

Flushed with victory, I left for the airport and for my next stop, which was Ecuador. As the plane landed in Guayaquil, I realized that I was in the hottest city, temperature wise, that I had ever visited. It was located right on the equator and was very, very humid. The sewerage system was open drains in the street, and just being outside was very unpleasant. We had seen customers from Ecuador in New York, but this was the first time that someone was coming to them. I know I have repeated this several times, but it was so important for everybody to see the effort that we were making for them, and was truly appreciated. We had a rather old Ecuadorian man as our agent, and he took me around to the customers. I did a little bit of business there, but the best part of my visit was that all the important clients came to see us on their trips to New York, based on my having visited them, and created curiosity about us. For some reason, the merchants of Guayaquil made much more regular trips to New York than any of the other countries in South America. I can understand why they wanted to get away.

The other city in Ecuador that I visited was Quito, which was at a reasonable high altitude and was quite comfortable. I did not have an agent there, as I was only seeing a couple of customers who had shirt factories, whom we knew from their previous visits to New York. I was able to do some nice business there as well.

Spending a month in South America was quite an adventure for me to experience so early in my career, and it was an opportunity that very few people have ever had. The traveling, along with my own knowledge and general confidence, had helped me very much. I flew home with a stop in Panama to change planes for a flight to Miami and another plane to New York to my loved ones.

Muriel had been staying with my parents at their house on Troy Avenue in Brooklyn during my trip. On the very first night home, I told the story of my experience in Lima, just as I have written it here. We then adjourned to go upstairs to bed with everyone believing the story, except for my mother who lingered behind, held my arm, and whispered, "You didn't really ask her to leave the room, did you, Alvin?" I was extremely innocent, as the story proves, and quite naive, but it has been a terrific story throughout the years. I believe now, fifty-nine years later, that my wife believed me then and believes me now.

When I left New York for the trip to South America, Ecuador was not on the schedule; but Uncle Joe decided that since it was "on the way" coming home, that I should stop off there, and he cabled me in Lima. He had never traveled himself overseas and didn't realize how it felt to make plans to be home on a certain date and then, a few days before heading home, to be told to go somewhere else for another four or five days. However, as I said, I did make the stops and then went home, though I was upset. What was particularly upsetting to me was that on my birthday in Cochabamba I received a cable from Muriel with birthday wishes and also the great news that I was going to be a daddy.

Being so far away at that time, the news was especially exciting, but I was also extremely anxious to come home. By the time I did get home, we learned that it was a false alarm, and our little baby would not be arriving as we thought.

I got home toward the end of June, and by the end of August, our little girl was conceived and subsequently came into this world on April 21, 1952. We called her Donna Caren; and she was the sweetest, cutest, smartest, most considerate little girl that was ever born. Muriel and I were late sleepers, and Donna seemed to realize this; for when she woke up in her crib, she would lie there, quietly playing and amusing herself. She was, and is, a tremendous joy and a great person for this world as she heads one of the largest adolescent AIDS clinics in this country at Montefiore Hospital in the Bronx.

After my trips to Ireland and South America, it seemed like it would be some time before I had the chance to travel to another market.

Most of the areas where we did business in Central America and the Caribbean had been divided between the brother-in-law of Lou Fisher and the brother of Willie Sachs. The firm had provided that when a salesman visited a market, that market became the territory of that salesman, who would receive a commission on any business done there in the future and half of the commission when the order was taken in New York.

As people from overseas started to travel more, that "half commission" became more important. Naturally, neither George nor Jack would be willing to give up any of their territories. For some strange reason, Costa Rica (right in the middle of Central America) had never been visited, as well as Panama, an important stop going in or out of Central America. In South America, Venezuela was also not on their list as it was considered too tough a market for the firm to break into. The other salesmen had already visited and would continue to visit Guatemala, Honduras, Belize (British Honduras), El Salvador, as well as Nicaragua and certain islands in the Caribbean like Puerto Rico.

The firm decided to take a chance and send me to Costa Rica, Panama, as well as Venezuela and any other markets that bought textiles but that our firm, Gulfstar Fabrics, had not ever done business with previously. In other words, I could have what was left over and not thought important enough prior to that. Since they had no idea as to whether or not I would be able to do business in these areas, they first prepared the samples for the other two salesmen so that they could leave, visit their markets, and have the merchandise shipped for the Christmas season.

After an uneventful summer of typing shipping documents, it was once again exciting to prepare for another trip, especially after the great success I had had in Ireland, as well as in South America. And so on October 2, 1951, I set out on another month-long trip to Costa Rica, Panama, Venezuela, and Cuba, and "on the way back" to the Bahamas and Bermuda.

The last two had been tacked on by Uncle Joe, who was beginning to feel left out of the decisions as Lou Fisher asserted himself more and more, and not always delicately. The Bahamas and Bermuda had been dealt with by the company via mail, with little samples being sent to little customers, and were not worthwhile markets to actually visit. As there were no direct flights from New York, I had to fly to Miami; spend the night there (or at least part of the night), as the flight left Miami for San Jose, Costa Rica, at 6:30 a.m.; and I had to be at the airport an hour earlier and up at about 5:00 a.m. I slept for a few hours at a small motel at the Miami airport. The thought of again selling textiles, spending time with customers and agents, and being able to practice speaking Spanish offered another new adventure for me. The plane to San Jose was flown by Lacsa, which was the airline of Costa Rica. It was about a five-hour flight on a DC-3, which was a two-engine plane and may be the most used plane ever, or at least it was before jet planes were put into service. The DC-3 was dependable and safe although not very comfortable. It carried about thirty passengers in rather narrow seats.

I arrived in San Jose at about 11:30 in the morning where I was met at the airport by our agent Gerardo Ducca, who looked exactly like you would expect a man from Central America to be, or at least what I expected. He was built fairly square, with black wavy hair and a rather large mustache. Gerardo was truly a gentleman and a pleasure to work with and, like most of the people that I worked along side of, became a friend through the years. He was a simple man, well liked, and respected by all the customers; and although he had never left Costa Rica, he knew *that* country very well. He made the appointments, took me to the customers, and then turned me loose to do my own thing.

I started off slowly, but soon things turned around, and I began to sell very well. There were some very large stores in San Jose, and we saw and sold to all of them. They were in a very concentrated area, so I had to be sure not to sell the same fabrics to those who were very close to one another.

The largest store in town was La Gloria, which was owned by a wonderful, kind gentleman named Santiago Crespo, who was a little older than my father at that time. After my first trip, I would visit Costa Rica about three times per year, and I would always start off my visit there with lunch together with Don Santiago and Gerardo at a lovely outdoor restaurant in a nearby town called Alajuela. The restaurant was alongside a beautiful high-narrow waterfall. After lunch we would go back to the store where he and his buyers would go through my samples. I became friendly with one of his sons (he had five), Rodrigo, who was about my age and was getting married the following year. I spent a lot of evenings with Rodrigo and his friends; and when Rodrigo and his wife, Maria, came to New York, Muriel and I would entertain them. We took them to wonderful restaurants in New York City and one evening to the famous nightclub the Latin Quarter. Entertaining customers was a very important issue with Lou Fisher, and he always wanted the salesman for that market to be involved in the entertaining of the customer in New York. Muriel, of course, would always be with me.

My friendship with Rodrigo lasted a very long time, and on all my subsequent trips to Costa Rica, Rodrigo made sure to spend time with me and show me around the country, once taking an antiquated railroad into the mountains and another time traveling for a weekend to the coast, where they had a home on one of the islands just off the beautiful beaches. (I believe they actually owned the small island.) The coast was not developed in those days. Today it is a tourist mecca, and many Americans have retired there.

Costa Rica was the only democracy and the only country in Central America that had no army. Most of the population was Spanish and somewhat different from other countries of Central America where the vast majority were Indians from those areas. After World War II there was a rather large emigration from Central Europe to Central America and particularly Cost Rica. Many Jews had settled there by the time my first trip took me there. The Europa Hotel, where I would stay, was an old, though very clean, place and certainly comfortable enough. Costa Rica remained a very good and friendly market during all the time that I solicited business there. Many evenings I went to the movies, walked around the central square, had dinner alone, and wrote home before going to bed. The hotel did not even have a bar or lounge.

From Costa Rica, I flew to Panama, which had a notorious corrupt customs department; and you knew that you would always have to pay off someone to get through with all your belongings, especially if you had samples. On my first trip, there they would not allow my samples to enter without a license, which I would have to get on Monday when the government offices reopened. I had spent five days in Costa Rica and arrived in Panama on Saturday night. The hotel El Panama was magnificent. It was new, the linens were luxurious, the restaurants were fabulous, and there was an exciting nightclub and gambling casino. All in all, not very difficult to take. I could not figure out why my firm had not tried to sell in Panama or send a salesman there, but I found out. I had a lovely weekend, just relaxing—and then wasted all day Monday visiting one government department after another, getting entry permits to work there and permission to take my samples out of customs. It took so long for this to be done that by the time the agent and me finally got all these documents, we found out that the office that had my samples had closed for the day. It was not until Tuesday morning that I was whole again and ready to work. However, it was not a very successful visit as Panama was a very poor country despite the presence of the Panama Canal and the U.S. army base. The customers only wanted cheap, cheap prices, and the quality and designs were not very important then. Price was the only thing that was important. And I did not seem to have much of that for them. While I did do a small amount of business, the best part of my trip there was that the customers did promise to visit us when they came to New York, which was great for me since this was now my territory, and I would at least get half commission if they bought. The market did improve through the years, the country prospered, and Panama became a very good place to sell textiles from the United States of America. Both Panama and Costa Rica became important markets for our business; and since I was visiting Costa Rica regularly, I would always stop in Panama, which kept it as my territory even though most of those sales were made in New York, when the market did turn around.

On one of the early trips, there was a civil disturbance in Costa Rica, and all flights had been canceled immediately after my arrival. I spent about ten days in Costa Rica, mostly with the Crespo family. I was able to leave on the first commercial flight out of San Jose, which was luckily headed to Panama, where I was going anyway. However, because of the danger implied with the uprising (there were some banditos in the hills separating the countries), the door of the plane was taken out and replaced with a large machine gun. We had to fly quite low because of the open door, and I felt like I was in a spy movie, playing the star.

Many years later, when I was in my own business, Muriel, Donna, and Richard spent two months traveling throughout Central America with me to every country there, as well as Venezuela and then some of the Caribbean islands. I was doing a lot of shipping to the area at that time during the family visit, and the most important steamship company was called Grace Lines. I, of course, was known to them, and they were kind enough to arrange a trip for my family on board one of their steamships that was going through the Panama Canal from east to west. I was working when they left on this side trip, but I often wondered why I simply didn't take the time off to go with them, as it was a special occasion for them and would also have been for me.

After Panama, on that first trip, I flew to Maracaibo, Venezuela. Panama was unbelievably hot. I would take showers in the morning, at lunch, before dinner, and before bedtime. The heat made you feel as if you were under the shower all day long, and the humidity, like Guayaquil, was relentless. Maracaibo was even hotter than that, and our agent there was not even very good, as I felt he was not taking me to good customers. This became clear to me only on my next trip, when I had a new agent and did very well.

On that discouraging first trip, after two days, I flew to Maiquetia, the airport of Caracas. One of the best agents anywhere was Georg Gluecksman, who was a German Jew who had luckily escaped Nazi Germany before World War II. Caracas was a large thriving city and was a big step up in terms of being full of promise for great business. I do not know why our firm had never visited Venezuela; but to me it seemed like it would be, or could become, one of our most important markets, and it did.

On those first trips to Central America, Venezuela, and the Caribbean, I almost always would have to start by going to Miami first and make a connection. Very often the connection would leave early the next morning, forcing me to sleep over in Miami. After the very first trip, I made sure to make arrangements to see our good friends, Ben and Thelma Morse, with whom Muriel had grown up and who had moved to Miami in 1952. They were generous with their time, especially considering I would rush in and rush out.

As I became more relaxed with the flying, I was able to really enjoy those nights with them. They would take me to a different restaurant each time, and of course, it is always better to be with someone and especially when they are supernice, as they were. They had two daughters, Amy and Susan, who were the same ages as our Donna and Richard. Muriel, one winter, spent a month with them in their house, with Donna and Richard, while I was on a business trip. Ben died quite young, but we have remained close to Thelma and the daughters throughout the years. In fact, the last three years we have spent the first night of Passover at Amy's house in Coral Springs, Florida. Good friends are a special treasure, and I consider myself very lucky having the ones I do.

Venezuela would eventually become our most important market. I was able to establish a very strong presence for my company and me, with the help of our agent, selling to wholesalers as well as manufacturers of men's shirts. In other countries, our customer base was mostly retail, so the orders here were much larger.

I was very new to the textile business; but the business itself, of exporting textiles, was a relatively new business, especially traveling overseas to the customers. There was no previous history to rely on; so many of the things that I did were being done for the first time. If we did not have a fabric that a customer wanted, I knew Lou Fisher would find it. It was really reassuring to know that Lou Fisher was there backing me up and that our customers believed in and trusted me. World War II had ended more than six years previously, and people would now be asking for more fashionable clothing, both men and women.

Up until that time, a man's shirt was almost always white with long sleeves. When different colors, stripes, and plaids were introduced, there was at first some resistance. But soon there was an eager acceptance, which helped our business to grow, as more demand was created for many different things. We were the first in our field and one of the first surely to bring fashion, at our level, to many people around the world.

Women were asking now for more colors and brighter patterns, as they saw magazines from other countries with different styles, and no one any longer was content to be wearing the same as the next person—always. Our theory of great variety was just perfect for these times. I feel very comfortable using the word "our" as I brought most of the ideas back to New York for Lou Fisher to act upon. Yes, there were two other partners, but they seemed to be involved more in the paperwork of the office and the warehouse. This, obviously, was not going to be a lifetime partnership.

Georg Gluecksman met me at the airport at Maiquetia. He was not the friendliest of men. He was Germanic, stern, and very rigid—all business, which was fine with me. He had given up all religion. He represented many firms from Europe, and ours was the first one from America. The Europeans, especially the Germans, were very exacting and efficient in their ways and habits while the merchants in the United States were a lot more relaxed in their ways, though not always correct, which often upset Georg but which he later grew to accept and appreciate, as he also relaxed and warmed up.

One of the firms that Georg represented was called Continental, a German rubber product manufacturer. Today, they are best known in the United States for the automobile tires that they make of very high quality. One of their featured items in the middle 1950s was rubber bouncing balls, and each year they came out with a totally different line of painted rubber balls in different patterns and sizes. When Donna was four years old, and Richard, one, I asked Georg to save the previous year's samples for me after he received a new line, which, of course, he did. There were about fifteen different sizes, colors, and patterns. I took them all back to New York in a huge sample case, and our little girl Donna was the absolute envy of the neighborhood, as no one had ever had a collection of rubber bouncing balls like she did.

Venezuela, obviously, became part of my regular spring and fall trips; and after Caracas, I would fly to Maracaibo where business, at first, was not nearly as good as it was in Caracas since most of the smaller stores were serviced by the large wholesalers from Caracas who had branches in Maracaibo, in addition to a few small wholesalers.

Maracaibo was the center for the oil industry; and with the passage of time, its population grew, and its demands grew into a very important business. It soon had its own large wholesalers and very large retail operations. Maracaibo was also very important to us as it had several shirt manufacturers, and we were slowly getting into the shirt fabric business because of these, and other customers, I was seeing. Venezuela was always a very rich country because of its oil production and reserves, so the hotels and restaurants were always great.

While the pressure to do business in Venezuela seemed greater because of the size of the customers, it actually felt easier for me to do business there because once the day was over (and they usually ended at 4:00 p.m.), you could relax in a beautiful swimming pool and be sure of an excellent dinner either at the hotel or one of the many fine restaurants nearby. Caracas was a large city, and the hustle and bustle that exists in the city was always there; but I reacted well to that, as I do in New York, especially at that time. The hotels were in the upscale neighborhoods, where you would find the better restaurants, and the taxi services were great.

Through the years, I expanded the area that I was covering and visited Colombia, which was just to the west of Venezuela, and also on the Caribbean. To the east was French Guiana, whose capital was Cayenne and had the notorious Devil's Island, just off its coast. British Guyana, known today as simply Guyana, had Georgetown as its capital city, and Dutch Guyana (known today as Surinam) had Paramaribo as its capital. They were all fascinating places, and we did business in all of them. In Paramaribo I had a dozen customers, all Lebanese and all from the same family. Four were brothers, each with their own textile store, then their sons and other cousins. Naturally, our agent was also from the Issa family. This family of Lebanese were warm, intelligent, fair businessmen and very much into family and overeating—very much like the Jewish people! I fit right in!

Throughout the years, I did business with every color of people, every religion that existed. I sold to Caucasians, blacks, Asians, Indians, and every shade in between. I did business with Christians, Jews, Hindus, Muslims, Confucians, Buddhists, Islamists, including nonbelievers, as well as every offshoot of every one of them. I was always Alvin Futterman, a Jewish businessman from New York, and everyone trusted me. I was completely honest, and if they did not know this at first, they soon learned it and appreciated it. They trusted me with their money, sometimes with their jewels, and always with their names and lives, as well as their business.

Everyone always wanted to have dollars in the United States, no matter where they lived, as the dollar was the most important currency in the world. I had more than two dozen bank accounts of various people from countries that we dealt with. This was not legal in their country, but they never felt totally secure, and there were no laws prohibiting this in the United States, as long as it wasn't an attempt to defraud the United States in any way. All the accounts were in the names of these customers, with me having their permission to sign on their account, and remove whatever I wanted. They had no receipt for this money and simply trusted that I would keep it for them. I never abused that trust, and it was especially important for those who lived in Uganda, when Idi Amin expelled all the Indian people that he could; and when they arrived to whatever country they were going, they were able to get in touch with me and get every penny that I was holding for them.

Sad to say, not everyone did the same. "What money?" was the response that some got from others they had mistakenly trusted. Some expressed their surprise and gratitude, as this was all they had after being forced to leave their country with hardly any possessions and certainly with no money or jewels. All the statements and mail from the bank were sent to my address, and we never charged a single penny for this service. I am very proud of that trust and the chance I had to help people in need.

A young gentleman from South Africa whom I had never met and whose name I did not know before he called me asked me to meet with him, which I did. He handed over to me a small bag full of diamonds and asked if I would please look after these for him. I told him that I did not want the responsibility, but he pleaded that he had no one else that he knew, and every one he had spoken to in Cape Town had said that he could trust me. I eventually agreed to take the bag and opened a safety deposit box in both his name and mine.

I later learned that his father, whom I subsequently met, owned more than one hundred small department stores in South Africa. Several years later, he asked me to sell the diamonds for him, and he would be very happy to pay me a commission. He was afraid to fly and could not make the trip over to New York. I found a diamond wholesaler through the jewelry exchange on Forty-seventh Street in Manhattan, received the price for the entire lot, reported it back to South Africa to him, and got the okay to sell at that price. I did not accept any commission, as it was an easy thing for me to do, and I was helping someone rather than just doing business. I hope that someone else might help my children or grandchildren in the future, if they needed that help.

It has been said many times, but never too many, that nothing is as valuable as a good name. I am very proud to be able to pass that good name onto my children and grandchildren, and maybe their children as well. Honesty, compassion, and love are the magic words for a wonderful life.

In the Caribbean I visited most every island, including Trinidad, Tobago, Barbados, Antigua, Martinique, Guadalupe, Jamaica, Dominican Republic, Haiti, Dominica, St. Lucia, St. Vincent, St. Kitts, St. Bart, St. Martin, Aruba, Bonaire, Curacao, Puerto Rico; and, of course, Cuba, the Bahamas, and Bermuda a little north of the Caribbean; as well as the U.S. Virgin Islands, the British Virgin Islands, and whatever other little specks that exist in that vast beautiful blue Caribbean. We did business in all of them.

I can only hope that I will be able to remember most of my adventures in these areas, but I am afraid it will be impossible to think of everything because every day was different; and with my insatiable curiosity, I would seek out something new all the time and learned so much. I was one of the first American salesmen in many of these places and was always received with great respect and, later, affection. Every place, everywhere, was fascinating to me, each with its own excitement.

After my first trip to Caracas, I flew to the then-Dutch possession, island of Curacao, which had a floating bridge that opened up rather than raised up. I should say that one end of the bridge floated to the same side as the other end, pushed by a motor, to allow ships to pass in between the two parts of the island. The bridge was used for cars and people so traffic would be completely stopped.

There were only retail stores on Curacao, but business was satisfactory, and it fitted comfortably with what we were doing. I made a side trip to the island of Bonaire, which was one of those tiny specks on the map. There were no hotels, one flight a day each way, and I wound up sleeping overnight in a hammock, which was in the government building in the basement. I called on the only customer there whose main business was raising pigs. Romer Boon was his name, and I showed him samples over the fence, as he stood in the pigsty; and I got an order. That night I went to see a movie *Jezebel* (starring Henry Fonda and Bette Davis), which was set up in the mayor's living room. Not too many people on Bonaire spoke English, as they communicated in Papimento, which was a local Creole from many different languages, including Dutch and English and the language of the original Carib people. Since the English spoken in the movie was not necessary for the people there, and there were subtitles in Papimento, they ran the movie at a slightly higher rate of speed, so I could not understand the English and certainly did not know the words that were written on the screen, but it was an adventure. It is not difficult to recall occasions like that.

I went back to Curacao the next day on the plane that had brought me in. Then I flew on to Aruba. All three islands (Aruba, Bonaire, and Curacao) at that time belonged to the Netherlands. In Aruba I actually had my own room in a tiny motel off the road. For that small island, I did very nice business, to my complete surprise and probably to the surprise of everyone at Gulfstar. Today Aruba is a very popular resort spot with several beautiful big hotels and gambling casinos. When I traveled there, a popular activity was watching the two-engine planes landing four times a day.

From Aruba, I left for Havana, arriving after midnight. I remember the lateness because the customs officials had already gone home, and we had to wait for them to come back. Cuba, in 1951, while being ruled by a dictator, Fulgencio Batista, was not an unpleasant place for tourists. I did not know how all the Cubans felt, but obviously, the arrival of Fidel Castro (about ten years later) was greeted with great joy by a vast majority of the people there. Unfortunately, it did not work out as well as it seemed it would under Castro, who was also in his own way a dictator. Life under any dictator has got to turn bad for a large part of the people, if not immediately then soon afterward.

In 1951 Cuba was totally corrupt, and the Mafia had great influence in Havana through its gambling casinos. Everyone had to be paid off for anything they did, even if that was their job. Cuba was our largest trading partner in the world at that time and was a fabulous vacation spot for people with money, and it was only ninety miles from Florida!

The Hotel Nacional was an international legend; the nightclubs, especially the Tropicana, was like what we see in Las Vegas today, and this was fifty-eight years ago! The island was beautiful with great beaches and wonderful people, the food was terrific, but the people lived under a dictator. Since it was so easy to fly to New York, most textile customers did that and used the business to make their own entertainment trips to the United States of America. Therefore, there wasn't too much business for me to do in Havana, once I stopped smiling and remembered that I was there to do business; but there were some accounts, large retailers, who had to fill in some of their stocks with new merchandise for quick delivery for the Christmas season. I was able to get at least those orders. I now had only two more stops to make before getting home, and I was quite exhausted. It had been a difficult and physically tiring trip.

My next stop was Nassau in the Bahamas, but I had to stop in Miami and wait a day for a connection. As I said earlier, Nassau had only small shops, with very small orders. I then flew on to Bermuda, which also had small shops and small orders. That trip ended as I arrived on October 5 at LaGuardia Airport, which was the destination for the Pan Am flight from Bermuda. The last six stops took about nine days, and I was excited to be home.

I was now a full-fledged official traveling salesman. After two months home, helping to make sure that everything was shipped as I had sold it, I was again sent out in January on another trip to Central and South America. My first stop, as before, was Costa Rica via Miami, then Panama, Caracas, Maracaibo, Aruba, and Curacao. On this trip in 1952 I also visited Ciudad Trujillo, in the Dominican Republic, and Port-au-Prince, in Haiti. The Hotel Jaragua in Ciudad Trujillo was new and similar to the Caribe Hilton and the El Panama, very luxurious for its time.

Our agent in Ciudad Trujillo, Dominican Republic, was Mr. Fuad Tonos. He was Lebanese, and in addition to the agency work, he also had his own store and was a customer. He and his wife were extremely hospitable, and I spent a full week there, spending a day in Santiago and another day in San Pedro de Macoris, both days returning home to sleep in Ciudad Trujillo. I traveled to those two other cities by jitney, with a salesman from the agency. San Pedro de Macoris has supplied the major leagues in the United States with some of its best ballplayers and, particularly, shortstops. Business was good in the Dominican Republic, and I then went on to Haiti.

Haiti was then, and still is now, one of the poorest countries in the world. I could not imagine anyone being able to afford my fabrics, no matter how cheap they might be. I did a little business and spent very little time there while suffering through a miserable hotel, which was the only one available as it was the height of the tourist season and the good hotels (of which there were very few) were fully booked. I could not imagine why a tourist would want to go to Haiti. The Dominican Republic and Haiti were two countries on one island, Hispaniola.

The trip lasted the full month, and I was happy to be home in early February. By May of that year, my company had me on the road again. No one seemed to realize how hard this frenetic schedule was. But I was earning commissions; and since we started our marriage with hardly anything and I was young, I wanted to build up something, and Muriel and I agreed it would be worth it. I went to Port-of-Spain, Trinidad, which was a direct flight from New York, and then visited Georgetown, British Guyana.

The people were all very hospitable, and the agent Frank (a former customs officer) was a partner in a firm called Merchants and Traders. The other partner was the financial arm and had several other branches in the Caribbean. Frank was very pleasant to be with, and we did some business; but British Guyana was a very poor country, so its funds were limited, and so were the orders. From Georgetown, I flew back to Trinidad to make a connection to Venezuela. Business in Caracas was excellent and growing due in great measure to Georg. With the new agent in Maracaibo, I started building a very nice business there too. That trip also lasted one month, as I had also stopped in Curacao and Aruba "on the way back," but I was back on the road again early in August. It felt like I had to reintroduce myself to my wife each time I got home.

Again, I visited Costa Rica and Panama since business was good there and continued to grow, and then I flew on to Haiti. Unfortunately, very unfortunately, Pan American Airways lost my large bag of samples after I checked in at the airport in Panama. I had arrived in Port-au-Prince, unable to work. The only fortunate part was that I was booked into El Rancho Hotel, which was a small luxurious, magnificent new hotel, located high above the city with fabulous views and every amenity one could think of. There was no menu in the dining room or at the pool. You just ordered whatever you wanted, and they would make it. You could have steak three times a day if that is what you wanted or, of course, anything else. That hotel alone would be enough reason to visit Haiti. The airline never found my samples, and it took a full week for Gulfstar to replace them for me.

In the meantime, I was a tourist at one of the most luxurious hotels imaginable, in one of the poorest countries imaginable. The airline paid for my hotel, my meals, laundry, and whatever transportation money was needed until my samples were replaced and carried free of charge by them to me.

The only problem was that I did not want to be a tourist without my wife—I wanted to work—but without the samples, I could not. I wound up staying in Haiti for two weeks, and with a different agent that I arranged, while waiting for my samples, I surprisingly did some nice business after the samples arrived. That was the first and only time my samples were lost in 150 trips, and I don't even know the amount of flights that were involved in those trips. If this had to happen anywhere, El Rancho Hotel was one of the best places it could take place.

Business was good in the Dominican Republic and Venezuela as well. Everything was building up nicely, but I did not get home until the middle of September. As Donna had been born in April, any delay was doubly painful, and disappointing, as I missed my two girls greatly. Donna was growing, and it was difficult leaving her when she was only four months old, but we knew we would go through certain hardships in return for success. Being apart from them was certainly a great hardship for me as well as for them.

Early in January 1953, I was once again traveling. Yes, my first stop was Costa Rica, then Panama, Caracas, Maracaibo, the Dominican Republic, and Haiti again. However, this time it was a very special treat, as Muriel was able to meet me in Ciudad Trujillo, where we had a fabulous time as I worked for the week, ending at 4:00 p.m. each day, according to local customs. Together, we left for El Rancho Hotel in Port-au-Prince. It was really our first vacation since our honeymoon, and we made the most of everything. We saw everything, we did everything, and were very happy together. We were entertained royally in the Dominican Republic by Mr. and Mrs. Tonos and some wealthy customers. Once in Haiti, we went to voodoo shows and danced every night at the Cabanne Choucoune, which was the place in Haiti for nighttime entertainment, that I never knew existed during my other visits. We spoke about Donna every day, and although the trip was amazing, it was great to get home to her and hold her and kiss her nonstop.

We were home for our anniversary and spent that as a family for the very first time.

In the early 1950s there were very few tourists traveling. Actually, there weren't many hotels for them; and there certainly was nothing for them to do in the evenings, especially for naive, recently married young men. During the day, of course, if you weren't there on business, you could do sightseeing and exploring, but there weren't many restaurants or any local entertainment that was yet organized.

In Central America the hotels were generally quite old, there were very few lobbies in the hotels, and certainly no bars where you could sit and have a drink just to pass the time after dinner before going on to bed. Traveling, while interesting for me and a great adventure, was generally a bore.

Once the sun went down, in asking what was available to do in the evening, I found out that the only places that had music were the houses of prostitution. These were big friendly places located on big tracts of land, with rooms for the customers set up like a motel if you wanted to use one, and many tables and chairs spread around the trees and the dance floor so that you could order a drink. The music was quite loud, as Latin music usually is, and the same for the islands in the Caribbean.

I would describe these places as a large ranch with a huge amount of young girls offering their services, in these basically Catholic countries, to mostly young men and well attended as you could not take out a "nice" girl since there was no place to go. The culture was such that young men regularly and routinely used their services and were almost expected to do so.

I did not learn any of this until I found out that you could actually go to these ranches and *not* hire female services but just have a drink, sit and talk, and listen to the music and watch the dancers. I ventured out to my first ranch to do just that. I found the people there extremely friendly, as I'm sure they usually are in that business. I could sit, have a drink, listen to the music, and watch the world go by. The girls working there were very friendly and would even sit down just to talk if you were not interested in anything else and if they were not out working.

That "action" suited me just fine and satisfied that need to be out and pass some time after work and dinner. For what it was, it was really an innocent time. I enjoyed speaking to the guys and girls, and they seemed to enjoy talking to me and having all their questions about the United States of America answered, as it seemed to be the case all over the world. In a couple of places, I got to know the workers very well, and it was really a lot of fun being an observer. I described all these places in my letters home and elaborated even further as I was questioned when I did get home.

On her first trip to the islands since our honeymoon in Puerto Rico, I picked up Muriel at the airport in the Dominican Republic. The next day I asked her if she would like to go to the National Library or the houses of congress; and she replied "No, no, no. I want to go to those ranches that you go to." We called for a taxi and asked him to take us to the house, or ranch, that I had been to more frequently. As we walked in, the music was blaring, there were some couples dancing, and I naturally said hello to those that I knew.

No one acknowledged me, and they all acted as if they had never seen me before. Obviously I was with my wife, and my friends there did not want to embarrass me. We sat down, had a few drinks, listened to the music, watched the "action," and went back to the hotel. I hope my wife believed in the "innocence" of that "ranch" of prostitution. I think she did. I hope she did.

During the time just before my trip, we had put down a deposit on a small three-bedroom ranch house in East Meadow, Long Island. As I was traveling quite a bit, Muriel wanted to be near people she knew, preferably family. My sister Honey and her husband, Hank, had decided to buy a house in a new community that was being built, and we decided to buy a house in the same community. When we put down our $1,500 deposit, our friends Morty and Bettye Friedman decided to buy a house in the same community because we were there. It was a much bigger change for the Friedmans, as they were coming from the Bronx and were leaving all their friends to be near us on Richmond Road. We, coincidently, all bought houses on the very same street, minutes apart.

After I returned home in early 1953, Joe Schwartz (our Uncle Joe) decided that I should visit what seemed like every small "mom and pop" store that sold textiles in the Northeast, as well as the central eastern states, down to North Carolina. I had to make these trips by car; and they were very difficult, tiresome, and not too rewarding financially either for me or for the firm. His ideas were both old-fashioned and showed a lack of understanding what the business could do and where it was going. He was at that time being totally overshadowed by Lou Fisher, who seemed to be making more of the decisions than anyone else in the company.

By adding on small markets when I was traveling overseas and, by now, requesting me to visit even smaller clients here in the United States, I felt that this was his way of showing that he was a decision-making partner also. Unfortunately, it was not a good decision, as the orders at most were for only a few hundred dollars and some even less than that. As they were all delivered via parcel post, that was the old Gulfstar, not the one that was being developed.

I made that first local trip within a month of having come home from overseas, and the results showed that it was not the business that would help grow the company. I explained this to Uncle Joe on my return and asked to have a long discussion with him about this. He obviously was under a lot of pressure, as the three partners were beginning to disagree on a number of items, and he never seemed to have the time to talk to me. On at least five different occasions, I requested the chance to discuss this; but it became obvious that there was nothing to discuss, in his opinion.

I simply could not physically travel that much and especially not if there was no chance of substantially increasing the business; and with the customers he wanted me to visit, there was not, which, unfortunately, was the type of business that he and Willie Sacks had before Lou Fisher joined them. I once again asked to speak to him, but he said there was nothing to talk about; and I guess out of simple frustration and desperation, I told him that if he didn't have time to talk to me about what was involved with these almost meaningless trips, although I didn't use those words, then it did not seem any point in my continuing to work there. Reading this, it doesn't tell how frustrated I really was and truly unable to do what he was asking me. He had hired me, and it certainly was my obligation to speak to him.

It was just a few months earlier that we had put down a deposit on the house and just about a year after our daughter Donna was born, and here I was foolishly leaving my job. The deposit was only $1,500; however, our daughter was growing and getting along with Muriel and me, and we were certainly living comfortably within our means. Without a job, we were in trouble, but I had made my decision, and I felt that was the correct one for all of us. Muriel was very understanding and supportive, even though it caused great problems with her mother's sister, Aunt Etta, with whom she was very close. Aunt Etta was a very strong lady, and I am sure she was pushing her husband in the matter of Lou Fisher. I was, of course, pictured as the "ungrateful in-law" in addition to a few other very choice words.

My mother-in-law was also supportive and told me I should do what I felt was better for me and my family. That was very reassuring and appreciated. It was very difficult finding another job, especially doing what I had been doing, since no one else in the textile business had the foresight to travel overseas, even for small and medium orders, which, of course, grew into larger ones.

A few weeks after leaving Gulfstar, I received a telephone call from Lou Fisher, who had seen my point of view but did not want to challenge his partner. He did, however, knowing I needed the money, offer me an opportunity to work in the evenings, doing what I had done in the past, which was typing their invoices and shipping documents. He said I could do this after hours and after everyone had left so that it would not be embarrassing for anyone, and I would be there alone. He said he had discussed this with his other partners, and they had agreed. Uncle Joe never called.

Of course, I realized the enormity of my mistake in leaving a job without having another one and gratefully accepted his offer, which would help pay some of the expenses, along with the unemployment insurance that I was receiving. They gave me $7 per shipment documents, and since there were six or seven shipments per week, it was enough to tide us over until something else (like another job) came up. However, there was the problem of our new house that would soon be built. I immediately contacted the builder of the house, a company called Klein and Teicholz, and met with Mr. Alvin Klein and told him that I had lost my job and probably could not afford to pay for the house. I asked him if it was at all possible to return my deposit, and he told me that the house would not be ready for several months and that after having had the conversation with me, he had confidence that I would find another job, probably better than the one I left. He also assured me that once the house was ready and it was my obligation to take it, and if I still could not afford it, he would then return my $1,500 and release me from all obligations, as he said that they already had a waiting list and would have no trouble finding a new buyer; but he would like to see *us* in the house.

In the meantime, he said I should keep looking for a job, and if he heard of anything for me, he would let me know about it. I could not have had better news than that discussion with Mr. Klein. I am sure it did not hurt that my first name was also Alvin.

1953: Starting Fresh—Dan River and Frank X. Maya

In May of that year, 1953, I answered an ad in the *New York Times* and interviewed for a job in the export department of a textile mill. Its name was Dan River Mills, and it was the largest single textile mill in the country. They made what was called yarn-dyed fabrics, where the actual yarns or threads were dyed before weaving rather than dying the fabric after it was finished. This way, you can produce stripes, as well as plaids or checks, that look much more natural than if you just printed those patterns on plain fabrics.

While the actual Dan River Mills was located in Danville, Virginia, the office was in midtown New York, where it employed hundreds of people in addition to the thousands of employees at the mill. The new job did not require any traveling at this point, although they had heard about all the traveling that I had done, especially when customers came to New York, although the future was certainly open for traveling.

The salary was $100 per week, and I, of course, anxiously accepted the position when it was offered to me. Our department consisted of four salesmen, or fabric department managers, as the mill preferred to call us. There was Jack Weisfeld, who was the head of the department; Charlie Gallagher, who was in charge of the ladies' dress goods; and Frank X. Maya, who was in charge of men's shirting; and I was put in charge of all other fabrics that the other salesmen did not cover, such as cotton pants material, denim, which was not popular as yet, and any new fabrics that the mill might produce. We each had a secretary, and there were three people in the traffic department who took care of the invoicing and shipping documents.

Charlie and Frank had each made some small trips to nearby places like Puerto Rico and Cuba, and Jack had made larger exploratory trips, like the one he took to South Africa during the time that I worked there at Dan River. The mill was quite unique and was one of the few producing what they did, the yarn-dyed fabrics, so its products were very much in demand. The new job was quite easy for me with all the help that is given at a large corporation and especially with a full-time secretary.

The textile business, like most businesses, is composed of many different levels and parts. At the top, you have the spinning mills—who take raw cotton or wool and, later, different synthetic fibers like rayon or polyester and sometimes mixtures of these—and spin them into long threads, putting them onto spools, which is why they are called spinning mills. Although some textile mills do their own spinning, others buy their yarn on cones or spools from the spinners in huge quantities. The textile mills have the machinery to either weave or knit fabrics out of the yarns. Sometimes the yarns are dyed into different colors, so the result is a yarn-dyed fabric, such as produced by Dan River. In order to make sure that the mill runs efficiently, they usually have to produce in very large quantities to keep their business going. They must sell very large quantities. They usually sell to large manufacturers, who take the cloth and manufacture it into garments.

Before selling a fabric, the mill or a converter usually dyed the fabric into various colors or print patterns on the raw fabric, which is commonly called greige goods. This is usually not enough to get everything sold; so there are wholesalers who also buy large amounts from the mills, or converters, who are like mills, except that they don't have the machinery. They buy the raw goods (greige goods) and convert it to a color or a printed pattern. A wholesaler usually sells the fabric to retailers or small manufacturers.

There is also another level called jobbers, who purchase excess fabrics from the mills, the converters, the garment manufacturers, or the wholesalers, who want to sell their remaining inventories of fabrics from that season. What these jobbers buy are therefore called job lots. We were both wholesalers and jobbers, as we bought regular-priced merchandise from the mills and converters, as well as job lots from either of those, or from a manufacturer who could not sell what he thought he would be able to when he purchased the merchandise. At that level, the fabric has been reduced considerably in price, which would enable the wholesaler or jobber to easily compete with the original manufacturer.

The United States, unlike many other countries, would make fabrics based on what the company thought they could sell, so they were producing on speculation, even though it was a well-calculated speculation. Other countries at that time, with textile mills, produced only against a specific order; and there was no excess ever. In the United States, however, much of that fabric was left over, unsold, and would have to be disposed of at the best price they could get so that they could go on to manufacture new patterns and colors for the coming season. That was the "niche" where we fit in, being able to purchase this extra merchandise at greatly reduced prices and resell it overseas at more favorable prices.

The fashions at that time usually got to the overseas markets the following year, so what we were offering was brand-new to them. We could sell to small stores and manufacturers, as we had the merchandise in stock, without requiring large orders to make up special for them. This existed at least throughout the 1950s, 1960s, and 1970s. Along with my boss Lou Fisher, we devised a method of selling all these extra job lots, which were not always consistent in quantities of each color; but since we were selling throughout the world to many different customers, mainly retail stores, we were able to make adjustments in the assortments and give everyone an equal assortment of colors and patterns.

By spreading the excess yardages over many different orders, we built up the confidence of the customers in our company and particularly in me since I was the one who was selling and then coming back to see the same customers for repeat orders. They bought from me usually on an assorted basis as I was able to convince them (and ultimately gave me their complete trust) or sold them to the idea that the widest possible amount of colors and patterns would be better for their selling since everyone has a different taste and all these patterns and colors had originally been selected by someone. We were therefore able to sell in advance, even before we knew what we would have, since the principle of every piece being different eventually appealed to everyone. Even though we might receive one thousand yards of a particular pattern or color, we could spread that out over twenty-five orders in different areas of the world so that each customer would only receive one piece of about forty yards. It worked very well because I made sure that we had the customers' interests in mind, as well as our own, while we ourselves were disposing of unbalanced yardages. I was able to convince the customer that all this was in their best interest since someone had designed a pattern, someone had selected it to manufacture, and another person decided to make a garment of it. Patterns we might never pick were obviously liked by some people, and surely others too would buy it.

Since all over the world, even people in the same community, have different tastes, and as long as the price was right and accessible to everyone, it would be profitable for everyone. The buyers were all older men with no knowledge of, or taste for, the new fashions. So they were satisfied for someone to make the choices and not take the responsibility.

Since my customers had to pay in advance by establishing a letter of credit through a bank, which specified that we would not be paid until the shipment was made, they had to trust that I would make sure they were shipped what I promised. They continued to buy from me for as long as I was in business, and that was the proof that they trusted me. If we had ever tried to get away with merely getting rid of patterns or colors of which we had too much, the customer would be heard from and would no longer want to buy from me. I therefore made absolutely certain that every order was shipped according to the way I had written it and had promised it!

I was able to continue doing the shipping documents downtown at Gulfstar in the evening as well. I would leave Dan River at about 5:00 p.m., have a quick sandwich, and then go downtown by subway to my other job. I would usually be finished by 8:00 p.m. and home by 9:00 p.m. The typing downtown was usually only three or four nights a week, so it really wasn't much of a burden. Since it was a large corporation, as Dan River was, you were not expected to work a minute past the 5:00 p.m. closing, and comments were made by fellow workers when I would decide to stay a little later to finish up something I had started. There was a whole new world out there, and I did not have to sweep up before the day started as I sometimes would do at Gulfstar, although no one there had ever asked me to do that.

At the time we were still living in Jackson Heights, Queens, and waiting for our new house at 636 Richmond Road, East Meadow, New York, to be completed. The house had three bedrooms; two bathrooms; living room; dining room; kitchen; and a full basement, which, in the course of the next couple of years, we had a carpenter completely finish with knotty pine walls and tiled floors. This gave us a long bar for entertaining, a large playroom, and an office, which made us feel and think that there was nothing more to be had in this world.

When I had spoken to Mr. Klein about the possibility of giving up the house, we had agreed to eliminate the fireplace, which we had added onto the living room, in order to keep the resale price as low as possible. In the meantime, we were living in our one-bedroom apartment, and my new office was only twenty minutes away in midtown by subway.

Many returning soldiers after World War II had to live with their new brides in one of their parents' homes or apartments. When Donna was born, she and her crib moved into our bedroom, which was reasonably large and accommodated us all very comfortably. The house we had purchased cost $15,900, plus $1,000 for an extra ten feet of land along the side of our plot, which went back one hundred feet.

At Dan River we all got along very well, and it was a great working experience for me in several ways. I learned a good deal more about the manufacture of textiles and also how a large corporation operated. After being there for about one month, and it became evident that I could handle the job capably, I was sent down to the mill in Danville for five days to learn everything I could about the working of a cotton textile mill and to meet some of the people with whom I would be in contact regularly. I went down by overnight train and was picked up by the company's white-gloved chauffer and driven to the company guesthouse.

By coincidence, the president of the mill was also staying there during my visit, as his house was being remodeled and his wife was with friends in Charleston. Every night we would eat together in the dining room and talk about business and life. He was a kind Southern gentleman, and he often asked me about the workings of the New York office. I think I was the first Jewish person he had ever met, so it was an experience for him as well, although I don't know what his ideas of Jewish people were before.

He still continued to ask about me at the New York office for some time after I was no longer working for Dan River. He loved to watch Western movies, and every night that became our entertainment after dinner, and he got quite enthusiastic over the films.

I learned to work with systems; cooperate with people; and, through Dan River, made great contacts throughout the world. Due to its special kind of fabrics, everyone in the textile business overseas, as well as domestically, wanted to do business with Dan River. All this later served me very well, as I was able to contact the agents that Dan River used for my own purposes. I had gotten to know them from their visits to New York, and through our contact through the mail, they were anxious to work with me when I contacted them after leaving Dan River.

In 1954 Lou Fisher telephoned me to tell me that he had decided to leave Gulfstar and start his own business. He was, of course, the main person there, and it represented a great loss for his two remaining partners; but he wanted me to know and offered me a position with the new company that he was going to start called Fisher Fabrics.

I was thrilled because I knew him, what he was capable of doing, and how he felt about me, as well as how he treated me. He offered me a much larger salary plus commissions, plus the independence to do pretty much what I wanted, under his supervision. He, as yet, had not asked anyone else to join him and was not going to take on any other sales help at this time. I, of course, accepted his offer and gave a full month's notice to Jack Weisfeld and then left Dan River when the time was up. It was a sad departure, though I had only been there for one year, forming new important business friendships.

Our handsome son, Richard Scott, was born later that year, on November 24, 1954, and Lou Fisher was his godfather. Richard was a very good-looking boy, smart, and quick learner. He was a perfect addition to our family. Somehow we knew that our first child was going to be a girl and only had a girl's name picked out, and we were just as certain our second would be a boy, even though we had not found out medically beforehand.

The year 1954 was truly a landmark year. We moved into our new house, I was now at a very different level in business, and I made my first trip around the world. In April of that year, our house was still not ready, but a strange happening pushed it forward. One night, while lying in bed, we heard what sounded like water coming into the apartment through what was probably a window left open in the living room by mistake. I got up to check and close the window and discovered that none had been left open, but the rain was coming in, pouring in, directly from above through a hole in the ceiling that had been caused by the heavy downpour. Luckily we did not have much furniture that could get ruined, but obviously, the apartment was no longer livable.

The very next morning I called Dan River to let them know that I would be in late that day and immediately left to visit Mr. Klein, the gentleman who had been so nice to me originally regarding the house. I explained to him the situation and asked for an exception to allow us to move in early, as neither the house nor the street had been completely finished and we ordinarily would need a certificate of occupancy to move in.

Under the circumstances, he made a very special request to the town board to allow us to move in, and we absolved them of any problems we might encounter other than what they would normally be responsible for; and within less than a week's time, we were in our dream house. We had very little furniture to move, so that part was easy, and at least we had a complete roof over our heads and were able to start life in our own home. (Eventually, we did get furniture!)

Donna loved her new little brother, and he seemed to be thrilled whenever she was near him. I left Dan River early in July and started working immediately for Fisher Fabrics. The most unfortunate part of this was that it made our relationship with Uncle Joe and Aunt Etta more bitter. They were upset that I had joined Lou Fisher, even though they had never offered me a job to come back to them. Jack Sachs also left to join Lou Fisher as head of the warehouse, leaving his own brother Willie; and strangely, George Babich stayed at Gulfstar, not joining Lou Fisher, his brother-in-law. I do not know if he had been asked or that he decided it was best to be separated and go his own way. He did not stay there very long and within two years had moved on to a completely different field.

We decided that I would not go to Central America and South America for the remainder of that year but would resume my relationships there at the beginning of 1955. At the end of August, after much planning, I left on a trip around the world starting in the Far East, then via India to Europe, and down through Africa, using many of the contacts I had developed in the year at Dan River. It was going to be a very long trip, but it would help set up a new company in many areas that we had never been before, and it was an important trip for me to take. Flights were not as frequent, and without jet engines, I would have to try very hard to stay precisely on schedule. The flying times were twice as long on propeller planes as on jets. Going across the vast Pacific were particularly long segments.

While I was flying in the Far East, Lou took a quick trip to Central America (which was very successful) and started the business very nicely, providing work for all the employees, including the warehouse staff. While my trip was for business, that would come a little later and continue the momentum. I flew to Manila in the Philippine Islands with stops to refuel in Los Angeles, Honolulu, Wake Island, and Guam before finally landing in Manila. I was seated throughout the trip next to a successful young businessman and politician from Indonesia. He requested that I come visit him in Jakarta, where he promised to be of considerable help to me. I explained to him that my trip was already overlong but that I would try to visit his country in the near future. Unfortunately, that didn't happen until many years later, and somehow the contact had been broken. I often read about him through the years, as he advanced to important positions in his country; but unfortunately, I never did see him again.

The trip was unbelievably long, taking about two full days; but the plane was very comfortable with every amenity you could imagine, including actual beds (where they now have the luggage racks above your head). They would pull them down at night so someone could sleep up above completely stretched out—a three-step ladder made it possible—and they made the very comfortable seats below into another full-sized bed. The space provided between seats, front and back, was so large that luggage racks above were not necessary. There was food and drink provided twenty-four hours a day, and it is hard today to imagine that they could do it then and not have gotten back to that comfort as yet.

F. E. Zuellig Incorporated, the agent in Manila, was a Swiss company that was known and respected throughout the world. They had a large textile sales force and usually only represented large companies. The exception was made for me, as we had developed a nice relationship through correspondence at Dan River, whom they represented. The customers liked working with them as their reputation was impeccable, and the manager of the textile department, Eric Gruenig, worked with me.

We visited every important customer there, and to my surprise, they were all Chinese; and we took several large orders for some very cheap fabrics that we were buying from a mill that manufactured the merchandise in El Salvador, Central America, who were friends of Lou Fisher, and allowed us to sell for them. Their name was Safie Brothers, and I often brought them Arabic food on my subsequent trips to Central America.

As an example, the price per yard at that time, for their cheapest line, was 15¢ per yard. So although I sold about five hundred thousand yards, the total dollar amount was $75,000.00. The Philippines had been a possession of the United States since a war with Spain many years before, but after their independence was granted after World War II, they continued to keep many of the customs that had been adopted from the United States and the many Americans who did business there previously. During World War II, Japan had invaded the Philippines and occupied the islands throughout the war until General Douglas MacArthur, in a very famous campaign, recaptured the Philippine Islands. The Japanese had been cruel conquerors, and thousands of Americans and Filipinos died during their occupation.

In the Philippines the most popular form of transport were converted jeeps, of which there were thousands in Manila left by the U.S. Army. The enterprising population would take a used army four-seater open jeep and build it up into a bus in which they would squeeze more than a dozen people. It was almost comical to see all these brightly painted vehicles with slogans and local words, as well as passengers hanging off the sides (and so many of them), simply clogging up the streets. Even the traffic today in New York City could not match Manila in those days, and I have been told they use the same transportation today!

During the war, Japan had taken over what was the most luxurious hotel in Manila, a huge city, for the officers of the occupying forces. It was still the Manila Hotel; and in 1954 it was still not available for guests, as once the United States took it back, we used it for the U.S. Army officers. I stayed at a hotel called the Bayview that first trip, but my next time back, I was able to get into the Manila Hotel, which was very luxurious even at that time.

Manila was a very flamboyant city, and the music was loud and played all the time, wherever you went. Almost all the merchants were Chinese; as I was soon to find out, that such was the case throughout many of the countries all over Asia. The Chinese have a history of being great traders; and with such a large population, they were always traveling and emigrating, seeking opportunities, and setting up businesses wherever they could. For me, the Chinese people as a group are my favorite to do business with, as well as to socialize. They are extremely generous and very gracious and honest in their business dealings. Their food is also my favorite cuisine. If I could eat only one type of cooking for every meal, I would choose Chinese for its unbelievable variety.

From Manila I flew to Hong Kong, which remains the most fascinating place I have ever been to this day. You can get whatever you want at any time of the day or night, more so than even New York City. It is one giant spectacle with every type of cooking in the world, not only Chinese, and all of it, the best possible. I could spend days talking about Hong Kong, the harbor, the people, the bright neon lights, the unbelievable restaurants, and nightclubs, the racecourse called Happy Valley, the world-class hotels, and the merchandise available; however, the most important is the Chinese people.

There are, of course, other people from every corner of the world trying to sell to the Chinese and also trying to sell Chinese goods made both in China and Hong Kong to every other corner of the world, and the mix of all this is almost too difficult to describe. I have visited Hong Kong more than fifty times—with my wife, with my daughter, with my son, and once all of us together—and the last trip there for me was just as exciting as the first one.

Hong Kong is composed of a strip of land called Kowloon, on the mainland of China, plus the island called Hong Kong, which is just across the bay and was reachable then only by ferry. They later built a tunnel under the bay from Kowloon, Hong Kong, to Hong Kong,

Hong Kong. Once it was built, I always stayed at the Mandarin Hotel on the island. Almost every one of the more than fifty visits was in room 1212. The hotel kept all those personal records and endeavored to make you feel that you were coming "home" with each arrival. The financial district and a lot of the textile companies with whom we did business were on the island, although there were many customers in Kowloon, which has a common border with China!

You could actually take a trip to the border and see the Chinese guards patrolling on the other side. At that time China was more than just a competitor of the United States, more like an enemy, and we were not allowed to travel there with a U.S. passport. I always felt comfortable in the company of Chinese people, and especially so in Hong Kong. Because we had customers on both sides of the water, I was constantly on the Star Ferry. It operated from 6:00 a.m. to midnight; was about a ten-minute ride across the harbor; and, if you had to cross after midnight, had to hire a small boat on which families actually *lived*. Then, usually a woman would row you across in whichever direction you were going.

These were called walla-wallas, and like everything else in Hong Kong, they were exciting. Our agent in Hong Kong, also from Dan River, was a giant Indian company Wassiamull Assomull, who had offices throughout the world and *owned a town* in India: Wassiamull City. None of the Chinese manufacturers at that time did business directly with the rest of the world, and in Hong Kong it was mainly large Indian firms who represented them and sold for them or, as in my case, represented me and sold to them. The Chinese did not speak English or felt uncomfortable talking in that language, even if they understood it. It was interesting doing business through an interpreter, as the Indian agents hired a Chinese person to interpret for me to the Chinese customers and vice versa. The Indians had the office and the means of doing the business in addition to the experience; but it was obvious to me as time went on, business would be done directly with customers, through Chinese agents, which at that time did not exist.

In fact, a few years later I hired a young Chinese man who was the interpreter for one of the Indian firms to act as my agent. His name was Au Lok Bun, but he adopted the name "Francis," so Francis Au remained my agent for forty years. We became very good friends forever after, and Muriel and I were invited to the wedding of his eldest son whom I had sponsored to come to the United States. It took place here in Chinatown in New York, and Francis eventually moved to New York as well, with his wife, Anna, since their three children had preceded them here.

Francis was also one of my favorite persons. He was an enterprising young man, with a lovely wife who did not speak a word of English; but I could sit next to her through dinner, and somehow we carried on a conversation, and I was never bored. Francis, who had originally come from China with his parents as a little boy, often traveled back there to set up contacts and sell fabrics from some of the European companies that he came to represent. My company was the first one that gave him the chance to go into his own business. Actually I encouraged him, and he never forgot that.

He always called me his teacher, and while I may have shouted some advice to him, he always listened and learned; but most important, he told me how to eat and enjoy the greatest of Chinese foods. He introduced me to cooking that I would never have dared try on my own, and often when I would ask what I was eating, he would advise me to eat it if I liked it and not worry about what it was called. He was absolutely right because some of the dishes I do not think I would have even tried had I known what they were.

Chinese people I have met value friendships and trust. Francis knew great Chinese food and was always willing to spend to enjoy it. He never let me pick up the check on any of my visits to Hong Kong, although I tried often. He introduced me to every delicacy, including shark fin soup, which even fifty years ago cost about $100 for a large bowl for the table. I did not meet Francis until about five years after my first visit to Hong Kong, so we were continuing to use the Indian agents with their Chinese translators. My first trip was only moderately successful, but I had such a great experience in this totally different world for me that I was pleased spending a week in Hong Kong in 1954, though it was much smaller then.

I was amazed at the things that were being produced in China and being shipped to various places in the world by Indian agents in Hong Kong. I brought back samples to show to various people who were producing the same garments in the United States with the idea of eventually starting an importing business. However, the vision of the people here at that time was not big enough to see what could be done. The thought of importing merchandise from halfway across the world was too frightening. In fact, I remember my cousin Sydney Jarkow, who was in the infants' wear business, telling me that he already had too much trouble with deliveries from Pennsylvania, so he could not possibly consider Hong Kong, although he did tell me that the prices were about one-fifth of what the merchandise cost in the United States. Imports from Hong Kong in 1950 amounted to about $80,000. By 1955 they were $800,000 and soon became $8 million, then $80 million, and I don't know how many billion today. Sydney later became a very large importer and a very successful one.

A great opportunity was lost there for me, but I did not have the experience at that time, and I did have a good job and a wonderful family to support so I could not devote my time to something that I felt could be wonderful as long as I had something that was already good. I have no regrets about it, but the size of the difference in volume with what I was selling and what I could have sold of imported goods into the United States is mind-boggling.

That trip of mine in 1954 really opened my mind and taught me that the opportunities that exist in this world are limitless. While I never put pressure on myself by setting goals, I knew that if I kept working hard, everything could be within my grasp. Working and building a reputation of trust and honesty have been the reasons for whatever success we have had. The Chinese always stayed together as a family, and you would always see the different generations of the family out together for dinner. There were the great-grandparents, the grandparents, the parents, and the children all at one table. The older people were never neglected, always respected, and were always included into every family activity. It was something beautiful to see.

During my first visit to Hong Kong, I was entertained very nicely by the Indian agents. I remember in particular one evening when I was invited out to dinner with a group of Chinese merchants and manufacturers along with the agents and me. There were eight

Chinese, three Indians, one beautiful Russian lady (who was the girlfriend of the president of the Indian company), and me. I was picked up by one of the salesmen and taken to the Star Ferry, as we were going to be eating dinner on a floating restaurant in Aberdeen Harbor, which was located on the other side of Hong Kong Island. I was staying on the mainland, so we took the ferry across, which was very simple.

We took another taxi across the island to Aberdeen. There were three huge restaurants afloat in the harbor, all lit up like Christmas trees, with streams of lights from the top of the mast to the bow and to the stern. When I say "huge," I mean that they could accommodate at least five hundred people for dinner. We had to take a walla-walla to the boat and then go up the gangplank to our table in a sumptuous room. Tables in Chinese restaurants are usually set up for ten people. We were twelve, and it was not a problem.

This night's dinner was truly a banquet; only I did not know the extent of it. There were going to be ten courses, which I also didn't know. The waiters would put out three dishes at a time—and very large amounts of each dish—on this huge lazy Susan so that it could be revolved around to every diner easily. I remember the first three courses consisted of platters of huge shrimp, fresh lobster, and scallops in a fresh fruit salad, and piles of giant crab legs, all caught right outside Hong Kong in the China Sea that very day. We had been on boats with friends and bought directly from the Red Chinese fishermen out on that sea.

It is most unfortunate that one cannot remember the exact taste or, for that matter, any ecstasy. You can remember that something was very good, but you cannot reexperience the actual feeling, or taste of something, without actually doing it again. But I do remember that I ate so much, which was not unusual for me, and that I was very pleased with how much I had eaten and how great it tasted. When I said something about how wonderful the meal was, it was then that I learned that there were seven more courses, and the proper etiquette would be to eat something of every one of them. I thought I was finished, and I had eaten too much already; but I dutifully tasted every other dish as well, each one as good as the first three, and was quite stuffed at the finish. Again, I was the first American guest, and they were very happy to entertain me.

Afterward my new Chinese friends and I piled into taxis while the Indian group left to go home and drove to the town of Stanley, not too far away, where we all got ice cream, which was also fantastic and a great topper to the meal, which I had enjoyed so much. Back in the taxis, I thought we would now be going back to the Star Ferry but not yet as we were driven to what looked like an old Chinese building housing another restaurant. The communication, of course, was not very good; but I went along happily, as the Chinese also drink a lot (as do some of their guests) with their banquets.

Once inside the building, we all sat in a spacious room, in a large circle, on huge pillows and were given menus. Oh no! There was no way that I could possibly put any more food into my mouth, even though it was probably a fabulous dessert, and so I gracefully turned down even looking at the menu. There was much gesturing and pleading on their part, but none of them spoke English very well, although I thought we did communicate surprisingly well, but I simply had to hold firm. They all ordered, and I was sure that I was going to have to share something with them. Five minutes later, to my complete shock, I was stunned to see eight young pretty Chinese ladies walk up to us and sit down, sharing the huge pillows, alongside each of us. The menus, which I hadn't looked at, had pictures and names of these young ladies, and the men were making their choices for partners to serve tea and cake.

Once it was obvious that I was the only one without a partner, every one of them offered their choice to me, as they were embarrassed that in their haste to place an order they had not noticed that I did not. I could not accept from one without also accepting all, but eight would have been too much. I think I explained that fairly well to them, and we all had a very good laugh, and the nine of us were served by the eight ladies that had arrived. I do not think that the ladies on the menu were there for any other purposes, but remember, I was still in my *very naive* period.

We had our tea and cake and left to go back to the ferry in order to return to the mainland and my hotel. By this time, it was quite past midnight, and the ferry was no longer operating; so they had to rent several walla-wallas to take us back across the bay, into taxis again, and to my hotel. It was quite a night and obviously one that I will never forget. Muriel and I, as well as Donna and Richard, visited Aberdeen and the floating restaurants on several occasions on subsequent visits and always had fabulous times, although we never repeated the visit to the teahouse, which I simply couldn't find while being sober.

Going back to Hong Kong, whenever we did, was something very special. After being introduced to all the different dishes by Francis

Au, we ourselves tried to eat as many different foods and cooking styles as we possibly could. I remember on one trip, Muriel and I having fifty-five different Chinese dishes that we had never had before, and there wasn't one of them that I would not order again. I wish that everyone I know could experience what we have seen and done in Hong Kong. I know that my children Donna and Richard; my wife, Muriel; and me have been blessed to have that experience so many times.

Although business on my first trip started out slowly in Hong Kong, it somehow felt like the right place for us and, at one point, was our most important market! From Hong Kong I flew back to Guam, an air force and navy base, as permission for me to land there was not ready on my way across the Pacific when we stopped to refuel. While in Hong Kong the office advised me that they had now received that permission.

Lou Fisher was stationed there in the U.S. Navy during World War II and, not surprisingly, had made some good friends there, especially with the other sailors. There was an American from Kansas called Jones and a native of Guam called Guerrero. Together they formed the business called the Town House or Jones and Guerrero. With such a great introduction, it is not surprising that I obtained a very sizable order from this large department store on the island.

From Guam I flew back to the Philippines and made a connection to Singapore. Singapore has gone on to become one of the cleanest and most pleasant places to be, but in 1954 it was not. The hotel was the Raffles, one of the most famous in the world (and the new one with the same name was built about forty years later), but at that time it was a little shabby and did not have a very good smell about it. It was musty, damp, and very hot; so conditions were not the very best. The agents there were the same as in Hong Kong, and even though Singapore was to become one of our best markets, on that trip very little business was done.

From Singapore I flew to Bangkok on KLM Airlines, a Dutch airline, which was probably the best in terms of service. They had a real lounge on the plane with a lovely table and chairs. Food and drinks were available at all times, and the service, as I said, was the best of any airline flying then. It is strange that Singapore Airlines today is probably the best airline to fly in terms of service and comfort but not in 1954. At that time everything was first-class (there was no economy or business class), and everyone was treated equally, all better than they are today. In another strange twist, I have been reading that some of the new airlines from the Middle East countries are probably the most comfortable today, especially Emirates Airlines, which we had the good fortune of flying on one trip.

Then and now, Bangkok is probably (certainly for me) the most interesting city you could visit. The culture is, of course, different than anywhere else, and the politeness of the people with their ever-smiling faces is such a pleasant sight to behold. The temples and government buildings, as well as some of the hotels, are constructed in Thai or Siamese architecture.

It is one of the friendliest, most exciting, most interesting of cities in the Far East (or the world); but it can also be one of the most frustrating. The people are all wonderful, the food is enticing and delicious, the temples and floating markets are magnificent, but the traffic and the heat are very close to being unbearable. It is a very hot and muggy city, and there was no public transport except for some very antiquated buses, which seemed to run down on every corner.

I remember my son, Richard, who was there on a business trip, calling me at the office in New York, almost in tears, from the Bangkok airport where he had just missed the plane. He had allowed four hours from the hotel in the city (the magnificent Oriental) to get to the airport but still missed the plane because of the traffic in the town. Most of Bangkok is below sea level, and when it rains, even a little downpour can cause havoc in the streets and bring traffic to a standstill.

It is a city today of more than nine million people. I understand that there is a transport system in effect now, but at that time you got around by a private chauffeured car or a very small taxi, none of which were able to move when it rained. Many families, even of moderate means, had drivers (if they owned a car at all). It was cheap by taxi, but going small distances could sometimes take an hour that should've taken, at most, ten minutes. The Oriental Hotel, where we stayed, was consistently voted the Best Hotel in the World by every travel magazine.

There was an unlimited selection of seafood wherever you went and at unbelievably reasonable prices. I remember one restaurant, the Fish Market, which was not only an actual market for fish but also an excellent restaurant. You would get your shopping cart, and the waiter would wheel it around with you as you chose your dinner from showcases with attendants. Salads, vegetables, seafood, or any other fish would then be taken to the cooks who would prepare the meal per your choice (boiled, fried, broiled, or any other way); and you could have them plain or with any one of a dozen different sauces from mild to fiery hot. It was a marvelous and exceptionally tasty experience.

We traveled by boat on the Chao Phraya River, which runs through the middle of Bangkok as a ferry system, with one of its stops right outside our hotel, which was on that river. We took a boat often to the floating markets, which were located on that river and its tributaries, where all sorts of produce and products were sold from the boats to local people by those who lived on those boats. It was amazing to see little kids swimming off their houseboats in a muddy river containing all sorts of refuse while their parents sold fruits and vegetables from the front of the boat (their living quarters being in the rear of the boat), which was floating in a wide section of the river. All sorts of household products, baskets, and everything needed by a family were sold in these floating markets that contain more than a few hundred boats in many different sections of the river.

Thai boxing was a fascinating sport to watch with the biggest difference being that the boxers could use their feet as well, in an artful way, as difficult as kicking could be artful; and before each match, the boxer would kneel and pray for the well-being of his opponent. I was able to do all these things with my family, which made these trips memorable. The Grand Palace, where the royal family lives, has the Emerald Buddha, made from jade and is, of course, a national treasure. There are many temples—or *wats*, as the Thai people call them—and I remember one of them had the amazing immense reclining Buddha.

I never tired of seeing Bangkok and all these wonderful places and experiences. Bangkok today has the unfortunate reputation of being a city that sells only sex, and while it does sell that commodity, there is so much more to it (although it is true that tours actually go there for just that one reason: sex!) There is now, and there was then, plenty of it in a district called Patpong, where it is difficult to walk ten feet without being offered a strip club, a sex movie, or the real thing.

I was taken on my first visit to Bangkok by my agent to a huge club in which there must have been one hundred young girls sitting in the back of a huge glass wall, on different levels, with numbers on them so that you could order whoever you wanted. It wasn't a nice part of Bangkok, but probably something like it exists everywhere; but by not looking for it, you are not aware of it. I recently saw a movie about Bangkok; and now it seems the girls are dancing on a huge bar that winds throughout the premises, the current music pounding away, and you make your choice that way. Some things never change. It is an interesting world, and I am very happy to be a part of it.

There are many things that go on in New York City, about which most of us know nothing, although today there is so much more that is out in the open. But several years ago, I, who thought I knew everything about New York City, was taken out by some visiting Japanese to a couple of clubs frequented only by Japanese, which were exactly like the drinking clubs in Japan—hostesses and all! I do not think I could even find them today or even the day after I was taken there, but you can be sure that they exist! There were no signs or nameplates, but those Japanese businessmen knew exactly where to go.

On that first trip to Bangkok, we did a certain amount of business, which required import licenses; and we were lucky that everyone was able to obtain their licenses, and all the orders got shipped.

I did not sell to them at that time, but the largest retail organization (not only in Thailand but throughout Southeast Asia) was Central Department Store. Twenty years later, they had seven large department stores that were comparable, each one, to some of the finest ones we had in this country. They were new and outfitted with the latest in cabinetry and design. There were escalators, as well as elevators, and they all had cafés and soda fountains, USA style.

Each store was at least five stories high and featured upscale merchandise for the middle—and upper-income classes of the country. A good deal of the merchandise in the stores came from the United States of America, which was, at that time, the most important supplier in the world for all types of merchandise. Oddly, sheets and pillowcases (simple and plain) were in most demand from this country all over the world. They had costume jewelry from the United States, imported groceries, and even toys from Mattel that were made in the United States; but most of the clothing was made in their own factories, and it was because I later sold shirting fabrics to their own clothing factory that I became personally known to them.

A little more than twenty years later, I became their official buyer for all the purchases they made in the United States of America. They paid me a commission, and we bought for them whatever they requested and also took their buyers to the various suppliers like Wrangler and Levi's jeans when they visited this country. They would send their buyers here regularly to visit our manufacturers, and then we would attend to the shipping and invoicing of the merchandise for them. They sent me the money in advance and gave me the prices that they wanted us to invoice them. Duties in Thailand were 100 percent of the cost, so there were great savings for them when the invoices represented only 50 percent of the actual price. We also gathered together various shipments from various suppliers so that everything could be shipped as economically as possible in large quantities.

After many years of doing business with them, selling fabrics to their factories, I had become very friendly with the chairman of the company, Samrit Chirathivat; and as their current buyer in the United States was retiring, he asked me if I would take over this important job for them. The chairman was the oldest of twenty-six children that the founder had with three different wives. He was the only one who had been born at the time that his parents came from China to Bangkok. They changed their last name from a Chinese surname to a Siamese name, and twenty-five of their children were in the business.

Three of Samrit's daughters were among the buyers who visited us and who all had been educated in the United States. The remaining child of the original founder, Samrit's father, a daughter, was a doctor who lived here in the United States in Washington DC.

In addition to department stores, the family owned a television station, select boutiques, magnificent hotels, and many other enterprises of which I am not even aware.

Again, always being totally honest and having the reputation of being trustworthy (which comes with the honesty) enabled me to represent this giant international corporation. Their name and their reputation were handed over to me as I represented them, and it was a great honor and a profitable business venture to be able to represent them and say that I did. It brought even greater respect to my company as their name and their reputation were handed over to me. I will come back to Bangkok later on and speak more about my association there, but for now I flew out of Bangkok and almost landed in Karachi, Pakistan, on the first try. That description may puzzle you, but as we came in for a landing, the plane suddenly took off again before touching the ground as there was a cow on the runway, and cows are sacred in India and Pakistan; and it would have been a tragedy had we mutilated the cow or the airplane. We did land the plane on the second time around where we refueled and went on to Cairo, Egypt. We stayed there only for one day before flying onto Rome, where I was to make a connection down to Johannesburg, South Africa.

As there were about four hours between planes, I quickly grabbed a taxi and visited the Vatican for the first time. I was fascinated there, as I always am whenever I visit St. Peter's Cathedral (which I have done many times) and often just between flights with the time allowed. I did not know too much about the Vatican at that time, so I wandered around looking up at this magnificent cathedral with its incredible stained-glass windows and the historical statues. I rushed back to the airport and caught my plane about midnight, headed to the Republic of South Africa.

From Rome the first stop was in Khartoum, Sudan; and as you stepped off the plane, you could smell the air, which was unique to Africa. It was so hot that with your first step off the plane, you could not help but begin perspiring. Somehow you knew you were on a different continent, and it felt and smelled like you would imagine Sudan would be. As these trips were always so long, often-unusual amenities were offered. In Khartoum we were told that we could take a shower if we desired, and I did! After filling up the tanks with gas, the plane took off again for our next landing in a town—or maybe it was the city—called Blantyre, in the country of Malawi. I had never heard of the city, and as I landed there, it somewhat upset me because I lack knowledge about it. From Blantyre our next stop was our destination: Johannesburg.

South Africa became my second home not only for the time I spent there over the next fifty years but also for the friendships that I was lucky to have, unlike anything else that has happened to me. In South Africa I was able to use the same agents that I had met through Dan River, and they were all very good. There were three separate agencies that had a loose association, which enabled them to offer a complete coverage of the country, each one having distinct areas without everyone stepping on one another's toes.

They knew what their territories were, and they all respected that. In Johannesburg the agent was Al Pollnow; in Durban it was George James; and in Cape Town it was Barney Elterman. For a first visit, business throughout South Africa was very satisfactory; and I knew that this country was going to be a great market, seeing that their taste, which was similar to ours, how they worked, and how easy we fit, becoming my largest one ever. I spent a month in South Africa and was starting to drag quite a bit. I worked with a salesman for Pollnow Agencies whose name was Gordon Robins-Browne, who was married to Carmen; and at that time they had two daughters, Denise and Patricia, and a few years later a third daughter, Caroline.

Gordon was one of the finest gentlemen I have ever had the pleasure of meeting, knowing, and loving. He was good-looking, built nicely, and with an excellent education and background. He was almost too nice for business, although he had the qualities that I look up to in every other man. He was honest and was willing to do whatever was necessary, working hard, to accomplish what had to be done. He was a great athlete: golf, tennis, cricket, and whatever other sports they played in South Africa. We worked together and got along famously. Carmen was wonderful and one of my all-time favorite people.

For the first three years, I stayed at the Carlton Hotel in Johannesburg; but after that (for the next twenty years), whenever I was in Johannesburg, I would be sleeping at the house of Gordon and Carmen. I never knew anyone named Gordon before him, so it is very interesting that in South Africa I met two other men named Gordon, Gordon Joffe and Gordon Jones, both of whom also became close brothers to me. Aside from my own brother Stanley, these three Gordons, all from South Africa, became the most important friends I have ever had. On that trip I also met another salesman who had just joined Pollnow, a young man named Harry Caganoff, who was a personal friend of Gordon Brown and became another close friend of mine. Harry was a bachelor, and he introduced me to the younger attractions of South Africa. He took me to music concerts given by black musicians and showed me a whole different side of young liberal South Africa. Miriam Makeba was one of the featured artists and later became extremely popular in her country as well as in the United States of America.

Despite its reputation for apartheid, my South African friends were all very liberal and against the government's policies. Living in South Africa during those early years was very difficult, especially for those who opposed the Nationalist party and their apartheid laws. Once Nelson Mandela was released from jail, South Africa was soon ruled by the majority, no longer by the minority; and none of my close friends ever thought of leaving their country for political reasons, although many others did. For various reasons, Alan and Di Reichman immigrated to Australia, following their two sons and families as keeping the family together was most important to them.

From Johannesburg I flew to Durban, a one-hour flight. In Durban I worked with George James who had emigrated from London, although he actually stayed on in South Africa after being discharged from the Royal Navy and decided to settle in Durban, which at that time was the most English and liberal city in the republic. George was an outgoing, good-looking, fun-loving big, six-feet-two-inch guy who never had the money that he now earned in the agency business. He was like a little boy let loose in a candy store with no one watching. He was married and had one son and had recently bought a large expensive home and was getting involved in owning racehorses (not a good sign). However, he worked hard and was entitled to spend his money as he wanted. He was fun to be with and was very successful in business.

I visited the land of "a thousand hills" and Pietermaritzburg in Natal, of which Durban was the capital, with its very picturesque racecourse, small and set in what was almost a garden but still a full-size racecourse. The three agents represented some of the largest textile people in the world and therefore did a lot of business, which earned them all a lot of money. The Zulu people live mainly in the province of Natal, and you could see many Zulu in their colorful clothing and beads in Durban itself. The Zulu were a great warrior people with a historic background of having fought the British very bravely and actually beating them in many battles.

There were no nonstop flights from Durban to Cape Town, so we stopped in either East London or Port Elizabeth on the way down to Cape Town. They were small country airports but interesting to see. I did not spend any time in the smaller cities on this first trip, but I did go there subsequently, usually stopping one year in East London and the next year in Port Elizabeth. I always did business in these towns although they were not major sales. Actually, it was a customer in Port Elizabeth who was my one and only account that did not pay his bill. I remember the name, which was M. Bettman and Company, and they went into bankruptcy before paying for the shipment.

In East London, about five years later, a young man who worked for our Cape Town agent married a young lady from East London; and since by this time he felt very close to me, he asked me to be the master of ceremonies at his wedding, introducing the speakers and making comments as I saw fit, hopefully funny ones. His name was Nissy (Nathan) Shapiro. Both his parents had died by the time he was twenty-one, and I guess I became a father figure to him. I had gone with him several times to visit his father who was in the Groote Schuur Hospital, which later became world famous as the first hospital where a heart transplant took place, performed by a South African doctor, Christian Barnard.

Nissy was a very smart young man and an excellent young businessman who worked very hard, which is all anyone has to do. I encouraged him to go into his own business and gave him the agency for our company, which was really a good start for him. At that time we did nice business in Cape Town, and the commissions he earned from us probably paid for all his expenses. But that was many years later; and on this trip, my first visit to Cape Town, our agents were Elterman Agencies, headed by Barney. Barney was the middle one of five sons. His two older brothers arrived with their father from Lithuania, and as they went through immigration, the officer entering their name listed it as Altman. It was strange to hear one brother called Altman and the other called Elterman, but I am sure that this also happened in the United States when families arrived at different times and did not speak English well, if at all. They probably didn't even notice at the time that they had been entered with two different names, and I guess it wasn't that important since getting out of Eastern Europe, and all the pogrom that took place against the Jews, there was only one important thing: getting out.

The wholesalers and clothing manufacturers that we visited in Johannesburg were all Jewish except for three Indian wholesalers. Our customers in Durban were mainly Indian, although there were some Jewish manufacturers of shirts. The shirt manufacturing business in South Africa was very large, and many of the popular brands in the United States (Arrow, Van Heusen, and Manhattan) were licensed to South African companies who produced under those American names. The manufacturers in Johannesburg produced the most expensive garments and in Durban, the cheapest. Cape Town was somewhere in the middle, and I would think that most of my buyers in Cape Town came from Eastern Europe.

The companies in Durban owned by large Indian families were generally the largest in the country, but the prices at which they bought for usually very large quantities had to be more competitive than we generally liked to offer, or even could. However, there were certain lines that could only be bought from the United States, and on those, we were very competitive and able to do considerable business. The bulk of the business in Cape Town was with small wholesalers and large retail stores, although there were a couple of large clothing manufacturers with whom we eventually made the right connections and did excellent business. Cape Town was the steadiest of all the markets, and business was continuous. South Africa was at the heart of our business for most of the next forty-eight years, so there was good reason for the more than sixty visits I made to that country. There were many other areas that also became important from time to time, but nothing was as consistent as South Africa, even though some of the other places were occasionally more successful. I do not want to minimize their importance to my business or my life, but it was South Africa and my friends there that made the greatest impact on the wonderful life that I have had.

During that first trip to Cape Town, I worked a little bit with Barney himself but mainly with his brother Dave Altman who was very pleasant to be with. Dave was the next eldest to Barney and had not yet been very successful. He had tried being a beautician, but it did not work out for him. He had a very easy personality and was well liked. Like most South Africans, he was very generous; and about two years later, he invited me to stay in his bachelor's apartment, instead of a hotel, that he maintained in a great part of the city, right on the Atlantic Ocean. While I was there, he went back to his parents' home and stayed there. Barney was married and had a family. Dave had never been married and went out of his way to make sure I was comfortable, kept busy, and saw everything in this most beautiful of cities, Cape Town.

Dave introduced me to horseracing, which he loved, and every Saturday would take me to the races at the most picturesque of racecourses. There were three of them near Cape Town, and the race meetings, as they were called, alternated between each course. All the betting was done with bookmakers, who stood up high in stalls with a board listing the horses and the odds alongside them, for the next race. The odds were written in chalk and were constantly being erased and rewritten, depending on what money was wagered on which horse. It was fascinating to watch and much more interesting trying to get the best odds before reality caught up, and every bookmaker, by the time the race started, would essentially have the same odds.

However, you could make a bet early on at great odds before the big money came along to adjust and lower the prices; but if your horse won, you were paid on the basis of what the odds were when you placed your original bet. It was so much better than everyone receiving the exact same payoff, especially if you had gotten the better odds. It could sometimes work the other way, where the odds could go up after you placed your bet; but if you won, you were paid at the odds you received when you made your bet.

I don't think I ever missed a race day on a Saturday in all the time I spent in South Africa, and yet I very rarely went to the races in the United States. Those first few years in Cape Town, I would have lunch with Dave at his parents' house; and he would then drive me to the races, introduced me to all of his friends (mostly racing people), and I was left free to do whatever I wanted until the races were finished. Naturally, I spent a lot of the time with Dave between the races, but I also developed friendships with people on the course as "the Yank," which was a novelty for them. Dave was not romantically involved with anyone, which was great for me also, as I wasn't the "extra person"; and we spent a lot of time together.

He later met, and was apparently quite serious with, a lovely young lady, Joan; but sadly nothing developed further. Although it certainly appeared that they would get married as they were very happy together, but I am sure her religion (she was not Jewish) acted as an impediment, especially in South Africa; but these things usually can be worked out. In this case, they were not. After work, the three of us would often go for drinks and snacks at a café called the Waldorf where they actually had live music from 5:00 p.m. to 7:00 p.m., and every young working person seemed to show up there.

Dave's most important customer was a shirt manufacturer called Coronet, and he spent a good deal of his time at that factory and was rewarded with most of its business. I was also a beneficiary of the attention he gave to them. Unfortunately, the owner of that business died at an early age of a heart attack, and the widow, Queenie, knew nothing about the business but was left with the factory. She had a young daughter, and Dave was very helpful to her since he had known that business very well. It wasn't too long after that, at Queenie's request, that Dave took over the running of the business and the running of Queenie's life as well. They married, and for their honeymoon, they drove from Cape Town to Johannesburg, a distance of a little more than one thousand miles.

They waited to leave until I had finished all my business on that trip. In fact, they had waited to get married until I had arrived in Cape Town! I was in the car with them on their honeymoon trip. We passed through the karoo, which was a large desert, on the route north. We made a stop in Kimberley, which was famous for its diamond mines, whose diamonds were so easily dug up out of the ground. All this happened, of course, several years later, but I mention it now so you can understand another of the relationships that I had.

After his marriage, on my subsequent trips, Dave would pick me up in his Rolls-Royce. He was now successful. He no longer was working for his brother, he had his own business, but our friendship continued. However, there no longer was a bachelor pad, and I was back to a hotel.

The first visit to South Africa was quite an eye-opener, even though I had seen so many different and exciting parts of life before that. Johannesburg was on a high plateau at an elevation of about seven thousand feet above sea level and was a big city, often referred to as the New York of Africa, but that was only by the people who lived in Africa. The capital of South Africa was Pretoria, about a one-hour drive from Johannesburg. Pretoria was a total Afrikaner city and the center of its most political and government offices, where Cape Town, as the legislative center, was where its parliament met.

Johannesburg, with its large Jewish population, was much more liberal than Pretoria. Durban was on the Indian Ocean and, as I mentioned earlier, was very English and also very liberal. The Indians, who were the largest group other than the native Zulu population, while allowed many more economic freedoms than blacks, were victims of the apartheid laws as well, as they were in the category of *nonwhite*. (Japanese were considered *white* for business reasons.) The Indians were not allowed to go to "white" restaurants or stay in "white hotels" or even go to the "white" beaches. They had separate beaches assigned to each color group. The cruelty and absurdity of apartheid, I think, reaches its height when a child could not cross an imaginary line in the sand to go in the water a few feet to the left or right. I can remember very clearly how upset Muriel became when she saw a police officer telling a young black child that it could not play in "that" sand but had to move five feet over.

I was entertained by Indian customers in Durban but only in their own houses, which was probably more interesting and comfortable than another hotel dining room. It was so wonderful when I was able to walk into a restaurant in later years with an Indian friend or couple, of which I had many. Cape Town did not have much of a black population at that time, although the "nonwhites" were the coloreds, who were various combinations of white, Malay, and the Dutch. Much Afrikaner blood was mixed in there as well.

Actually, there were no blacks in any of the cities as they were forced to live outside of town in what were called townships where the conditions were simply awful. Even those who were successful businessmen, or professionals such as doctors and lawyers, could not live outside the townships if they were black. There were no black businesses outside those townships. So aside from the domestic help who had to carry their passes with them and generally lived in small houses or shacks outside the main house, you could not come into contact with 90 percent of the people who lived in the country.

We started off doing some nice business in Cape Town, and it continued to grow throughout the years. Nissy Shapiro worked as an office boy for Elterman Agencies; but it was very obvious even then, when he was sixteen, that he would eventually have his own business, and I am very proud that I was able to help that come about. He always had questions for me, and although I was only eleven years older than he, he always looked up to me like the father he never really had.

I had spent a full month in South Africa, but it was time well spent, both financially and socially; and the very many trips made thereafter were all successful, and the closest friendships in our life were developed there. Adding up all the days I spent in South Africa comes to a little over five years of my life!

Onward to the Rest of Africa

When I first arrived in Johannesburg, it was one week before Rosh Hashanah. After getting along so famously in the first few days with Gordon and Carmen, we decided we could spend time together and have some fun over the Jewish holidays. That year they happened to fall on a Monday and Tuesday; so we packed up and left early Friday afternoon (which was always an early day in South Africa), got into their car, and headed to Lourenco Marques, in Portuguese East Africa (it is now called Maputo).

The Polana Hotel in Lourenco Marques was well-known to the world travelers as a great vacation spot and the place where South Africans could act like normal human beings and not be subject to apartheid laws. The food there was fabulous, as I generally have found Portuguese food all over to be (including Long Island), and it was a long day's drive down to the Indian Ocean coast where we were headed. We took a little bit more time and drove through the exciting Kruger National Park, which was on the route down to Lourenco Marques.

It was my first time in Kruger; and I was simply blown away by the animals, the jungle, the desert with the lakes, and the people. Of course, the huge attraction is the animals, and we were not disappointed. It was an exciting trip, and we slept at a lodge in the park and simply enjoyed the day. Portuguese East Africa was also a revelation after the rather staid Republic of South Africa where the movie theaters could not even open on Sundays.

It was a playground where the races mixed and seemed to party all night. The hotel was great, and the five days we spent together, in close quarters, provided a very solid foundation once Muriel met them for a wonderful lifetime friendship.

Although my original plans were to fly home from South Africa, Lou Fisher requested that I stop off in the Belgian Congo and Liberia, which were actual regular Pan Am stops on the flight home, for a few days in each place. I know that these business trips were very expensive, and you have to maximize your time along with the cost of the plane trip; but this request was a little unreasonable since Muriel was pregnant and due the latter half of November. This was the very first day of November; and since I was an employee, being well paid, and I was ten thousand miles away, I flew directly to Leopoldville from Johannesburg.

From the air it was startling to see what looked like a little village in the middle of the jungle with nothing else within sight. From the ground that is exactly what it was. Even though the city of Leopoldville was well-known, it was essentially one long street, with the jungle starting and ending at each end. The Belgian Congo was the private property of the king of Belgium, but while it wasn't known at the time, the people there were mistreated and used. Private homes were spread out somewhat and occupied mainly by Belgians. The native Congolese lived in nearby villages and serviced the town.

We had no agent in Leopoldville, so I had to call on customers on my own. I do not remember what the hotel was like, but without too many people visiting the Belgian Congo, it could not have been very special. We did have names of customers, and Lou Fisher knew several of them. He seemed to know people all over the world; and it always surprised me how well they remembered him from what, I am sure, were sometimes only brief encounters. It seemed to me that he always stored every single person in his mind, thinking that some time in the future he was going to do business with them.

It was rather easy to put myself in touch with the merchants since it was essentially one street, and easy to find every possible buyer. The customers in Leopoldville were mostly Belgian Jews, Sephardic, and business there was very good. They were very hospitable to me as they rarely had the opportunity of entertaining anyone. When they wanted to speak about a pattern or a price of something that I was showing them and obviously did not want me to know what they were saying, they would speak in a Sephardic language spoken only by the Sephardic people called Ladino.

It was a little embarrassing to me because I understood every word they said that I was not supposed to hear since the language was very similar to Spanish. The Sephardic Jew originated in Spain and Portugal, and during the Inquisition, many left that country and traveled toward the Middle East. I had to tell them that I understood what they were saying as I understood Ladino, and I think they really appreciated my honesty as I could've easily kept quiet and used it to my advantage.

I think in the end it worked out better for me this way. I remember the nicest and most important customer there, whose name was Leon Hasson. His younger brother, Ari, worked for him, and they were extremely successful and wealthy. Their business was called Au Chic. They were both in their early forties; and if you wanted, in those days, to live dangerously (and I mean dangerous parts of Africa), it was almost guaranteed that you would be successful financially. Your family wasn't always with you, or you with them, but the business was guaranteed. Other parts of Africa, that while colonies of European nations, with Algeria and Morocco on the Northwest Coast, Rhodesia, just north of South Africa belonging to Great Britain, as well as Ghana and all the other countries on the West Coast. The French colonies, like the Ivory Coast and Morocco, were generally the safest as France accepted all the local people as French citizens and was certainly the best in their treatment of the people, allowing them to come to France for their education and freely enter the country.

The other colonies eventually revolted or were so threatening that they received their freedom and are independent today. Many of the French colonies decided to stay aligned with France, and although they may be independent today, they depend on France for their protection and economic well-being. France was great that way all over the world, wherever it had a colony, and the people reacted accordingly. In the Belgian Congo, every time there was a hint of unrest, the women and children of the Belgians would immediately flee to Europe; and it did not seem to me, even on that first trip when the families were all there, that it was a safe place to be.

There was always an undercurrent that existed throughout West Africa, as well as Central Africa, although I never felt personally threatened or endangered. Maybe again, I was just too naive; but I often made friends with the local people, in addition to my customers. I always felt comfortable having a drink with them and spending time, whenever I could. The local people were, of course, the most interesting part of their country, not the ones who came to colonize and take advantage.

The proof of my success in that field was Tanzania and also Uganda, both of which were extremely rewarding to me, particularly after they received their freedom and the local people were running their own countries and favoring me with their business. Native Africans were extremely important to the development of my business.

I flew to Monrovia in Liberia after three days in Leopoldville, where I was also on my own without an agent. Liberia had been settled by former American slaves who returned to their country once they were freed after the Civil War. The main business in Liberia was owned by Firestone who had thousands of square miles planted with rubber trees from which they tapped and obtained the pure rubber. When you left the grounds of Firestone, the rest of Liberia was not very attractive. It was difficult getting around, and the roads into the town from the airport were not in good condition. The airport was about sixty miles from town, and no transportation was available when I arrived; but I was lucky to hitch a ride in the back of a small pickup truck, and I'm sure my back has never been the same again after those sixty miles of bouncing on a dirt road.

I did business in Monrovia as I had done in Leopoldville, and as I have said many times before, I am sure that being the first textile salesman to visit there was the main reason for the wonderful reception I received in both cities. The hotel was just awful, but in three days, I was back at the airport and on a plane to the United States. We stopped in the Azores to refuel before arriving home to my two girls and my son, who was about to be born in a little over two weeks. It was a very happy time arriving home after such a long time away; but in hindsight, despite all the loneliness and suffering we all endured, it turned out to be a good decision to make that trip, which provided the basis for the future of our lives.

On November 24, 1954, we became a family of four, and the thrills of that day I can still feel today as I write about it. Richard arrived on Thanksgiving Eve, and it was our first Thanksgiving as a complete family, and we certainly had a lot to give thanks for then and for all the years that followed. Everything was very good and remained that way for all our lives, even up to today. There have been a couple of hiccups along the way, which every family experiences, but again I must say it has been a wonderful life.

I was only home a little over a month and a half, and it was time again to start a Central American trip. I had not traveled in 1953 while I worked for Dan River or made this trip in 1954, but with my first stop, it felt like I had not skipped a beat. I started off in San Jose, Costa Rica, to my usual success, and then on to Panama; this time I went to Trinidad before Venezuela where I did some nice business, all subject to customers obtaining licenses. From Trinidad I flew to Georgetown, British Guyana, where I arrived at the same time as the new salesman from Gulfstar who, of course, was working with the same agents.

We worked with a different salesman from the same office, and I outsold them by a large margin, which was doubly satisfying. Visiting Georgetown was never a pleasant trip as the hotels were awful with food to match. I would always read a great deal on my trips and finish many books, wherever I was, and Georgetown was the best place for this. There were no direct flights to Venezuela, so I returned to Trinidad for a day and happily learned that they had received licenses for the business I had done the previous week.

I would really work the agents very hard during the time that we had, and I am sure they were happy when I would leave but would probably be even happier when they received commission checks to cover the nice orders we had taken.

From Trinidad I went on to Caracas, and the new Tamanaco Hotel on top of a hill overlooking the city was absolutely beautiful. Since the Pan American flight was not until the next day from Trinidad, I had taken a local airline, and we had made six different stops before arriving at Maiquetia. Needless to say, it was good to see Georg again and work with him. From there, I went on to Maracaibo.

New hotels were being built all over the region, except for Georgetown, and it made traveling now that much easier and more pleasant. It had become much more difficult being away from my family and having my children growing up without me being there all the time, but I have no doubt that every business has its own drawbacks, and we felt that our lives were steadily improving. Business in Venezuela was okay; as I have been away for two years, the customers would have to get used to us again. My next stop was Aruba before going on to the Dominican Republic and Haiti. The trip had been successful, and I arrived home on the day of our fifth anniversary, February 12, 1955. It was so great being together again. All these exact dates had been stamped in my passport.

However, my job was traveling too much it seemed, and a month later in March (after receiving a cable from other friends of Lou Fisher in Tahiti), it was decided that I would take a trip to the South Sea Islands of the Pacific Ocean. Tahiti, whose capital was Papeete, was one of the islands of a large group, French Oceana or French Polynesia. Some of the other island groups in that area were the Cook Islands, Tonga, the Solomon Islands, the Marshall Islands, as well as several other groups. Tahiti is due south of the Hawaiian Islands. Tahiti had received licenses from France, of which it was a possession, allowing it to purchase $55,000 worth of textiles from the United States.

Bertrand and Josephine de Marigny, who were the friends that sent us the cable informing us of the issuance of the licenses, owned one of the five companies who had received their share of these licenses about $11,000 each. The five companies were owned by Frenchmen, originally born in France and later settled in Tahiti to keep up the French presence in that area. This would not be considered a large amount of money today, but in 1955 it was a good amount for our business, and it was worth the trip for me to take to see if I could obtain orders for the entire amount.

As we were the only American company willing to travel that far, it was pretty certain that I would get it all. The owners of the stores, to whom the Frenchmen allotted their licenses, were all Chinese. Although the overwhelming portion of the residents was Polynesian throughout the Pacific, in Tahiti, of course, they were Tahitian. The Tahitians themselves were not really interested in business as they enjoyed an easy, relaxing life on their island in ideal weather all the time. Unfortunately, this all changed when jet planes came into service in the late 1960s, and tourists everywhere wanted to visit every part of the world that could now be reached easily by jet; and Tahiti was one of the most renowned, exotic, and beautiful destinations.

At that time in 1955, the only way to get to Tahiti was by seaplane or on a freighter carrying cargo to the various islands, making as many stops as possible to make it a profitable trip for the steamship company, so they were usually very long trips. Cruise ships were not yet popular, or available, and the freight ships rarely carried passengers. Sailing leisurely in the Pacific, for obvious long periods of time, was not a luxury that many people could afford. If the freight ship did have accommodations to carry passengers, they were limited to twelve; otherwise (according to the maritime laws), a doctor was required to be on board. For twelve or less passengers, a nurse would be sufficient, and she could also perform other duties on board.

There was generally not that much business to do in Tahiti, so regular business trips were not worthwhile. There was no manufacturing there, but the island and the entire area was appealing for its beauty and completely laid-back atmosphere; and Tahitians, being brought up in that atmosphere, appreciated it and took advantage of all the natural bounties of the sea and the lush vegetation that grew there.

Breadfruit, which was grown on trees, was a staple of the diet and grew in great amounts on its own and, of course, was free. I am sorry that I cannot describe it better, but breadfruit was shaped like an avocado, same color with a bread-type consistency. Anyone could take a breadfruit from a tree and eat it. I did not find the taste appealing, but I'm sure if I had been brought up on it, I would have been very happy with it. And then there were all the fish in the stream, which seemed to be limitless and probably was. At that time the famous book (which was made into a movie, plus two remakes of the original movie *Mutiny on the Bounty*), written by two authors named Nordhoff and Hall, told of the urge in the 1700s by the British to get breadfruit trees and plant them in their other colonies so that it would be cheap and easy to feed all the local people throughout their empire. The *HMS Bounty* was the name of the English ship, whose captain was Mr. Bligh, and the officer who led the mutiny because of the cruel treatment and irrational actions of the captain was Fletcher Christian. It was a true story of a real event. The authors of that book also wrote several others that took place in that area, and they were all quite interesting and very well written. Clark Gable portrayed Fletcher Christian in the original, and Marlon Brando had the role in the remake.

Tahitians had it all and therefore were willing to leave the small retail businesses, as well as other menial jobs that had to be performed, to the Chinese immigrants who came there. Whatever little was imported was brought in by the French, and Tahiti was regarded as the true paradise of its time. Unfortunately, over time the sailors brought in diseases and other problems. In 1955, though, it was one of those trips of a lifetime.

It was something that I remember today, almost as if it had just happened last week, and it was one of those great experiences, tremendous for me. I mentioned earlier that you could go to Tahiti by seaplane, which was serviced by New Zealand Airways, who flew a double-decker aircraft. Frenchmen, artists, scientists studying the Pacific, and its peoples did visit but certainly not a businessman looking to sell. I was once again probably the first to visit Tahiti with actual textile samples. Pan American Airways flew across the Pacific at that time, from Los Angeles to Honolulu, Hawaii, on its first leg of its round-the-world flight. I made a connection there to a side flight of Pan Am, from Honolulu to Pago Pago in American Samoa. Pan American was known as the flag carrier for the United States and the only American Airline flying around the world. It was up to them to provide service to every American area outside of the United States, even though they were not always commercially profitable as I am sure the flight to Pago Pago was not, but I was on that flight. And what a thrill it was to be there. Pan American Airways would carry the mail from the United States to all the U.S. possessions, so it did get some remuneration from the government. Very few people had ever spent much time in the South Pacific at that time, except for the navy, or on the freight ships, which also carried provisions, mail and all the necessities, to all the islands from all over the world.

We arrived in Pago Pago (which is pronounced as if it were spelled "pango pango") in the afternoon, and those people going on to Apia (in Western Samoa, which belongs to the British) as I was caught a flight on a small plane to the city of Apia, which is where the TEAL seaplane would leave from. We arrived about 8:00 p.m., and it was a short bus ride to a very old-fashioned village with a lot of huts (our motel), where we were able to change our clothes and take showers. We then had dinner and were treated to some Samoan hula dancers who performed for us. The Polynesian hula is danced at a much faster pace, with a much quicker drumbeat. At midnight they drove us all to the double-decked seaplane, on which there were about twenty passengers on each level. It was surprisingly very comfortable and spacious. We always had access to our baggage and were advised to keep a change of clothing near the top.

The plane had been readied and gassed up by hand, and at 2:00 a.m. we were ready for takeoff. We had been told beforehand that we would be making a stop to refuel at seven in the morning at a small uninhabited atoll in the Cook Islands, which belonged to New Zealand, the owner of the airline. The atoll was called Aitutaki. I was seated next to a very good-looking and interesting Frenchman, Guy Theron, about thirty-five years old; and it was an extremely pleasant and informative trip, talking to him for the next twelve to thirteen hours. It turned out that he was the publisher of a magazine in France called *Paris Match*, which is still popular today as one of the leading magazines of Europe. He was, at that time, the boyfriend (for lack of a better word) of Francoise Sagan, a young woman who had written a world best-seller called *Bonjour Tristesse* (*Hello Sadness*).

Before we left Apia, the airline had advised us to leave out of our overnight bag a bathing suit, as we would be landing in a lagoon with a beautiful white sandy beach where we could swim and have breakfast during the two hours it would take to refuel the plane by hand pump. This little island was uninhabited, and Polynesians from the nearby islands would row over with fresh fruit and juices and other breakfast foods for us while the plane was being serviced. (I never found out why they used an uninhabited island.)

Soon we were again ready to take off at 9:00 a.m. for Papeete, the capital city of Tahiti. The flight was pleasant and very comfortable, and after being served lunch on board, we landed in another lagoon at about 3:00 p.m. Six hours seems to be close to the limit for flights at that time, and the Pacific was so vast that numerous stops had to be made on any long journey. Even going across the Atlantic Ocean, it was hardly possible to fly a much longer distance than those five to six hours, depending on the winds.

It is certainly amazing to consider that Charles Lindbergh flew from Long Island to Paris, nonstop, in 1927. But, of course, his single-engine plane with him in it alone was loaded with an awful lot of gasoline, and it was the first time it had been done. As larger planes and stronger engines were built, and especially the jet plane that we all take for granted today, of course, the distances covered became larger as well.

We landed in this lagoon of Papeete and disembarked from the plane by getting out of the door onto the wing and then were helped down to a motorboat, which took us to shore. We climbed up steps to the pier and started walking toward the custom shed where we would pick up our luggage and my samples. As I walked alongside Guy, I saw in front of us, about one hundred feet away, a very beautiful young Tahitian lady running directly toward me. I had been very happily married a little bit more than five years at this time and was hoping that Lou's French friends and our agents were not being too hospitable, according to all that I had read about the hospitality and the South Pacific and the absolute openness of the local people. But here she came, running directly toward me. I do not remember at this time if I was happy or sad; but when she came to about ten feet in front of me, she made a sharp right turn, jumping into Guy's arms. Well, of course, she was there for him and no one else but him, and she was the reason he was coming to Tahiti this time, and he had never mentioned her in the previous fourteen hours; but she was an absolute beauty. I later found out that they had used Tiare (that was her name) on all posters and advertisements about Tahiti and, in fact, for the entire South Pacific. For me, my welcoming committee was Bertrand and Josephine, a good-looking young French couple. After a brief hello, as they also knew Guy and Tiare, and then an all-too-quick good-bye, the three of us—my agents, of course, and me—drove into town.

The accommodations were not very good as there were rarely visitors in need of a hotel coming to Tahiti. It was a square concrete building called the Hotel Tahiti, and the rooms were rather basic; but I had my own bathroom, and the mattress was comfortable. After a quick dinner, we said good-bye and made arrangements for them to pick me up the next morning. I unpacked my clothing and went to bed; it had been a very long day.

The next morning, after breakfast, Bertrand picked me up, and we drove to his office. I was going to work with a different agent each day who would bring in their customers: the Chinese owners of the retail stores. That first morning he called in five of them, showed them the groups of samples that we had laid out, and allotted to each of them a different amount that they would be able to purchase. They would have to pay him a commission, as we also did, for the license was really a gift from the French government who wanted to keep that French presence in Polynesia and tried to make their countrymen comfortable. Bertrand allotted the amount, depending on his experience with each one.

The merchants quickly went through the samples, made their selections, and the $11,000 was taken up in a little over an hour; and we were finished even before lunch. We had a very leisurely lunch in an informal restaurant on the water. I had realized immediately that it wasn't even necessary for me to be there with the agent to record these sales; and so the next morning, when I went to our next agent Tracqui et Fils, I explained to Pierre Tracqui that all the prices were marked on the samples and he could call in his customers so that they could make their selections, place their orders, and I would be back again in the afternoon to pick up my samples and go over the orders with him. We had the same arrangement with all five agents regarding commissions; and I would wait until the customers came in, greet them, and then leave to return that afternoon.

Tracqui et Fils was also the agent for Vespa scooters, which were made and shipped from Italy. Before I left that morning, I asked if I could possibly rent a scooter for the next twelve days, and he graciously offered to give me his as they did not rent them. Not wanting him to feel insulted, I quickly graciously accepted his kind offer. Only a rather short set of instructions and explanation was necessary, and I was on my way to explore Tahiti on my scooter. I could not believe my good fortune, but like everything else that has happened to me, it was all good luck and a great adventure. I repeated the same routine with the three other agents and their customers for the next three days and was able to receive orders for the entire allotment of $55,000 that was available.

Pierre turned out to be another of the wonderful people that I met on my travels, and his offer of his Vespa added to my wonderful life and stay in Tahiti. The Vespa was the most popular means of transportation throughout Europe, as well as most places in the world at that time and probably still today, as long as there was no more than two people involved; and so I was freely able to get around the city, which was quite small, as well as explore the entire island of Tahiti.

If you are not familiar with the Vespa, while I call it a scooter, it would be best described as a smaller, slower, and safer version of a motorcycle. However, it was a legitimate vehicle; and while it was not allowed on the highways of New York at that time, it could be driven through the streets; and it did require a motor vehicle registration, a license, and of course, *insurance*.

I rode over every road and visited every corner of the island. I was always by myself, but I made many friends almost every time I stopped to see the view or to have some lunch. There were no other tourists that I saw, so it was mainly with local Tahitians that these friendships developed. In the evenings I would usually be invited out by the Frenchmen, our agents with their wives, for dinner and sometimes afterward to a local bar. When I wasn't seeing them, I usually had an invitation from the locals to join them in their evening activities, which usually ended up at the local bar.

The French painter Gauguin had gone to Tahiti on a trip—for what I am not sure—when he was of middle age, I think about forty. After being on the island for a relatively short time and living among the wonderful people there, he decided to abandon everything he had in France, including his family, and live the rest of his life in Tahiti, among the Tahitians, where he eventually acquired a new family. There is a museum there where he lived, from which you can imagine the simple life he enjoyed, as well as many paintings that he did while he lived in Tahiti. Most of his paintings today are spread throughout the world, in museums and wealthy homes; but there were quite a bit at his home in Tahiti, and that is the kind of art that I truly love (impressionism), although all the art of that time and the artists appeal to me very much. On my very first day of traveling around the island, I met some Tahitians my own age at the museum, and they invited me to have a drink that evening with them and listen to Tahitian music.

There were no real restaurants in Tahiti, and when I wasn't invited out to dinner, I would usually eat alone at a luncheonette-type place where I would have an omelet each evening along with French-fried potatoes. This one particular place was owned by a French man, and soft popular music was always in the background. My taste for food was not very sophisticated at this time. The Tahitians ate whatever they could get from the land and the sea, but I was not yet ready to make that commitment.

I arranged to meet my new friends that first night after meeting them at the museum, at the most popular local meeting place that existed in Papeete. It was called Quinn's Tahitian Hut. It was much larger than a hut, and I would best describe it as a huge barroom.

It had a very large rectangular bar in the middle with tables and chairs, as well as couches and large pillows along the walls. There was entertainment going on all the time, and it consisted of the Tahitians themselves who would jump on the different parts of the bar and, accompanied by Tahitian music played on drums by the local people, would do their hula dances. As I mentioned earlier, the Tahitian hula dance was much faster than its Hawaiian relative and very animated. It was a very noisy bar, catering mainly to the local people, as well as some sailors off ships, and some of the French people who lived there.

My new friends, actually two couples my age, were very protective of me. My friends made sure that I was looked after; and if any Tahitians approached, asking me for a drink, they simply told them that I was with them and was not to be disturbed. That sounds rather formal as I write it now, but it was in a much more relaxed way than it was said and done. It seems that all over the world local people at bars can spot a stranger immediately and are never bashful to ask for a drink. We would sit and talk and drink, as different quality hula dancers would jump on the bar and do their thing, as every night was "amateur night."

It was the local law in Papeete that within the city limits everything had to be closed by midnight. As it got close to midnight and I mentioned that I was going back to my hotel, my friends advised me that we were now going to pile into different expanded jeeps, somewhat like the ones I had seen in Manila, although not nearly as big or garishly decorated, and would be going on to a similar place that was outside the city limits and could stay open until dawn. It sounded like the thing to do. As the evening grew later, the noise grew louder, and the drumbeating got faster, along with the hula. The jeeps drove us to our next stop, which was called Lafayette, and due to the extra alcohol in everyone, it seemed that the noise and drumbeating knew what they had to do. The décor was a little bit more natural, and less comfortable, which was not very important at this hour.

In those years Tahiti was spoken of as the utopia of the world, and from my overall experience, on that first trip there, I would have to say that it was. It was a wonderful week although very empty and lonely when the night ended.

On the Saturday of my first week there, I had lunch with Bertrand and Josephine and was invited to join them and friends of theirs for a visit the next day to the beach and lunch again with them. We were going to visit and spend some time with my friend from the plane Guy and the young lady Tiare, which meant "flower" in Tahitian, who had greeted him so enthusiastically upon our arrival. They picked me up before noon on Sunday, the next day, and we drove to a most beautiful black-sand beach. The black sand was the finest volcanic ash, and it was on this very private beach that Guy had rented a house for him and Tiare.

I had never seen a setting as beautiful as that part of Tahiti, with the island of Moorea directly in front, several miles away. I asked Bertrand if he could find me a little house on some part of a beach, black sand if possible, for the next week that I would have to spend in Tahiti without any business to do since my plane was not due in until the following Sunday and I was, therefore, "forced" to spend that next week on the island. After lunch on the beach, consisting of barbecued fish that had just been caught, breadfruit, and other vegetables, locally grown, and after answering at least one hundred questions about the United States and particularly about New York, we all decided to go for a swim.

We all went into the water and swam out to a safe distance, just beyond where the waves would break as they came to shore. As we floated there, bobbing with the tide, without warning a huge series of waves, some of them at least twenty-five feet high, rolled in just about on the line where we were all swimming and drove, I believe, all of us (certainly me) down to the bottom of the area of the sea that we were in. I truly thought that at best I would be badly hurt and I was forcefully pushed under, and in my mind, I almost gave up. I raised my hands above my head and luckily floated upward to the surface, only to be hit again by another huge wave. It probably was only a few seconds, but it seemed like a lifetime. Luckily, the second wave, while pushing me down again, also pushed me in the direction of the shore.

Our entire group had been just about wasted in a few moments by the fierce action of the ocean. Although the eleven of us were originally spread about thirty or forty *feet* wide, we wound up being separated by about thirty or forty *yards*, all of us lying exhausted on the beach from our experience. After taking the headcount to be sure that all eleven of us were there, we discovered that one of the men had a broken leg and one of the Tahitian girls, in great pain, had two broken ribs, while the rest of us were very much shaken up as the ocean tossed us around like little toothpicks. Despite the bad experience, I still wanted to rent a house on the black-sand beach, and the next day they found one for me. The furnishings were nothing to speak of, but it was on the black-sand beach and definitely an improvement on the hotel in town. Along with my Vespa, I was able to "endure" the next week. I felt sad and found that with Muriel not being there with me, along with Donna and Richard, it made the time away from them a little bit more difficult, especially since I was in this idyllic place. Not every place was like Tahiti, but even there it was lonely without them, and I knew that they were just as lonely at home without me.

I had gone to college and graduated with a BA degree in romance languages; but if you did not have a profession such as doctor, lawyer, or accountant, you had to do whatever it took, like traveling alone, to be able to accomplish something in the business world. I knew that, Muriel knew that, and since we had started our married life without any money but thrilled to have each other, we were both willing to sacrifice; and I don't ever want to minimize that sacrifice. As I write about all my adventures, I never forget how much of a huge sacrifice it was for her, and me, to be apart as much as we were. Muriel had the additional job of keeping things together at home and seeing that the children were happy, which she did better than anyone could have done, which gave me the peace of mind to make me a better businessman and a more successful one, since she did all the extras that allowed me to concentrate on business and develop a reputation that was the cornerstone of our success.

The rest of my stay in Tahiti for the following week was just as pleasant and exciting as the first week. I managed to see my Tahitian friends and my French friends and made sure not to go out very far into the ocean. I drove all over the island on my Vespa, came home, went in for a quick swim, and would write a letter to my family every day, even though I could not mail it. Only certain freight ships carried mail, so it was going to be easier to mail a package of all these letters when I reached Hawaii. Many nights I went back to Quinn's and Lafayette with friends, but by now, the time was starting to go slowly because I had very little to do.

During that week in Tahiti, however, I did have the good fortune to visit the island of Moorea, whose mountain peaks one could see so clearly from Papeete and especially from the house that Guy had rented. The peaks loom high and dark, and though they are very impressive to look at, the island itself had a couple of small villages and seemed to be untouched. In that last week I also made arrangements with Pierre Tracqui to buy a Vespa from them and pick it up at the New York distributor for Vespa. This was April, and it was due to arrive in New York during the late summer about three months later, which was just fine with me.

I also learned that Johnny Wanamaker—the young main heir to the Wanamaker fortune, which included many different holdings and especially some large important department stores in New York and Philadelphia—had taken a trip around the world immediately after graduating from college. This was a gift from his family and was not an uncommon occurrence with families of means, when a son graduated from university. Tahiti was one of his stops, and he, of course, met the beautiful young Tiare—yes, the same one who was spending time with my French companion Guy. Johnny immediately fell in love, which was rather easy to understand, but what wasn't easy was that he proceeded to marry Tiare in Tahiti. The Wanamakers were a very conservative, old-line, wealthy family from Philadelphia; and Johnny's mother ruled it with a very strong hand. You can imagine how shocked she was when her twenty-two-year-old son came back from his around-the-world trip with a wife and, although very beautiful, was not of the color that she would have imagined. It was a very beautiful copper color, but the Wanamakers wanted white, white, white. The sad end to the story for the young couple was that the marriage was annulled. Tiare received a very nice settlement and was literally sent home to Tahiti. I do not know who Johnny eventually married, but she could not have been a nicer person than the Tiare that I met.

I came back to town on Saturday to check in with the airline and make sure that everything was okay for the next day's departure. Guess what? It was not all okay. I was informed by the airline personnel that the plane was not going to arrive the next day as it was being serviced in dry dock, back in New Zealand, and would not be coming back for another two weeks on its regular schedule. I, of course, panicked as it was impossible for me to stay for an additional two weeks in Tahiti, even though it was *Tahiti*.

Unable to make a telephone call or even mail what was now a huge letter that I had been writing (which would soon be as big as a book), I asked if there was any way possible for me to get off Tahiti and head back to the rest of civilization. A private plane? A private yacht? Anything that could help me? I was told that there was one possibility, and that was a Danish steamship that was coming through on Sunday, the next day, and leaving Monday. However, no one knew if they could accommodate passengers, or even if there was room if they did, and there was the problem of the maritime laws regarding doctors and nurses and the limits of twelve passengers, if they were allowed.

I anxiously awaited the arrival of the steamship the next morning. I was there as the boat pulled in and gleefully found out that they did have passengers and there was one empty small cabin as someone had not shown up when the ship left California. I was very lucky to be able to board the boat; and the other eleven passengers, the crew, the officers, and me left the next day after some warm and sincere good-byes to everyone I had met in Tahiti, plus a few tears. I, of course, did not know if I would ever be able to show Tahiti to Muriel, and I wanted to take her there more than anywhere else in the world.

We sailed at midmorning on Monday from Tahiti, and we were headed to the Tonga Islands. The island we were going to with some cargo was Tongatapu, whose capital was Nuku'alofa and was west of Tahiti on a straight line through Aitutaki and the Cook Islands, and then just slightly south into Tonga, just on the other side of the International Date Line. As you cross the International Date Line, the time remains the same, but the day goes forward to the next day. The freighter was going to drop off a load of lumber in Tonga for the Mormon Church, which I was discovering was very active proselytizing throughout the islands of the South Pacific.

It did not help my anxiety of being away so long to lose another day, and frankly I didn't even know what day it was. If you went around in a circle and crossed the dateline several times, you could gain a day, then lose that day, etc, etc. We arrived outside of Nuku'alofa on Wednesday afternoon, local time, about 4:30 p.m. I am sure of the time as the ship required a local steamship pilot to lead it into the harbor. Most all the islands in the South Pacific are surrounded by coral reef, and without an experienced person who knew how to navigate into shore, it could be very dangerous as the ship's bottom could be easily destroyed on the reef. In this instance, however, the pilot had gone off duty. Even though I am sure he knew we were arriving, his tour finished at 4:00 p.m., and he probably had a date for a drink or some other very important thing to do in Tonga. We would have to wait until the next day to be brought in through the opening in the coral reef. Unfortunately, the next day was Holy Thursday, then Good Friday, followed by Easter Saturday, Easter Sunday, and Easter Monday, which is celebrated in Great Britain and all its possessions. Tonga was a possession of Great Britain and therefore celebrated the same official holidays.

Nearly a week later, on Tuesday morning, the pilot came on duty very well rested and brought our ship into the shore. We had been anchored outside of Nuku'alofa for five days. However, while we were there, we had a motorboat available to everyone that took us to shore every day. Many stayed on board, but I chose to go on to the island each day and learn as much as I could about Tonga and its people and the way they lived. Most of the officers of the ship's crew also went into Tonga, and some evenings we even slept on the island.

We became friendly with very many people, including the royal family of Tonga. Queen Salote was a six-feet-tall lady and became well-known throughout the world during the inauguration of Queen Elizabeth when she would appear at many of the functions wearing huge hats, which made her seem even taller. The houses in Tonga, as in most of the islands in the South Pacific that I visited, did not have any sidewalls. There was a thatched roof, which was generally held up by huge trunks of palm trees at each corner so that the breezes could blow through easily. Of course there, was very little privacy, but the breezes were obviously more important to the people.

Family, love, family. All one big family, all one big love. Children are the most important part of their culture, and every child was loved dearly. They considered themselves one huge extended family and sometimes raised other islander children as their own. If one family, for example, had all girls and the next family had all boys, they very easily could exchange children to balance out the mixture in a family, of course, with the child's permission. The children, of course, knew who their birth parents were and which were the parents that raised them. They were all loved equally, and it was wonderful and amazing to me to see how these people could live together.

You were always welcome in their home, and they were willing to share everything they had in addition to adopting one another's children. If a child was born out of wedlock, that child was never embarrassed or looked upon as anything less than every other child, as there were always others, with or without children, who were willing to take another baby into their family as their own without going through the formality of adoption. The baby was then part of that family. You could see this and feel that by just being with the people and have it confirmed when their customs were explained to you. It was such an honor to be taken into their homes and practically be made a part of their family. Life was a lot easier then, and I hope it remained essentially the same through the years for them.

Though it was difficult, traveling away from my own family at that time, I quickly gained a great benefit of being able to spend time with other peoples and cultures and learn from them. I often have tried to apply some of the things that I saw to my own life.

The food on Tonga was similar to the food on Tahiti as nature supplied it all. We, the crew and I, and sometimes some other adventurous passengers, were invited several nights to have dinner with some Tonganese families. Of course, we accepted, and they were always interesting experiences.

When we slept on the island, they provided us with mats that were placed on the ground, and the sky was our cover. When we were on board, some of the crew members actually fished over the end of the boat for sharks, especially when we were out on the ocean. There were always a number of games of darts, at which I became quite proficient. We went to church on Easter Sunday and generally became Tongan for five days. It is hard to believe that I had this opportunity so early in my life.

It only took about three or four hours of work to unload the lumber for the new Mormon Church, and so on Tuesday before 4:00 p.m., we left Nuku'alofa and Tonga for our next stop. On board the ship, there was a small swimming pool, but I don't think it was large enough for all twelve passengers to go in at one time. The eleven other passengers were all friends of Ronald Reagan, from California; and although he was not yet governor, he was, of course, well-known and was starting to make noises in politics. His initial fame came from being a well-liked actor and a spokesman for General Electric on television. At one point he was a Democrat and was president of the actors union, which makes his conversion to being the idol of all the real conservatives in this country almost difficult to believe.

All the passengers on board ate at two large roundtables together with the captain and the officer crew, along with the nurse. The food was very good as the ship was Danish, and the smorgasbord was excellent. I, of course, continued to write my letter every day. I still didn't know how I was going to use the Vespa I had ordered, but I was really carried away with my use of it in Tahiti. Except for the valuable time that was wasted, the trip on board the boat was delightful, though uneventful.

After Tonga, our next stop was Suva in the Fiji Islands, a short distance northwest of Tonga, where we again dropped off cargo and continued on our trip to Pago Pago, American Samoa, arriving on a Saturday, two weeks after we left Tahiti. The boat trip took the same time as if I had waited for the airplane, if it actually came on the new promised date. The flight leaving American Samoa, back to Honolulu, was only once a week and was the return trip of the flight that I had taken down, one month earlier on Pan American.

We had one customer in Pago Pago, and due to the plane's schedule and my late arrival for the connection, it was not going to be possible to take my samples to his store. From the boat I had made arrangements with him to meet me when we docked so that I could see him and talk to him. He was there with his wife, and as we drove to the airport after leaving the boat to make my flight, he and I sat in the back of the car going through the samples as his wife drove. He made his selections, and unbelievably, I had another order.

Naturally, the clothing worn by both men and women in all the Pacific Islands was very colorful and the designs unique to that area. I made sure to bring back many of the very special patterns that were very popular there as I was sure they would also sell in the Caribbean and other markets as well. We eventually incorporated all those designs and colors into a regular line of "island prints." Throughout the Pacific, especially in Hawaii, these prints were called pareu designs; and the women wore them as sarongs, wrapping the fabric around their body and tucked in at the top, while the men wore the same patterns for their shirts. Of course, these are all very common today, but in the fifties you never saw that type of clothing unless you were in the South Pacific.

When I introduced these designs to the Caribbean islands, I was known as the "hot shirt" man. Honolulu was due north of Pago Pago (Pango Pango), and the flight again was almost six hours. I spent three days in Honolulu working with an agent, Bill Nelson, who had formerly lived in California many years before, and together we did some good business. I stayed at the Moana Hotel, which was one of the very famous hotels on Waikiki Beach. The most famous one at that time was the Royal Hawaiian, which was very formal in its dress code and its much older guests. It was a very elegant hotel, but I think I was better and happier at the Moana. Hawaii was wonderful.

During my stay in Tahiti, and on the Danish freighter, I continued to write home every day. By the time I arrived in American Samoa, there were about 270 handwritten pages, which my customer there promised to mail for me. I, of course, was able to speak to Muriel from Honolulu and explain more fully to her what had happened, although she was kept as up-to-date as my office was by the cables that I was able to send.

It was unbelievably lonely not being able to speak to her for a full month, for both of us, and I can almost remember that pain today. As always, she was very supportive and encouraging, and she wanted to make sure that I would not worry while I was away. I could not have done any of these things without my wonderful wife and her belief in me.

As I speak of all these places that I have visited, I am talking about things that happened fifty years ago, and I am sure that today nothing resembles what I saw or did except maybe the black-sand beach. The world changes all the time, but it is wonderful to think back and be thankful for all the opportunities that were given to me to enjoy and remember what they were like then.

From Tahiti to Japan

Leaving Honolulu again on Pan Am, we headed west, stopping at Midway Island and Wake Island to refuel at each stop. Midway Island was just east of the International Date Line, and Wake Island was just across that line. As you head west, it becomes earlier with each time zone being one hour, and the time zones were each fifteen degrees. Of course, you cannot simply keep on getting earlier, which is why they set up this International Date Line. So, as I mentioned earlier, as you cross that line, it becomes the corresponding moment of the following day. I find all this extremely interesting, although, of course, nothing actually changes, just the date, but to think of how somebody worked this out in their mind and got the rest of the world to accept what was very different in thinking, but very simple and obvious.

After Wake Island we landed in Guam, where I had been the year before. It was on these three islands (Midway, Wake, and Guam) that memorable battles were fought with the Japanese on the islands, as well as the Japanese Navy in the Pacific Ocean in that area. The United States was, of course, victorious in all these historic battles, but many Americans and Japanese had died there; and now some sixty years later, as the two countries are very large trading partners, it seems like a lot of young wonderful lives were wasted. But that is true for every war. They should make the older generals and the older politicians who declare war do the fighting and let all the young people live their lives.

My accommodations on Guam were still in a Quonset hut, which had been left over by the U.S. Navy. It was a metal structure, built like a half a circle, and was very easy to erect. Many movies were made about World War II and the battles in the Pacific, and as I watched them, it always occurred to me that I was actually there. It was now more than ten years later, and a lot safer, but not very much had changed.

I again did nice business with Jones and Guerrero and then flew to Tokyo where I was going to visit the army PXs (post exchanges), which were like today's Wal-Mart. There was still a huge contingent of army soldiers and their families living on U.S. army bases in Japan, and still do today; and shopping for American products was made easy for these people at the PX, which were the huge stores that had been established for this purpose. They carried everything from peanuts to furniture and appliances.

I was not too successful as I learned that most of the buying for the stores was done in the United States, but I did have one very amazing experience in Tokyo, Japan, on that trip.

There are two rituals that were always followed for business visitors. One was that you were taken to a Japanese steakhouse where you enjoyed probably the best steak in the world called kobe beef. It's from cows that received very special treatment, being fed beer with their meals and receiving a massage every day so that the fat was spread throughout the meat. The meat is known to be well marbleized and was unbelievably tender. I did not try it, but I'm sure you could cut the beef with your fork. I used a knife.

The other absolute ritual for visitors, since the only visitors at that time were businessmen, was that you would be taken to a club where you were assigned a geisha girl in a traditional kimono; and she would serve you a drink and offer a hot towel, which was very relaxing. But don't get too used to it because the girls were changed every twenty minutes, so there would not be any misunderstanding regarding the purpose and the relationship with these young ladies. Obviously, you could not get too familiar with any particular girl since very few of them even spoke English, although I am sure that there were other more friendly-type clubs as well somewhere in Tokyo. Since you couldn't communicate, except through some hand signals, one of the most popular pastimes was playing jacks, the old-fashioned little girl's game.

Japanese men, although they like to drink, cannot hold their liquor very well; and before nodding off to sleep as they often did, they would sing quite loudly very old-fashioned songs as they thought the people in Texas probably did. I later learned on subsequent trips—and there were many subsequent trips to Japan—that many of the important Japanese businessmen, high executives in the company that was usually a multibillion-dollar trading company, had very serious relationships with a lot of these young club women, keeping them for the very little extra time that they seem to have.

The first two women who sat with me could not speak a word of English. Amazingly, the third geisha girl spoke very good English, and this third young lady I learned as we spoke was *Jewish*.

Her parents had come from Europe, many years before, along with their parents. She did not look very Jewish, or what I thought was Jewish looking, but dressed in the traditional kimono; and with the makeup in a Japanese club, it would never have occurred to me that she was anything but a different-looking Japanese girl. She invited me to visit her home to meet her parents on the following Friday night, as they too observed Shabbat, and she said they would be thrilled to meet an American Jewish visitor; but as I was leaving the next day, I could not continue my Jewish-Japanese experience. She was so happy to meet another Jewish person, aside from the small community of which she was a part of. And it was an amazing twenty minutes, but only twenty minutes. The rules are the rules, even for Jewish businessmen with Jewish geishas.

The Japanese people have always been a great mystery to me. One of my closest friends, and most important business client, Yuichi Kashiwada, of Kampala, Uganda, and Tokyo, Japan, is Japanese. Yet when it would ever come up in conversation, he would always say, "No, I am African, not Japanese." This seems to be a total inferiority complex from a people who are extremely abrasive, overbearing, and even bullying.

People from the United States acquired the description of being an ugly American, but in the Far East, the Japanese are disliked by almost everyone. Their personal hygiene, their personal possessions, their personal living space are immaculate; yet among the dirtiest public places that I have seen are the floors of a movie theater, if a large group of Japanese have attended a screening. The floors are littered with the skins of fruit that have been peeled, papers, candy wrappers with half-eaten candies—whatever garbage you can think of—because the public place is not their home, which they religiously cherish. Of all the places in the world that I have visited, I have never been invited to a Japanese home. They are usually extremely small spaces, and as recent as forty years ago, the Japanese would put down a tatami mat in the tiny living room at night, and that became their bed and bedroom. This is an economy that is second or third in the world, so I do not think it is a question of money but something that I somehow cannot work out in my own mind. They spend a fortune of money on making electronics, on building better machines to build better products, on providing themselves with the best quality of everything they produce; yet so much of what they do is unexplainable and very difficult to understand.

The waitresses and waiters in the new international hotels are told to immediately pour a cup of coffee at breakfast time. I do not drink coffee. I have never drunk coffee. But there is no way that I could ever get away with not having my cup filled with coffee. I would say, "No thanks." I would try to explain that I do not drink coffee, but as soon as I turned my attention away from the cup, it got filled with coffee. It was almost like a game of who was going to win. They always won.

The Japanese love to play games. They spend hours in "pachinko parlors," an old-fashioned game arcade, although I am sure they have all been updated electronically by now; but hearing that constant clicking and seeing grown men in their business suits and ties, sitting and playing, was always mind-boggling.

After a while you stop trying to figure it out and just accept it; that's just how the Japanese are. They have silly childish games that the hostesses play with the customers at very expensive and exclusive bars and nightclubs. They play jacks! They play "paper, rocks, and scissors"! Paper is represented by an open hand, and that beats the closed fist of rocks (it covers it) but loses to two separated fingers, which looks like a pair of scissors. The scissors beats the paper, which it can cut.

These are games that children played sixty or seventy years ago, and the Japanese were entertaining their overseas guests with these same games. At the end of the evening at 11:00 p.m. you can see a line of at least one hundred taxicabs in the nightclub area, waiting for their customers to be led out of the clubs and into the taxis to be taken home, either asleep or drunk. These were the bosses! I don't know who it was, who first thought that part of a good massage was to have someone walk on your back, digging in with their toes or heels; but you can imagine the surprise you would feel when someone would get up and walk on you, and that was part of every Japanese massage.

The cost of living in Japan has always been extremely expensive, and there didn't seem to me any sense as to what was being spent or how it was spent. From the lowest-paying jobs to the highest, no one seemed to know or care what the cost was. You simply watched in wonder as all these contradicting things took place. When you are presented with a bill at an upscale restaurant or nightclub, it is given to you folded over so that all you can see is the total and the place for you to sign. It would be highly insulting if you wanted to check the bill, or even look at it, and everyone seemed to accept this.

I never could figure out the purpose or direction that they wanted to take, and it wasn't only that I didn't understand the language. After awhile you simply said, "Well, that is the Japanese way!" It was very nice to be entertained where nothing counted and nothing mattered, but it really was very confusing to me. The Japanese could be absolutely perfect in so many things that they did and then so very childish in all the others.

The subway was the most modern in the world and also the most crowded. They would have these big strong guys who would stand by the open doors of the subway cars and literally *push* as many people as they could into the cars. These were the employees of the subway system! As the economy in Japan improved and more of the Japanese wanted to travel overseas, the government held classes to teach the people how to behave in foreign lands. I honestly remember that one of the courses involved instructions that you were not to run around in the hallways in only your underwear. I swear this is true, and I had seen many Japanese walking in their underwear!

I think I stopped questioning everything when someone started to explain the Yakuza to me. The Yakuza was the equivalent of the Japanese mafia. They kept order in the neighborhoods, controlled the crime, killed who they wanted to, and collected taxes and protection costs from the local people. I found it incredible how this was all accepted and explained to me. Without the Yakuza there would be chaos, so it was important to have a good Yakuza. There was no point in asking any of the questions.

I flew home from Japan as the extra two weeks that I lost in Tahiti were making the trip last far too long. I explained this to Lou Fisher and asked for his permission to come home. He said he understood my feelings completely, and I returned from my extended Pacific trip.

The mid-1950s:
Africa, Asia, and Hardship

For the rest of 1955 and then into 1956 and 1957, I continued to travel quite a lot. At this time I was no longer going to Latin America as the markets in Africa and the Far East were much larger and more important to us. Lou Fisher had hired another young man, John Cageao, to cover Central America and the Caribbean. John's father had been in business with clients from Central America for many years, especially Santiago Crespo of Costa Rica, although Santiago worked directly with me. John was a gentleman and a good guy. Central America had become routine by now, so it was easy for John to step right in.

My trips during this period to Asia and Africa were, of course, very long, both in distance and duration. Each trip was better than the one before as I traveled back to Manila and Hong Kong; and the markets of Singapore, Malaysia, and Thailand were also developing nicely. In Africa, the better that I did, the more places that Lou Fisher wanted me to visit.

The trips, however, were becoming a great burden both physically and mentally on my family and me. I would start out in the Far East, spending time in every market, and then travel to Europe to make a connection on my way down to South Africa and other countries in West Africa. While business was good, there were too many dark clouds looming ahead. Traveling in Africa in the late 1950s was difficult physically and mentally, and there were so many problems. Even to put a telephone call through to the United States, you had to book one in advance (sometimes as early as twenty-four hours ahead), and of course, the time the call came through was never the time the call was booked. My children were growing, and I was losing my edge and was not always happy and thrilled as I had been in the past.

Lou Fisher, my boss, was also under a great deal of pressure. His wife, Esther, was very ill, and he had two young children with whom he should have been spending more time with. But as the business got bigger, he enjoyed the role of being a big buyer and often would buy too much, which would put the pressure on the sales as we could not deliver in the same fashion as the business had originally developed, mainly of giving people excellent and diverse assortments.

The success had truly gone to his head, and as good as he was (and certainly he was great to me), he became very difficult and would not listen to any advice or complaints from customers. Since his purchases now were larger than ever, they were also more uneven, and so deliveries to our customers started to become uneven and not as honest as we had been in the past. Lou Fisher's father owned two textile stores on the Texas border with Mexico: one in Laredo and the other in McAllen. Lou had two sisters, and the father had given a store to each of the son-in-laws; and Lou was the buyer in New York for the stores, which was, of course, the center of the textile wholesale business. In 1957 Lou's father passed away, and as his desire had been to be buried in Israel, Lou took the body there and saw that he had the proper Orthodox funeral that he wanted in the Holy Land.

However, Lou's buying habits, even for those stores, were becoming so erratic that his two brothers-in-law informed him that they no longer wanted him to buy for them and they would travel to New York at different times to do their own buying. This was a terrible blow to Lou Fisher, and added to his other personal problems, he became even more difficult and even irrational at times, which started to worry me.

The "look" that we were selling was something new to the areas of Asia and Africa, and so we were very popular, plus the fact that I was selling myself to the customers and promising that the orders would be looked at very carefully. Unfortunately, I was traveling a great deal and most times had no control over the shipments, and I started receiving more and more complaints as I returned to those places for additional business. It took a little time for all this to catch up with us, but when it did, there were many unhappy clients. I remember how upset I was and was starting to regret having to face my previously enthusiastic customers who I had been forewarned by the agents had many complaints and were unhappy with previous shipments.

I knew we had problems that were only going to worsen as Lou did not recognize that he simply could not ship what *he* thought was best rather than what the customer wanted, which I clearly wrote on the order. He actually convinced himself that he was doing better for the customers that way, and I knew by early 1958 that this wonderful run that we were having was going to come to an end unhappily. This did not have to happen except that my boss was losing his sense of reality and hurting his own business.

All my traveling over the past three years had been mainly in Asia and Africa, and since it took so long for merchandise to arrive, there were not too many early signs. In any event, I continued to travel during the previous three years, building what I thought was a very solid base and making many friends along the way. Hong Kong, Singapore, Thailand, and South Africa became the most important markets of the business; and the quantities we were selling were huge. My relationships with our customers were terrific, as they were very pleased with the original shipments and felt they could trust me forever. Unfortunately, I was not being backed up as I was originally. Before the real difficulties started, it was all a wonderful experience, and there were *many* wonderful ones.

One of the most exciting experiences for me was in the fall of 1956. With the permission of my wife, I think, I was allowed to also love Marilyn Monroe. I don't think I was very unique in this, as probably most every man in the world was in love with Marilyn Monroe, including the soon-to-be president of the United States John F. Kennedy (as well as his brother Bobby). On this particular evening in October or November 1956, I was returning home from one of my trips. I was flying on Pan American Airways, which stopped in Shannon on the west coast of Ireland to refuel before flying on to the United States. I think I knew every crew member of the airline (pilots, copilots, engineers, and cabin crew) as with all my flying I had the chance to fly with almost every one of them.

Pan Am used to fly to South Africa once a week (a very long flight), and then the crew would have one week off in South Africa before flying back. The flights took thirty-seven hours—New York to Johannesburg, with stops in Lisbon, the Azores, Monrovia, Lagos, and Leopoldville—before finally reaching Johannesburg. The crews usually changed in Monrovia, about halfway, with a fresh crew taking over. My friendships in South Africa by now were very strong, and I introduced many of the crew members on the various flights to my wonderful friends in South Africa who always were the best of hosts and looked after the Pan Am people very well. They made arrangements for short safari trips and, in general, kept them busy during their week in South Africa. The Pan Am people were very appreciative and, whenever possible, took very special care of me on their airplanes. I would sometimes even wait an extra day for a Pan Am flight if they were not flying on the day I wanted because I knew that they would look after me, and with the flights being so long, every extra comfort and convenience was important. At that time all passengers flew first-class; but later on (even before the jets were introduced and different classes were a part of regular flying), I never left New York without being upgraded to first-class, even though my ticket was economy, and the same courtesies were extended to my wife. If the flight was going to be full, the special services of the airline would call and ask if I could delay myself one day so that Muriel and I could be upgraded to first-class.

Marilyn Monroe had just completed filming *The Prince and the Showgirl* with Sir Lawrence Olivier in England and was returning home on the same flight as me! She had gotten off the plane, along with her husband Arthur Miller (the famous playwright), to do some shopping at the duty-free airport in Shannon, just like other humans; and the airport there was by far the most beautiful and extensive duty-free shop in the world.

My great relationship with Pan Am even extended to its photographers, whose job at every important airport was to get a picture of the Pan Am plane in the background along with the important people, statesmen, as well as celebrities, who would be boarding that particular flight. I prevailed upon the Irish photographer, whom I had brought various presents on each trip of hard-to-get items such as chocolates and nylon stockings over the previous few years, and asked him to take a picture of me as I walked alongside of Marilyn so that it might have the appearance that she was with me, and that is exactly how it all came out!

He sent the pictures to me in New York, and they were fantastic, and it did appear that she and I were walking together, and her husband Arthur was a few steps farther back with the packages. When I received the photos in New York the following week, no one could believe that it was me and her! In fact, Lou Fisher pasted the pictures in the windows of our storefront with a huge sign reading OUR ALVIN, and many strangers came into the store, literally asking to meet "Alvin" and to shake my hand. It was a great laugh. What most people did not know was that the stewardesses had asked me, once we were on the plane, if I would like to meet Marilyn Monroe. And guess what? I said yes! Marilyn was traveling in a separate compartment in the forward part of the plane, and even though the entire plane was first-class, she had a private area with her husband and hairdresser. My friends in the flight crew brought me up front and introduced me as one of Pan American's more important accounts. Being that close to her was very special, and she was every bit as beautiful as you could ever imagine, the most beautiful person I have ever seen.

During April 1956, I had also spent a lot of time in the Far East on a very successful trip before flying all the way across to Europe; and on this trip I made stops in Frankfurt, Dublin, London, and Lisbon before heading down to the Belgian Congo and South Africa.

Later in September, I basically repeated the same trip, leaving out the European part but included some countries in West Africa. The year 1957 was a replay of 1956, except that there were more complaints, and I knew that I would have to make some kind of a move as I did not think that I could convince Lou Fisher that he was doing anything wrong. It was his business, and I was an employee.

I had to explain what was happening because the agents were getting very upset and wanted to resign, so on an informal basis, I discussed with some of them the possibility of their working with me, if I were to do this on my own. The responses were always favorable, and by June 1958, I told Lou Fisher that I could not do the traveling anymore; and since I realized that this was the most important part of his business, I would resign. I offered to stay at least three months to give him time to replace me or make whatever plans he wanted. He, of course, was not very pleased with my decision, but there really wasn't very much else that could be done since I was determined that I could no longer travel for him (although I blamed it on the pressure of traveling).

Leaving Fisher: A New Path, 1958

I knew that Lou Fisher would be hurt by my decision to leave, and I did not believe that he would simply allow me to go into my own business. I therefore did not tell him of my plans, but before leaving at the end of September, I had already started the foundation for my own business. I had interviewed with a large textile converter, A. Steinham & Company, and was able to convince them that I could run their export department without spending a full day with them each day. I would then be able to start my own business and get it running while earning something from Steinham, to whom I planned on devoting about three hours each day, sending samples and taking care of the mail from overseas. I would then have the rest of the day to visit other suppliers and prepare samples to send to my overseas friends.

When other people in the area downtown by Fisher Fabrics heard that I was leaving him, they approached me as to what my plans would be and asked if I would like to run their export department on my own. Jack Abrams Incorporated, the next-door neighbor, was an important one; and Marty Rieber and Dave Falk of that firm became very good friends, and we did a lot of business together, shipping exactly what I sold.

I felt pretty confident that things would work out once I got past the initial wrath of Lou Fisher, who had been extremely good to me, but yet I knew he would try to prevent me from going into my own business. Immediately after leaving, I sent a cable to Tahiti asking Bertrand and Josephine de Marigny if they would be willing to work with me if I made a trip there within the next two weeks. I knew they would advise Lou immediately, which was the purpose of my cable because I intended to go to South Africa where I had been asked to come by both agents and customers, who wanted to be the first to buy from me in my new business. That feeling existed in all the places I had been and simply reinforced my belief that honesty was the only path to follow—always. Just as I had believed the De Marignys would, they advised Lou Fisher that I was making a trip to Tahiti, and he immediately made plans to get there either at the same time as I did or even before me if possible. (I still had friends advising me from within Fisher Fabrics.) He felt it would be easy to mentally overpower me and make sure that I did no business. I, of course, had no intention of going to Tahiti at that time.

I left for South Africa and had a wonderful initial first trip in my own business. I never intended to leave Fisher Fabrics or had the burning desire to be in my own business, but I always felt that I was forced into the situation by my employer's actions. He had always treated me extremely well, and I was unhappy to make the decision I felt I had to make when I gave him my notice. By the time he found out that I was not going to Tahiti but had actually gone to South Africa, he finished up in Tahiti and left as soon as he could (which was not that easy, as you might recall!) for South Africa. Fortunately, by the time he arrived, I was finished with my trip and, with good sales, was on my way home to take care of the orders. I do not remember what happened to Lou Fisher's business, but he started to neglect it; and with all his personal problems, he had a very hard time.

He was the best boss anyone could have, and I will always remember him that way.

Marty Rieber and Dave Falk were both very helpful in getting me started. They knew what I could do, and they supported and vouched for me, as did others, with merchandise and credit to buy it. I made sure that the various suppliers shipped exactly what I had sold, and I was soon able to recapture the customers I had been so close to losing.

Late Fifties and Sixties: A New Era

On East Fifty-fourth Street near Third Avenue was the bar and cocktail lounge known as Stella's. Every time we had a visitor from overseas, you can be sure that some time during the evening we had to make a stop at Stella's.

They did not serve dinner, and I'm not sure if they served any food except for maybe the pretzels or the nuts at the bar. We went there quite often in the late fifties and early sixties, as it was a great, fun place. It was noisy, always crowded; and while the drinks were no different than any other bar, this one had Stella, and no one else did. Stella was quite a character, and I am sure not to everyone's taste. She was a grandmother, probably in her mid—to late fifties, who had started out at a speakeasy during Prohibition and worked in burlesque afterward before opening her own bar. Her language was as raw as it could be, and every four-letter word in existence was in her vocabulary, and she used them all in normal conversation. If Stella knew you, she greeted you with a warm smile, and you went to the bar or cocktail table in a normal way. However, if she did not know you, a greeting would consist of either baring her breast and offering it to you or grabbing you in the most surprising part of your body. Seriously, she did exactly what I state here, as the idea was to shock; and that is exactly what happened every time, as you can easily imagine. People who had never seen her before and who she, of course, did not know could not have been more shocked. As you entered the bar, usually with a smiling face because of the noise and obvious festivities, your mouth was soon wide open from the total surprise of being grabbed. It was all in fun, and everyone laughed uproariously, except maybe the "grabbee."

I remember many times taking friends for a drink after dinner, and I am sure that forty years later every one of them remembered the experience. On one occasion, before leaving on a business trip, I noticed a huge sign above the bar, inviting everyone to come to Stella's birthday, which was to come about two weeks later. I left on my trip a few days later, to Africa, and from every stop I made, I sent her a birthday card or postcard wishing her a happy birthday and merely signing it "Love, Alvin Futterman," She, of course, did not know my name and wouldn't know who I was, though she did know my face, and I was only grabbed once!

When these cards started coming in from so many different countries with funny-sounding names from West Africa, I knew it would puzzle her, and I would have loved to have seen her expressions; but I got my reward upon my return a month later. We dropped in at the bar for a drink after dinner; and Stella, as usual, was at the door, greeting people. I walked up to her and said, "I am Alvin Futterman." She stared at me for a moment and then screamed "You son of a bitch, you are Alvin Futterman. You drove me crazy, but I love you, you bastard." She then took me by my hand; dragged me to the bar; and then, throughout the cocktail lounge, screamed all the way, "This is Alvin Futterman. This is the guy that drove me crazy with birthday wishes from all over f—ing Africa, but I love him, the bastard!" Knowing her personality, I could imagine how she was, receiving all these cards (about ten of them) and not knowing the person who was sending them to her. Every subsequent visit to that bar was like a homecoming party.

Another very interesting restaurant at about the same time was one called Nicholson's. Unless you knew about it, it would be very hard to find as it was located in the shadow of the Fifty-ninth Street bridge, just before you make a turn to get onto the upper roadway. It was furnished in a strange Hollywood-type way, with large chandeliers and dark spaces.

The food was very good; however, if the owner did not feel like working that night, he simply didn't open the restaurant, even if he had reservations. Sometimes you would call for a reservation and be told that the restaurant was full and then just at the last moment turn up and find that it was practically empty. The whole operation was very strange, and even though the food was excellent and fairly expensive, everyone who went would rave about it; but the owner was simply too eccentric to have a successful business. I think it could have been full every night if he put his mind to it, but he obviously had different interests. There were very many interesting restaurants, bars, and meeting places in New York at that time; and the greatest thing about it is that almost anyone who was working, at any job, could at sometime celebrate an occasion and be able to afford it.

After the 1939-1940 New York World's Fair, there was a mad desire for top-scale French restaurants. The big hit of the fair, regarding food, was a French restaurant called Le Pavillon. Its owner was a man by the name of Henri Soule, who became legendary and was known as the father of all the great French restaurants that followed, as many of the new ones were owned by people who apprenticed at Le Pavillon. Although we had only recently been married and did not have that much money for entertainment, we were able to go to that restaurant and enjoy it along with the top society people of New York.

Everything seemed to be affordable, just as long as you did not overdo it. Today a working-class couple cannot afford to go to the finest restaurants in New York City. Some of the wonderful classical French restaurants that followed were La Caravelle, La Cote Basque, and our favorite Le Grenouille. Maybe the most outstanding was Lutece, whose chef was Andre Soltner. The Four Seasons was an exceptional American restaurant during this fancy French time, as well as Windows on the World on top of the World Trade Center where Muriel and I had taken our grandsons, Evan and Matthew, just two days before 9/11. We discussed that day how difficult it would be to get to the street from the top in case of an emergency. Maxwell's Plum was a wild young meet-your-bride bar and restaurant with a totally new and out-of-this-world design and was owned by Warner LeRoy, who later rebuilt the fabulous restaurant in Central Park, Tavern on the Green. It was a dressier time, and it would be rare to see someone in any of these places without a jacket and tie. It didn't mean that they were any less relaxed, or cool, but such rules were stricter then.

We went to the very ritzy Le Cirque, as well-known for its celebrities as its excellent food; we went to places like El Morocco and the Stork

Club, which catered to the very wealthy, chic, and exclusive crowds; and we also entertained at Sammy's Romanian Restaurant, on the Lower East Side, which featured Jewish music and Jewish food, along with chicken fat for the mashed potatoes, the largest Romanian tenderloin steak you have ever seen (oversized for the plate), and egg creams to finish it all off. There was no greater heart-attack food in New York, as all that fat surely had to stick to your arteries. The egg cream was a New York invention that had no eggs or any cream. They simply put a bottle of seltzer (soda water that was made in that bottle), a bottle of chocolate syrup, and some milk on the table and let you mix them all together into one of the most delicious drinks ever invented, along with the martini and the Manhattan.

The non-Jewish visitors, especially our friends and customers from Ireland, enjoyed the visit to Sammy's more than any other fancy place we took them. It was truly a dive, down about six or seven steps from the sidewalk, in an awful neighborhood; but the atmosphere and the food were truly great fun. It was Donna's choice for her sixteenth birthday; and when we planned on having Richard's twenty-first birthday at the Harvard Club, he insisted that it be at Sammy's, and it was a fabulous party, and the food tasted great! Probably our favorite restaurant at that time was a small reasonably priced French bistro, Le Veau D'or, on East Sixtieth Street near Bloomingdale's, and we tried to eat there regularly.

The 1940s, 1950s, and 1960s were the golden age of entertainment in New York and its surroundings. The six or seven leading movie theaters in the Times Square area not only showed the top new releases of movies, but they also had stage shows between the showing of the films, with the stage shows being the real attraction. The first film would start about 10:00 a.m.; followed by a live stage show at about noon, which lasted about one and a half hours; followed by the reshowing of the film and the repeat of the stage show. The film was shown usually about five times per day and the stage shows four times. The stage show consisted usually of one of the big bands such as Tommy Dorsey or Les Brown or Glenn Miller, Artie Shaw, Vaughn Monroe, and even the great Benny Goodman—oh, there were so many, and the sound was so great! The bands usually had featured singers. Frank Sinatra and Jo Stafford sang with Tommy Dorsey's band before they went on their own to become the huge attractions. Particularly Sinatra, probably the biggest entertainment name ever at that time. Doris Day was with Les Brown, Glenn Miller featured Tex Beneke and the Modernaires, and Bob Eberle and Helen O'Connell sang with Jimmy Dorsey's group.

The bands usually consisted of about twenty musicians, and you could sit through as many showings as you wanted, as it was continuous; and the theater was not emptied for cleaning or for any other reason, so you could bring your lunch and sit through the films in order to get to see the live entertainers. In addition to the bands, the stage show always had a name comedian and tap dancers or magicians and every other assortment of entertainment. They were the best and the brightest available at that time, and they were all excellent. Dean Martin and Jerry Lewis, as big an act as there ever was, played the Capitol Theater. Frank Sinatra always played at the Paramount Theater, and the lines of screaming young bobbysoxers was legendary. Other stars appeared at the Roxy and the Strand Theater. Of course, the incomparable five-thousand-seat movie theater in Rockefeller Center, Radio City Music Hall, had its special Easter and Christmas shows, as well as its other spectaculars, throughout the year in addition to the Rockettes (a precision-tap-dancing, high-kicking group of about fifty beautiful young ladies) and always one of the top movie films of the time.

I do not think the admission price was $1; it was probably much less. Other theaters, which could not afford to show live entertainment, would show a second film, usually of equal importance. The Catskill Mountains, as I mentioned earlier, also had every important act in the country; and there was not a single comedian who did not perfect his act "playing the Borscht Belt," as the Jewish-influenced Catskill Mountains was known.

Stand-up comics, although not called by that name at that time, included people like Phil Foster, Henny Youngman, Jack E. Leonard, Buddy Hackett, Red Buttons, and Alan King, all of whom were typical Catskills-type comics. Then other different comedians, some more cerebral like my favorite Mort Sahl, would carry that day's newspaper on stage and, just referring to the day's events, do an entire routine with his very wise comments. Zany Jonathan Winters and brilliant Mike Nichols and Elaine May.

I have not named half of the stars of the time because there were so many—Bill Cosby and, of course, the brilliant Woody Allen, still as strong as ever. Television was just in its infancy, and not many people had a TV set in the early 1950s, but you could see it all in person at a movie theater. It was also during these years that nightclubs came into fashion, again with entertainers.

Today everything is in Las Vegas, but then everything was in New York. The Latin Quarter, with its spectacular costumes and shows, was easily affordable for dinner and dancing. The Copacabana was the in place for the best-known singers and comedians in the country. Billy Rose's Diamond Horseshoe was a pretty good imitation of the Latin Quarter. Fifty-second Street between Fifth and Sixth Avenues had at least twenty-five different jazz clubs. When you think of it now, it is almost overwhelming as what was available to even an average person as Muriel and I were able to enjoy all this. Even the hotels had name acts in their dining rooms and nightclubs, and the number one band in the country, Glenn Miller, appeared at the nightclub on the roof of the Pennsylvania Hotel across the street from Penn Station. Overwhelming!

Not everybody wanted all this "show business," but if you did—and we did—you could have it all. In 1960 a fairly unknown local entertainer by the name of Chubby Checkers came out with a song called "The Twist" that changed the way people danced. Up until then, you danced together with your arms joined with your partner's; now for the first time, you danced by yourself, even with a partner, but no touching as you introduced your own "moves" to the infectious music. A very popular nightclub opened in New York City called the Peppermint Lounge, and for the first time, you had to know someone to enter or wait outside patiently for someone to leave to make room for you to get in. It did not have the glamour of the previous nightclubs, but it sure was popular with the young people of the time.

As the music increased in volume and speed, drugs and pills (uppers and downers) were introduced for the first time in large numbers. I am sure that they were always available, but it wasn't such an open business as it became. That probably culminated in the immense success of Studio 54, which had been the theater on West Fifty-fourth Street and became the center of wild sex, unlimited drugs of all kinds, and nonstop dancing and drinking. It was an absolute "must" for every celebrity visiting New York to make a visit to Studio 54. It was an incredible scene compared to the rather tame nightlife that had preceded it. The owners of Studio 54 became multimillionaires, probably as much for the drugs as the success of that club; but New York had definitely begun to change, in many ways, along with its dance habits.

You don't realize these things are happening as you are living inside it, but forty years later, it is so obvious what changes took place and when and how it happened. The type of club that was now opening was trying to emulate Studio 54. Many private clubs with membership lists started to spring up. New York was slowly losing its place at the top of the live-entertainment world to television, which was free, to Las Vegas, which could also be free as long as you could gamble for hours, and to the Caribbean, where every island seemed to have its own casino and you could jet-set all over the world easily at no tremendous cost. But that live entertainment in intimate clubs and hotel rooms, holding at most two hundred people, was, for the most part, lost.

I was thirty-one years old, it was 1958, and I was in my own business. I did not expect to have my own company so early in life, but circumstances seemed to bring everything about much more quickly, and I was forced to make the move. With the encouragement of my friends from overseas, especially in South Africa, I was able to start off running, and the business got going immediately. My friend Gordon Robins-Browne had left his company to start his own business in Johannesburg, and I, of course, immediately appointed him as my agent for that area. Elterman Agencies in Cape Town and George James in Durban both left Fisher Fabrics to work with me as well. The customers in South Africa knew only my name from all my visits and were quite happy to turn over to me the type of business that we had done in the past, as well as any new items that I could introduce.

It was very encouraging to get the support of everyone, and now I had to go about building a business. I did not have enough money to start my own office, so I used the room we had built in the basement and had outfitted it as an office. However, it wasn't businesslike enough or confidence building to have mail, cables, and phone calls coming to my house; so I hired a service where I had a post office box number in New York City, as well as an address there with a New York City telephone number, and used the name "Donna Shipping" as my cable address. I took the train into New York every morning, checked my post office box for mail, called the telephone service to see if there were any messages, and then spent most of the day visiting suppliers and friends and staying aware of everything that was happening in the textile market.

Every day I spent at least two to three hours at A. Steinham & Company looking after their export department, sending out samples to overseas agents, and doing whatever had to be done since they were paying me a salary, plus a commission on what I sold. During the day, I also picked up samples from old and new suppliers and took them home where I would relabel them with my own names and a sticker with my new name of "Futterman Fabrics." Bettye Friedman used to work for me, part-time, as they lived on the same street and her children were in school, so she had the time and loved the work. Before going into the city in the morning, I would leave work for her, telling her what I needed and then send it out the next day.

Everything began working out well, and the business started to build up with each passing day. I had wanted Frank X. Maya, my fellow worker at Dan River, to join me; but he had five children, and it was too much of a risk in his mind for him to just give up a good job on the hope that he would do well in his own business as I had offered him a full partnership. Frank was a very hardworking young man, and very-good looking, so people enjoyed being with him and working with him. It took me about a year to convince him to take the big step and join me as a partner, but I had also guaranteed a salary to him as he needed that reassurance for his family obligations.

I knew that he would be a good partner, and I was very confident that we could build a very good business together. In the spring of 1959, I went back to South Africa and had another successful encouraging trip. As I was doing everything myself, it was not easy to add many different things to the business, but we were selling and making money. In September 1959 I heard from friends that Australia was looking to start doing textile business in the United States, and I was given the name of a very good agent in Melbourne, Doug Willy. At the time he was representing a very large textile company in New York called Cohn-Hall-Marx, but I telephoned him; and although he was reluctant at first, he agreed to meet with me if I came to Australia with samples, and he would then make a decision.

I obtained a few other names of agents, but I felt that Doug would be the one. He was a very demanding and strict person but extremely honest, though difficult at first. He became a very good friend and was an excellent agent, respected by everyone in Melbourne, and did business with all the important textile companies and clothing manufacturers there. Doug had a brother, George, who lived in Sydney and became our agent there, who was completely different in personality and capability, Doug being by far superior in both.

Their parents, who were originally from Sydney and founded the agency there (many years previously), were members of a religious sect called the Brethren. It was a very rigid Protestant religion, and the true Orthodox believers could not associate socially with anyone who was not a member of the Brethren. Doug was not an observer, and we had dinner together most nights. He lived in a beautiful home in a wealthy section called Toorak in Melbourne. His wife had taken ill a year before and died suddenly, and he was just coming out of his deep sadness. I like to think that I was responsible for part of this because he did not have too many personal friends, and I am sure that I was the first Jewish one that he got close to. His brother George would not even have tea with me, even though it was a very common custom in Australia, like in England and South Africa, in the late morning as well as early afternoon to have a cup of tea and cookies. I did not realize that his brother was not having tea with me as I joined everyone else in the office and thought he was catching up on paperwork in his own office until someone told me that he was not allowed to have a cup of tea with us or eat with people not of his faith due to his strict observance of his religion. I was quite surprised, and he is the only agent with whom I never had dinner or tea. But that was fine with me as I very quickly gained many friends in Sydney.

I had flown all the way from New York to Melbourne through Sydney, and the entire trip was fifty-two hours. Doug looked through my line of samples and decided he would act as my agent. I did not see him the first few evenings as he was otherwise engaged, but he had a young salesman about my age, Paddy Lewis, who was extremely kind and concerned over my welfare. He would take me to his club where everyone would sit with a beer and drink and drink, etcetera. The bars in town were not allowed to serve alcohol between 6:00 p.m. and 8:00 p.m. in order to make sure that the men went home for dinner, but they could get their pints at their private clubs.

I also met a salesman from an Italian textile company on that first trip who shared the same agent (George Willy) with me, and we wound up spending a fair amount of evenings together. I started selling and was very successful with some of the new items that I had brought with me from different suppliers. I was very happy with Australia, and Australia seemed to be very happy with me. I had taken a chance on coming to a market that I did not know and spending the money to go there, but it was a good investment. After the first week, Doug seemed to warm up considerably, and he was a very gracious host. As business was surprisingly very good, I realized how important it was for me to have someone else with me, even if it meant giving up half of my business, and Frank Maya was still the one I thought would be best.

He was being very helpful and contacting people in New York for me while I was traveling, which was certainly encouraging.

Through Doug, I was meeting some very important businessmen. As a matter of fact, I was the guest of honor at the most exclusive men's club in Melbourne, the Kelvin Club, of which Doug was a member, and was called upon to draw the tickets for the sweepstakes on the big race of the year, which is run on the first Tuesday in November, a public holiday. I was also invited to be the guest of the club at the races, with the feature race being the Melbourne Cup. The club had its own private section at the racecourse, and the champagne started flowing at 10:30 a.m.! As the first helicopters and limousines arrived, I was very far away from home, on the other side of the world, missing my family; but the Australian people were so wonderful and warm that I was also able to enjoy the good business that I was doing.

I was very happy that the largest order that I was able to obtain in Melbourne was on merchandise that was owned by the company Jack Abrams, where Marty Rieber and Dave Falk both had important positions, though minor partners. I spent the first two weeks in Australia, in Melbourne, and in just a very short time, I was made to feel welcome and developed excellent relationships there. The largest order I had taken up to then, I received there, and the customer became my most important account anywhere for the next few years. Frank continued to be very helpful throughout this entire trip; but I felt that if he could not join me, I would have to get someone else as there was just too much that could be done, and I could not do it all, especially if I was going to also have to travel, which was the most important part of the business. Business in Sydney, with Doug's brother George, was also very good; and the entire trip to Australia was immensely successful—more than I could have imagined.

After two weeks in Sydney, I came home via Hong Kong, where I stopped off for five days, and good luck continued there as well. I was very happy to be on my way home, but I knew that there was so much to do and decisions to make for the future, as I needed help, as well as much more money for the business. My family never looked better, and the business never looked back as we went from success to success.

One of the first things I did upon my return was to look for an actual office in New York City, as customers were going to be visiting, and I certainly could not meet them at my little post office box. I was lucky to find space in a prestigious building, Number One East Forty-second Street, right on the corner of Fifth Avenue. I also hired a secretary for all the work in the office. We were taking on additional expenses, but the business warranted it; and best of all, I, with the help of the results of my trip, was finally able to convince Frank Maya to leave Dan River and come in as my full partner. He would do a good share of traveling while I would be in New York, and then he would be there when I was traveling. I was financing the business, up until then, on the basis of my reputation, and the credit that was given to me by the businesses from whom I was buying. As the business was obviously growing, the next problem to solve was financing a larger business.

In Sydney, where there was zero social contact with Doug's brother, I was fortunate to quickly meet some very nice people to spend my evenings with. On my first evening in Sydney, I saw an ad in a newspaper stating that a new restaurant and nightclub was opening that night. I called for a reservation for dinner, only to be told that it was one of the biggest nights in restaurant history in

Sydney, but they would be happy to accommodate me some other evening. While I was on the phone, I could hear a voice asking in the background as to who was calling. It turned out to be the owner of this new restaurant and nightclub, Sammy Lee, who unbeknownst to me had the reputation, well deserved I am sure, of a gambler and nightclub-type owner. When he heard it was an American looking to come for dinner (he was originally from Canada), he insisted that they make room for me, "the Yank," even if they had to put a table on the stage, and insisted that I come over as soon as I could as he would like to spend a few minutes with me on this very busy night. For the next two weeks in Sydney, I had to report into Sammy every night, if not for dinner then at least for a drink afterward, before going to sleep.

Sammy was quite a Damon Runyon character and known throughout the country, not always in the most reputable way. I don't think my new friends in Melbourne would have quite approved of Sammy Lee, but my friends in Sydney were very impressed with my influence when they wanted a table at the Latin Quarter, Sammy's instantly successful new nightclub.

Big-name American nightclub performers, especially from New York, were starting to come to perform in Australia and either starred at the Latin Quarter or ended up there after finishing an appearance or concert somewhere, even at a football stadium sometimes. It was very heady times for Sammy and his partner, Reg Boon. I remember one night I had been to dinner with customers and was quite tired afterward and went back directly to my hotel and fell asleep almost immediately. At 3:00 a.m. I was awakened by a knock at the door; it was Sammy Lee with half a dozen showgirls and several bottles of champagne! I had not reported into him earlier, so they came to me! His business was such an instant success, and he was so thrilled by it all he felt that I had brought him this good luck on opening night when I had shown up.

It was quite a trip to Australia, meeting the total extremes of people while having a great business trip. Wherever I traveled, I always met wonderful people, almost all of whom became very good friends. I cherish their friendship, and they were a very important part of my life as they filled in the time from what was otherwise a very lonely time when I was away from my family. I missed Muriel, Donna, and Richard every moment of every day; but these friends enabled me to keep going although I was always thousands of miles away from where I had left my heart. It is very hard to describe the loneliness every night and every moment during the day that was left empty and allowed my mind to think, and it was always about my family and the sacrifices we were all making. You never know when you are doing something if it is the right thing to do, and sometimes you're not even sure after the fact; but Muriel and I had decided that we would be able to handle being apart, even for long periods of time, and in exchange we had our deep and real love to keep us going. The traveling I did gave us many comforts in exchange for the loneliness, but not knowing what the alternative would have brought, you never know if you did the correct thing. It was all very difficult.

Although the title of these memoirs could be *What a Wonderful Life*—and it certainly was adventurous and exciting and always extremely interesting—it was at the same time very difficult and extremely lonely, feeling helpless when there was so much to do at home with my wife and two children. As I have mentioned many times before, in addition to the adventures, it was friends and good friends that made life bearable. All this is evident in the letters I wrote every day to Muriel and the children. I was crabby and always complaining, not only about my aches and pains (real and imagined) but also when the mail was delayed, through no fault of anyone, but just accenting the pains of loneliness and missing everyone.

George Bloomfield and his wife, Shirley, were two of the wonderful friends I met in Sydney, probably my closest. George had a manufacturing business of ladies' garments. We did not do business since I was not selling the type of merchandise he needed, but nevertheless, he was there for me from the day that I met him, almost as if he and all the others knew how important they were to me. George was always at the airport to pick me up and at the hotel to take me back to the airport when I was leaving. Even more important than Sammy, they made Sydney so great for me. If I didn't have an appointment for dinner with businesspeople, I was with them and their family and friends. Sometimes it was an informal dinner and other times more formal, often joining them even when they had prior arrangements. I want to jump ahead a little bit because this involved George Bloomfield. In November 1961, I had met a gentleman in New York, Elmer Finn, who had a product called Permachem, and we obtained the rights to this product for Australia; and it seemed that Frank and I had something very special. I spent a lot of time with it in Australia and together with Frank in New York. I had hoped to do business together with George on the Permachem product, and he arranged many interviews on the radio for me as well as articles in the newspapers. Permachem was this super antigermicidal product that eliminated 99 percent of the bacteria in the air and in products, and it could be combined safely with other products to make them antigermicidal as well. It was eventually bought by Lysol, a huge company here in the United States, and, of course, my rights to it in Australia disappeared with that purchase. Unfortunately, none of our great expectations came through, but at the time it was very exciting as we were talking millions. However, the textile business was very good; and as we took good care of the business, it took good care of us. Elmer Finn also was a decent man and an honest businessman. He reimbursed us for any expenses we had with Permachem.

I truly regret having lost contact with many of the people that I met over the past fifty years, although that is probably not too unusual, considering the huge amount of wonderful people there were, although spread across the world from one end to the other. But I am still in contact with many of them and see several every year and certainly speak on the phone to a good many others. Unfortunately, some of the real great ones like George Bloomfield are among that group that I no longer see. However, I do intend to make an effort to speak to all those that I met along the way and were so good to me when I was without my family and so important to me and my state of mind. All of them. Every time I mention great friends that I have not seen enough of, the name Alan Reichman comes to mind.

Australia is, of course, the most isolated of all the continents, being so far away from almost everywhere. When you are there, you just feel that everything is so far-off, somewhere else. It is a beautiful country, and it is a relatively new country in the sense of development, although, of course, it is just as old as everywhere else; but the people seem to have a pioneering spirit, and you can feel the country pulsing, building, rushing forward, accomplishing as quickly as possible. The native people, the Aborigines, are generally limited to the area outside the cities, and the spaces, from one end to the other are vast and cover every possible geographical description. But it is a different place, with animals there that do not exist anywhere else such as kangaroos and the cuddly koala bear, as well as many others. It is very hot in the northern region and can get cold in the south. It is huge. It is, of course, surrounded by water and has fabulous beaches along its vast coasts. It has great deserts, and you can ski in Australia, either on water or snow.

Sydney is one of the physically most beautiful places in the world. Rio de Janeiro and Cape Town also come to mind for their beauty. All three have great harbors, with Rio and Cape Town having the dramatic mountains that come right down to the sea. But the harbor of Sydney is difficult for me to describe (always extremely busy, yet calm and under control) because of its beauty, with its exotic coastline and the flora that exists in Australia and nowhere else. Sydney is surrounded by beaches and little islands, with some of the nicest beaches anywhere. Bondi Beach is a part of the city of Sydney, easy to get to, and very important for the people of Sydney. Along the harbor, there are dozens of ferries that take its passengers to near and far beaches, many of which can only be reached that way. I myself have been to more than half a dozen beaches by ferry, which have great restaurants and very interesting towns of which they are a part. Sunday morning at the harbor is fascinating, with all the people boarding the ferries and disappearing for the day.

The weather in Sydney is usually great, and it seems like a fabulous place to live. It has a tremendous mixture of immigrants with a lifestyle similar to America, probably more to our West Coast in climate and laid-back attitude. The time I spent in Australia was always spent with the wonderful friends that I met there and always such gracious hosts to me. It seems that the more isolated geographically a country is, like South Africa and Australia, the more anxious to please visitors are the residents of that country. As far as business is concerned, it was a successful place for me and helped me along the path to growing up. I spent mainly my thirties in Australia, so there was much for me to learn and see and experience.

In the early 1960s Muriel and I spent a lot of time in New York City, and since we were both big fans of Frank Sinatra, we tried to see him whenever he appeared in New York throughout the fifties and sixties. We were mostly there with visitors from overseas but often met friends for dinner and fun there. We often heard that Sinatra would be showing up after a performance at some theater or club, at Jilly's, a very popular bar at Eighth Avenue in the west fifties. Jilly was a friend of Sinatra, and the rumors of his showing up or any of the other members of the Rat Pack was, of course, excellent for business. The chance of getting a glimpse of Frank was more than enough to send us, and many others, running to that bar and having a couple of drinks while we waited; but, of course, he was never there (or at least never showed up when we were there). The Rat Pack, also known sometimes as the "clan," consisted of Frank Sinatra, Dean Martin, Sammy Davis Jr., Joey Bishop, and later Peter Lawford, a brother-in-law of President John F. Kennedy, who was an actor of not much talent. With the exception of Joey Bishop, they were a boisterous, free-drinking, loudmouth group of fun seekers; and they found all the fun they wanted and did it all. They were great tippers. Many $100 bills were tossed around freely. But they were all great entertainers, so most everything of the boorish behavior was excused.

For more than twenty years, Frank Sinatra reigned as the leading person in the entertainment world; and there was no one else even close to him until Elvis Presley, and then later the Beatles, came upon the scene. His bad behavior and almost dictatorial attitude toward those he didn't like was always excused by his legion of fans. I too loved him in the sense that I thoroughly enjoyed listening to him and everything about him: his many affairs with some of the most glamorous women of the day, including Lana Turner, one of the most famous and beautiful actresses of our time, and his up-and-down, tempestuous marriage to the gorgeous Ava Gardner, the Angelina Jolie of that time. If Sinatra was in a bad mood or having trouble with his romance, the audience knew it and commiserated with him. If he didn't smile, they didn't smile. It was surely a cult, and Muriel and I were a part of that cult. As he performed and worked himself out of his funk, the audience, who had been tense, relaxed with him. I don't know which entertainer today has that power, but Frank Sinatra definitely had it!

He had grown up in Hasbrouck Heights, New Jersey, in a lower middle-class neighborhood and was always a champion for the poor and underprivileged. He fought against segregation and all forms of racism, even in the songs that he sang and, of course, in his deeds. He stood up to local governments and foolish laws. It was nice having him around as I proceeded into adulthood. While on a trip to the Caribbean, I heard that Frank Sinatra was making his final appearance in New York at the Copacabana as he would not appear again, he said, as he refused to be fingerprinted and get a cabaret license every time he came to New York to entertain, which was required by law from anyone who worked in a nightclub where alcohol was sold.

His very last show was taking place in two weeks—on the very day that I was due back from my business trip. I sent a cable immediately to Mr. Jules Podell, the owner of the Copacabana, in which I stated that I was flying into New York on that particular day specifically to see Sinatra's last performance and I was bringing along five friends with me from Trinidad, and requested a ringside table. Immediately upon arriving in New York that day, I telephoned the Copacabana and asked if my cable had been received. They assured me that it had been and that Mr. Podell had reserved the table for me. I reminded them to make sure that it was ringside, as I had flown in especially for this, and they promised me they would do their best on this biggest night in show business history. It really was a big deal. It was a very big night in New York, and every columnist and news report was reporting that it was the event of that decade, and it would be impossible for almost anyone to get in who wasn't a big name in New York. We invited two other couples, who, of course, accepted quickly; and after a shave and shower and change of clothes, we were all on our way into New York City and the Copacabana and Frank Sinatra.

It was a freezing cold night in February, and long lines had formed up on East Sixtieth Street to Fifth Avenue and down Fifth Avenue to Fifty-ninth Street. It would've been impossible for all those people to get into the Copa, but hope dies last. We parked the car in the garage across the street and entered the club. I introduced myself to the person in charge at the door who was very familiar with my name and welcomed me on behalf of Mr. Podell, who was otherwise busy, and then proceeded to lead us all into the nightclub, which was already packed. He led us past several other well-known performers and professional athletes including Joe DiMaggio, Judy Holliday, many movie stars, and other people who would easily be recognizable at that time. Yes, our table was right down in front of everyone next to the stage, one of the best tables in the house. It was a thrilling evening, and seeing Sinatra perform from that close, at what was then the height of his popularity and power, was truly something else. He never again performed at a nightclub in New York.

Partnership

Frank Maya had been with Dan River for a little over six years, selling fabrics that were very much in demand; and during that time, he had made some very good connections with Latin American customers and also with other mills in the United States. One of those mills was a smaller version of Dan River and was called Mission Valley Mills, located about twenty miles from San Antonio, in a small town (New Braunfels, in Texas) originally settled by immigrants from Germany. Because of his reputation and his experience with yarn-dyed fabrics, we obtained the representation of this mill for all their export sales.

This was a terrific opportunity for us and helped launch our new partnership, giving it legitimacy. We were immediately able to do business for them since Frank had been doing exactly the same type of fabrics for Dan River. Soon after joining me, Frank took a trip to the Caribbean and Central America. His parents had come from Ecuador and Columbia. He was, of course, immediately successful, and we were very happy. I continued traveling to Africa and Australia, and the partnership worked out very well from the very beginning, as I knew it would. We needed more money so that the business could grow, and we tried taking in another partner who happened to be my cousin, Karl, son of my mother's sister Molly. I should have learned not to get into business with family after Uncle Joe, but I never learned; and, unfortunately, when Karl did not work out (although we mutually agreed about it), it again caused great hard feelings as my mother was very close to her sister who was desperate to see her son in a business, and there was great drama. My mother understood and told me I had to do what was best for my family and me; but I am sure she suffered for it, as my mother-in-law, Evelyn, did when I left Gulfstar Fabrics and later joined Fisher Fabrics.

We then decided to use what is known in the business as a "factor." In markets that were close geographically to us, we had to extend credit to customers as everyone else did. In markets like Australia and South Africa, we were paid by letter of credit or by letters of confirmation from banking houses, where we received our money immediately after shipment and enabled us to pay our suppliers quickly. With the factor, we would receive 80 percent of the value of the shipment once it was made, and the client had been previously approved (as all our clients were) for a relatively small commission to the factor, and this enabled us to expand. We received the balance of 20 percent when the customer paid the bill to the factor. This was a new concept in export, and the factor, a division of a bank, used *our* experience and knowledge to grow this part of *their* business.

In July 1960, the young man who worked in Barney Elterman's office in Cape Town, Nathan Shapiro, got married in a small town up the coast from Cape Town on the Indian Ocean called East London. I was honored to be both a master of ceremonies and the toastmaster, as these positions are usually shared by two of the closest friends of the groom. That is how much Nissy thought of me. Everyone in East London knew everyone else, except me. The bride's father had, at one time, been the mayor of East London. It was quite a novelty to have an American at a wedding in East London, and that added to Nathan's decision to have me speak. I even got invited to several other weddings in East London! Nathan, whom everyone called Nissy, was a very sweet young man who was very conscious of his religion and belonged to several Jewish groups. In later years he moved to Israel with his wife and three children, and they settled in a beach town called Netanya. He was thrilled to live in Israel and was very proud of being Jewish and Israeli. He had two sons and a daughter, and they all served in the Israeli army.

After our entertaining trip with the entire family to Israel, I explored the possibility of our doing business there since it had been such a great place to visit. After Nissy and his family moved there, I asked him to find a good agent for me, as he himself was no longer in that business. He did some investigating and came up with a very good salesman who seemed to have all the good connections, and I was soon on my way to Tel Aviv. The wonderful warm feeling never leaves you as you arrive at the airport of the homeland of the Jewish people. We were able to do some business, but it never amounted to very much, and it was too difficult getting the proper licenses and making shipments. I did get the chance to visit a large part of Tel Aviv and Haifa, and, of course, it was extremely interesting.

I was disappointed that Israel—which I had read was a young, vibrant, and exciting new country—did not seem that way to me. It felt more like I was in Williamsburg, Brooklyn, the Bronx, or some other poor Jewish neighborhood. I made mention of this to the agent, and that night he quickly corrected my impression. He explained that the "with it" crowd generally congregated in one particular area, and he took me to one of the best-known "hot" places. We spent an entire evening in one building. The first floor was a huge bar filled with pounding music and young good-looking Israelis, three deep at the bar, no different from Manhattan. The second floor was an elegant French restaurant, very expensive, very beautiful; and the mood here was much more subdued and the people a little bit older and very well dressed, no different from Manhattan. The third floor was an ultramodern discotheque, the music was loud and strong, the young people were dressy and aggressive, and the atmosphere was charged and electric, no different from Manhattan. It was like a different world existed in this relatively small place, in this relatively small country, the homeland of God's chosen people. The entire building was owned by Mandy Rice Davies, who together with Christine Keeler had been a part of the largest sex scandal in London, featuring one of the members of the House of Lords John Profumo. Mandy had married a rich Israeli, and this was the result of all her great experiences. I did not think I was happy about finding the "with it" people in Israel no different than Manhattan, and I think I might have been happier going home thinking of Israel as the land of the kibbutz and the homeland of the Jews different from Manhattan.

August 1961, I visited Tahiti again; and while it will always be fabulous, civilization and all new facilities had arrived, and it was different from that first trip. What an opportunity it was to see Tahiti before anything changed.

By mid-August 1961, the airplane service to Tahiti had improved greatly, and you could fly in and out at least every other day. From Tahiti I flew to New Zealand. My agent in New Zealand was originally from Australia, met and married a pretty young lady from New Zealand, and moved there. His name was John Mingaye, and he was about my age, and her name was Roddie. He was a wonderful guy, and like with so many other of my business acquaintances, he became a good friend. Together we traveled from Auckland to Wellington and then to Christchurch. New Zealand is a magnificent place consisting of two islands, and while business was not as great as in some of the other areas, it was a very interesting and informative trip. We later developed a nice regular business, but New Zealand never became an important market. John was visiting New York and staying with us at our house in East Meadow on the day that we actually sold our first house.

I then flew to Australia, where business again was very good. A new hotel had opened in Sydney called the Chevron, and it really was something very special. It was in a great location overlooking the harbor, which, as I have said, is one of the most beautiful in the world. In Sydney a great many of my friends were in the entertainment business, either owning the nightclubs or the best restaurants or starring on TV, which had really hit its height in Australia at that time. One of the entertainers with whom I became very friendly was a young man, again about my age, from London, England. His name was Digby Woolfe. I had met him one evening at Sammy Lee's club where he was a stand-up comic, and now, one year later,

219

he had the most popular program on TV in Australia. It was on for one hour at 8:00 p.m. on Sundays. It was a variety show very much like the *Ed Sullivan Show* here, and he was the host, talking to and introducing different entertainers. When I was in Australia, he would always have me at the taping of the show, and we often would spend weekends together at his house on Palm Beach. It had been a gift from one of his sponsors and was perched on top of a hill overlooking the ocean.

Because of its location, it had a very narrow road coming up to the house, and you could not turn the car around on that road. They had built a large lazy Susan in the floor of the garage; you would push the car around on the lazy Susan, and you would then be facing out and be able to drive down the road. Digby later came to New York and became the chief writer of a very successful comedy show on TV called *Laugh-In* with Rowan and Martin and Goldie Hawn. We saw him in New York, but when the show moved to Los Angeles, like so many other of my great friendships, the distance made it difficult. I haven't seen or spoken to him in many years now.

In 1962 we were approached by a manufacturer in Germany, a friend of a customer of ours, to see if we would be willing to import a cheap three-wheeled automobile. It was called a Messerschmitt, as it actually consisted of the cockpit of the German fighter plane used during World War II, which was called a Messerschmitt. It had one wheel in front and two wheels in the rear. There were two seats (one in back of each other), and it was well stabilized and not uncomfortable. I don't remember the exact price, but I know it was less than $750. You got into the car the same way that you would've entered the plane, by lifting up the top, which was on a hinge and was made of Plexiglas, and then stepping into the interior. It had a very small engine, probably the same as the Vespa, so we didn't go too fast but fast enough that you could get about one hundred miles per gallon. Gas was not very expensive in those days, but the car would have been fabulous today, and I believe that they are making similar ones for local use. It was a nice little car to drive to the railroad station for commuters and was also handy around the neighborhood. I think that someone in Germany must have found a huge warehouse with these cockpits and came up with the idea of using these thousands of old airplane parts as the foundation for an automobile. We got one to try out, each of us (Frank and I), having a Messerschmitt for three months each; and it was a lot of fun. I used it to go to the station a few times, but mostly it was to give my children and their friends rides around the neighborhood, just as I had done with my Vespa seven years earlier. Either we were just too busy selling textiles, or there wasn't enough interest. But after about a year, the project was dropped, although it was an enjoyable experience.

Early in the spring of 1963, we decided that during July and August of that year, while it was school vacation time, as a family, we would take a long business and pleasure trip to Central America and some of the islands of the Caribbean. School ended near the end of June, and we left right afterward on our journey. We took a nonstop flight from New York to Guatemala City on Pan Am. During the week, throughout the trip, I would work from eight in the morning until four o'clock in the afternoon when all the stores would close. While I was working, Muriel, Donna, and Richard would take various tourist trips, seeing ruins and all the sights. We were together for dinner every night; in fact, we had lunch together every day as the stores were closed from noon to two o'clock. If the hotel had a swimming pool, we certainly used it; and if there was no pool, there was always something else to do.

Donna and Richard learned to eat many different foods on that trip, not always happily, and I vividly remember the looks on their faces as some of the dishes like arroz con pollo were served, when they thought they were just ordering chicken and rice. I do think they enjoyed most of them. It was a fabulous two months for all of us. In Guatemala, besides the capital Guatemala City, one Saturday we visited the very interesting and old town of Antigua. We had hired a car and a driver and had the unique experience of seeing our car run over a large snake that was lying in the middle of the road, cut it in half, and then we watched as each half went off in a different direction! Business was good in Guatemala, as it was at every stop we made on that trip. We had wonderful agents, and they would see us many of the evenings; and that is, of course, the way to feel a part of a country, being with the people who live there.

After a week in Guatemala, we left for El Salvador where several of my textile customers also had coffee plantations or, as they call them, fincas. Donna and Richard both rode horses on the fincas, and all the customers were delighted to see a supplier bring his young family on a business trip. Not too many salesmen did that. In Salvador, Donna and Richard went to their first and, I believe, only "piñata birthday party" at the home of Pedro Schmid, our agent, who had been educated in the United States and who was married to an American with whom they had this cute young daughter, whose birthday we were celebrating. A piñata is usually an animal made of paper containing many little presents inside its body. The piñata is hung from a tree; and the children, usually blindfolded, take turns hitting this very colorful decoration until it breaks apart, and all these little presents and candies fall out.

Among other things, Pedro, thanks in good part to his father, owned the land on which the airport was located. Pedro was about my age. Richard was not yet nine years old, and Donna was eleven.

The hotel accommodations in Central America were not very luxurious; but our next stop, Managua, Nicaragua, was really the bottom of the barrel. The room they first took us to was filthy and messy from the previous occupants who had very young children, and the condition brought real tears to everyone's eyes. The hotel manager changed our room, and everyone's outlook improved immediately. Our agent, Mr. Levy, and the customers entertained us magnificently; and we spent one day on a close friend's boat on Lake Managua, and it was fascinating. Rodolfo Jerez, our friend, was the most engaging person with the friendliest smile and the biggest heart. He had a shirt factory, and I met him through Frank Maya. He was a very liberal person, and he opposed the dictator of the country, Mr. Somoza, who was ruthless and made life miserable for Rodolfo, even up to putting him in jail on several occasions. He never broke Rodolfo's spirit, but he made his life very difficult including, eventually, destroying his business.

From Nicaragua we flew to Tegucigalpa, Honduras, and also visited San Pedro Sula in that country. Our agent in all of Honduras was Egidio Tentori, a partner in the business, together with Pedro Schmid of El Salvador. The business in both countries, as well as in

Guatemala, was Schmid and Tentori. The Tentori family was Italian, and we spent a couple of fun evenings at the Italian Club. Both Egidio and Pedro and their families were wonderful people, excellent agents, friends, and hosts. It was great being in their company, and they seemed to be very happy with us. I was very proud to be able to show my family to everyone.

From Honduras we flew to San Jose, Costa Rica. A volcano, not too far from the city, had recently erupted; and the ash was still falling every day, all day. At the end of each day, our clothes were so dirty from the falling ash they had to be scrubbed. We took a ride and then a long walk to the lip of the volcano and looked down at this tremendous occurrence of nature. It was awesome. In San Jose, Muriel and I were guests at a cocktail party where the president of Costa Rica was also present. Business continued to be good, and we were all having the time of our lives.

Our next stop was Panama, and I had made arrangements with the Grace Line, which was the steamship company we used for all our shipments to Central America, to have Muriel, Donna, and Richard take a trip on one of their ships through the Panama Canal with its famous locks and lakes. As I mentioned before, I don't know why I didn't take a few days off and go with them, but I continued working while they had this tremendous experience of passing from the Atlantic Ocean to the Pacific Ocean. Unfortunately, Muriel burned her hand on the flash of the little camera we had as she was taking pictures to show to me, all the more reason why I should have been there. But we had so many stops to make, and we were keeping to an exact schedule, and that was probably the reason why I did not go. I did business, but I wanted them to see everything.

From Panama we flew to Port-of-Spain, Trinidad, where the accommodations were excellent at the Trinidad Hilton. It was a new modern hotel built into the side of a mountain overlooking the city. I had previously been staying at a very old hotel in town, so this new one was built just in time for my family. The lobby was on the top of the building, and you went down to your floor. It soon became known as the upside-down hotel, and it was excellent, and we all had a great time in the pool and large modern dining room.

Richard and I took a side trip to Georgetown, British Guyana. The hotel was awful, and the food was worse; but I think that Richard was very happy to be away with me, just the two of us. We came back to Port-of-Spain, spent a few more days there, and then flew on to Barbados. We stayed at the Sandy Lane Hotel, which has always been one of the finest hotels in the world. It has just recently been rebuilt, and I know that many, many millions of dollars went into that project. The hotel was right on the most beautiful beach, and Barbados is one of the greatest islands in the West Indies. It has many terrific beaches, restaurants, gorgeous scenery, wonderful people, about fifty world-class hotels, most with great dining rooms and night-time entertainment.

In later years, we rented a house right on the beach next to the Sandy Lane Hotel and spent about a month in January to February in three different years. Our family at that time included grandchildren who we were thrilled to entertain in Barbados. The house was right on the beach, which was our backyard. When we rented the house, it came with a car, a cook, a housekeeper, and a gardener. "Flying fish" was the specialty of the house, and we bought the fish fresh as the fishing boats came back in the afternoon. They were fried the *bajan* way, in the islands' spices, accompanied always with rice or potatoes and fresh vegetables. Everyone, including Evan and Matthew in later years, looked forward to those dinners. Lauren was very young.

Our next stop on that summer long trip was Antigua, another wonderful West Indian island; and we stayed at a hotel, again on the beach. I only had two customers there; so after two days, we left for the Dominican Republic and the Hotel Jaragua, in Ciudad Trujillo, the capital, named after that island's dictator. The hotel was new and modern, and everyone was happy. In the Dominican Republic, Donna and Richard were thrilled one evening as we walked in town after dinner, and they saw labels on the rolls of fabrics that we had shipped previously that read "Another Fine Futterman Fabric." We finished our trip in San Juan, Puerto Rico, staying at the Caribe Hilton where Muriel and I had spent our honeymoon in 1950, being the first guests to ever sleep in our room as the hotel just opened the week before we were married. It was our greatest summer ever, up to then, and I hope that everyone else remembers it as well as I do. It was a great business trip and a fabulous family trip! At the Sandy Lane Hotel, in Barbados, breakfast was only served in the room; and even the toast was made in the room, as each room had its own toaster. The children ordered pancakes but were a little disappointed when they were brought crepes. It was a hard sell, trying to convince them that the crepes were a fancy version of the pancakes they had ordered.

New Home: A Dream Come True

In 1964, by coincidence, both Frank and Janet Maya, Muriel, and me bought new houses (or maybe it was the good business). Muriel and I had discussed the possibility previously; and although we were very happy in our three-bedroom ranch house at 636 Richmond Road in East Meadow, I felt that something larger, and on a bigger piece of land, would be nice to have. Muriel was not as anxious as me as she was very content and happy where we were, as I was also, but I was looking forward to a change. Late in June of that year, while looking through the real estate section of the *New York Times*, I saw an advertisement for a colonial-type house on two acres of land on the North Shore of Long Island in a village called Sands Point, in the town of Port Washington. I knew nothing about that area, but Muriel said it was quite expensive and, supposedly, extremely nice. She had been doing informal modeling shows, and one or two had been at the club in Sands Point. The house was advertised for $110,000, and although our high price that we could afford was only $75,000, I suggested we take a look to see what houses like that were. After a lot of good-natured pleading (on my part), she decided to waste the time and satisfy my inquisitive nature. I called the agent who had put the ad in the paper, Ruth Leonard, and Muriel and I traveled to Sands Point.

The house was lovely but old and in need of much work. Ruth offered to show us other houses, and as long as we were in the area, we agreed to look. Sands Point was, and is, a very exclusive neighborhood with magnificent homes on large pieces of land. The agent showed us a very modern home, which was exciting, on a secluded piece of land. She then showed us a very different home, which had been built by a Dr. Mendelson, as a one-bedroom house on six acres of land, with the property going right down to Long Island Sound and having its own sandy beach. The house had been bought about five years previously by a Mr. and Mrs. Auerbach, who had two sons and a large apartment in Manhattan, and used the house in Sands Point mostly on weekends and holidays, as well as the summer, as it also had a swimming pool plus the beach.

Dr. Mendelson had the house built in 1950, the floors were all slate, and the walls were practically all huge glass windows held together by wooden beams; and except for the main bedroom, which was the only original bedroom (and was located on a separate floor), the rest of the house was quite open with a high-pitched, two-stories-high ceiling, which I would loosely define as contemporary (in the Frank Lloyd Wright fashion). The doctor used to travel to the house and, wherever his work took him, by a single-engine seaplane, which he kept on the property per photos that I saw. The Auerbachs had added two bedrooms and a small laboratory to the side of the house. The laboratory was for Mr. Auerbach, who was an inventor and was responsible for the automatic tote boards that one can see with constantly changing odds and numbers of all sorts at racetracks throughout the world. He had also invented something for the telephone company, which brought great rewards to them. However, Mrs. Auerbach, who was a writer, preferred to spend all her time in New York City and wanted to sell this extra home. I got the impression that he was not too happy with that idea but had decided to go along with her in order to keep the peace.

I immediately fell in love with my "dream house" and knew I would never have another chance to buy something like it. The style was nothing like what Muriel wanted, which would have been a design much more traditional, but she could see and hear how thrilled I was with the possibility of this being our home. In order to keep everyone happy, after long discussions, she agreed to make me very happy. Now all we had to do was find a way to buy the house closer to what we could afford to spend as the Auerbachs were asking $115,000.

We made an appointment for the next week to see the house again, and this time, we brought along Donna and Richard. After looking over the house again and being more thrilled than a week before, I told Mr. Auerbach how happy I would be to be able to give this to my children but that unfortunately, I could not come close to what he was asking. He asked me what I was looking to pay, and I told him $75,000. That was a lot of money for us, and although the house was worth more than what he was asking, I told him we simply could not pay it. He told me there was no way he could sell "my" house to me at that price and asked if I could raise my offer. I do not think that the money was an issue with him, but he could not accept my first low offer.

I pushed my offer to $80,000, and somehow he accepted, to my total surprise. I was thrilled. This was my dream house and property, and we deserved it. Now we had to find a way to get the money to pay for it and also get a mortgage that we could afford to pay every month. We had almost $25,000 in the bank, and we were able to sell our house in East Meadow rather quickly for $27,000, so we had a down payment of $50,000 and easily got a mortgage for the balance. As I mentioned earlier, John Mingaye, my friend from New Zealand, was staying with us the weekend that we sold the house in East Meadow. Our accountant, as well as our lawyer, both told us that we could not afford the house; it was obviously not their dream. I knew in my heart that the house was worth considerably more and that I would be earning more money in the future, and it never was a problem. It was the best investment that we, or anyone else, could have made in their lives, and for the forty years that we lived there, we were thrilled and very proud. Muriel, Donna, Richard, and I loved living in that house, on that land. And so did Sandy, the golden retriever we soon got. We enjoyed every summer at the pool and swimming in the sound from our own beach as well. Our families, our brothers and sisters and their children, were able to spend time with us; and we had many celebrations and happy occasions at Fifty-seven Cornwells Beach Road, Sands Point, New York 11050.

Although we had agreed on a price, Mr. Auerbach was not very happy about selling and was very uncooperative in letting us show the house to our parents, family, or friends. Until we actually closed on the house, he would not let anyone else in. We had visitors from South Africa, Gordon and Carmen Robins-Browne; and although they would never have another chance to see the house, he would not let us show it to them. As I said, even our own parents were not allowed in until we actually took title. We wanted to move in before the beginning of school for Donna and Richard; but all of a sudden, the very difficult Mr. Auerbach, who had no need for the house after the summer, would not allow us to take title until October 1, 1964. We registered the children in Port Washington's schools and stayed at the Bayberry Hotel in Great Neck, almost half an hour away, for the month of September. Muriel drove the children to school and picked them up afterward for the entire month. It was a great inconvenience for her and the children, and very difficult, but it was a small price for the prize.

Donna loved horses, riding them and taking care of them, and spent two summers at a horse camp, Rawhide Ranch; and it would take another two months to get the smell of the horses out of her completely. In the back of my mind, I had hoped that we might be able to keep a horse on the property for her as there was a small barn on a neighboring property that kept horses there. Other neighbors owned horses and would ride on the beach along the shore. Unfortunately, this dream never happened; but I think that we were all very happy to be where we were, and it was one of the few dreams not realized.

Soon after moving in, we replaced the laboratory with another bathroom and shower, which was used by Donna and Richard. We had our own bathroom as well, upstairs, and in the middle of the house on the ground floor was the main bathroom for guests and visitors. There was a small kitchen, a medium-sized dining room, a very large living room, down a few steps to what was called the music room, and a nice-sized den. It all looked out onto this long stretch of land that was ours, to Long Island Sound, and across the sound to Westchester and Connecticut. The nearest neighbors that we could see were in those communities on the other side of Long Island Sound. Since no one could see us, there was no need to have curtains, and we had this magnificent view through floor-to-ceiling windows all the time. We would wake up to the sunlight, and it was almost like living outdoors. The house was built with steel beams and poles all exposed, so what you saw was what you got. It was all wood, steel, stone, slate, and glass. There were fireplaces in our bedroom; in the den below us; and in a huge beautiful stonewall, floor to ceiling, that separated the living room from the kitchen. The living room rose to two stories high, and overlooking the living room, before entering our bedroom, was a long wide balcony. It was a simple house, but it was a classic and very comfortable and easy to live in.

The stairway leading up from the living room to the balcony and our bedroom was against the wall on the right side, with no railing or anything else on the left side, so you made sure to walk closer to the right. It was like a free-floating staircase. The land was six acres, which was split up the middle by West Creek, a narrow stream of water that ended on the left side of our property. On the other side of the creek, it was mostly beach grass and then a sand dune before getting to the beach and the water. Coming back on this side of the creek was a rather steep incline. With our house situated on the highest point, we walked down a wide winding pebbled staircase to the swimming pool, and then it was down a similar type set of stairs. Once we built in a tennis court, that was used constantly by us, friends, and family.

It was hard to believe that this was all ours, but I thought that even though our accountant and lawyer did not believe we could afford it, there was no reason to think that we wouldn't have it for a very long time. We eventually sold the house, forty years later, as it was just too much to take care of for Muriel and me; but it was the love of our life for every minute that we were there. We moved into our current apartment in September 2003 and are truly thrilled to be here. It is a new building, and we have no responsibility except to pay the bills. Everything is done for us, and at this time of our lives, it is exactly what we want. It was originally planned by the architect to be a four-bedroom apartment, and we had them build it into a two-bedroom apartment, doubling the size of the master's bedroom and the living room, making everything quite spacious and extremely comfortable. Because of the original layout, we have three and a half bathrooms. We have a terrace that is sixty feet long, and we overlook the seventeenth hole (a water hole) of a beautiful golf course, three floors below us, with this fabulous view.

We have been very lucky, wherever we have lived, since the day we got married; and I'm sure this has contributed to our peace of mind and our wonderful marriage. Seeing the expressions on the faces of Muriel's mother and my parents, once they did see the house and the property, was worth the world to us. My father, in the first year, must have walked on every square inch of that land (trees, bushes, and marshland) at least a dozen times.

We were very fortunate to be the guests of Julia and Herb Zack on three of their sailboats for extended trips. Herb was, and is, a very enthusiastic sailor, and we became very friendly with them. About 1969, they invited us to spend a week that winter on the *Julia Lee*, their forty-two-feet sailboat, which was at a marina in the U.S. Virgin Islands. We flew down to St. Thomas; went directly to the dock where we met them; and then sailed (just the four of us) to the British Virgin Islands, as well as to St. John and St. Croix in the U.S. Virgin Islands. We would anchor at a different island each night and would have either lunch or dinner onshore, do some sightseeing and shopping, swim off the boat in the lovely Caribbean Sea, and had a great time. We visited another of our neighbors, the Freemans, who lived right next door to us and who had a condominium in a community called Secret Harbor in St. Thomas. The Zacks told us of their intention to redo the lovely house in which they lived, which would've been an expensive undertaking, and they were on a rather small plot of land.

I remember Muriel, one of the top real estate brokers in Port Washington, suggesting to them that as long as they were willing to spend that kind of money, they should consider buying the four acres of land that was next to us and was available. They became intrigued at the idea, and soon after we got home, they purchased the acreage through Muriel, who that year sold more real estate than any other realtor in Port Washington. They proceeded to build the most beautiful modern home, with the novel idea of a tennis court on the roof. They remained our next-door neighbors for four and a half years and bought and sold a few other houses in Sands Point always through Muriel. The following year, they bought a fifty-two-feet sailboat; and we were invited once again to sail in the Caribbean with them and another couple, Bob and Emmie Carras, also neighbors. Bob was a neurosurgeon and head of that department at North Shore Hospital. He was the most caring doctor and a dear, compassionate friend. He operated on my back twice and once on Muriel's, performing laminectomies skillfully and successfully. It was a great week on that trip, getting to know the Carras and spending the time with our wonderful hosts. We sailed to different islands and had a wonderful time, continuing to have one meal on board and another onshore each day. The Caribbean is truly a wonderful place to enjoy. Two years later the Zacks had a sixty-two-feet sailboat, and we joined them this time on the island of Rhodes from where we sailed with a captain and mate. It was a very luxurious trip; and the four of us sailed to Turkey, the eastern most part of the Mediterranean, where we took a day trip to Ephesus, which was once a thriving city on the trade route from Asia to Europe.

Now, it just had the ruins from that time, when it was so important. The ruins were fascinating, similar to some of those in Rome, and St. Peter had actually preached in the coliseum at Ephesus. There is something very special about being in a place like that, and you can feel a part of the history being there. We have had many great times together with our friends, the Zacks. They have joined us in Barbados, at our home; and we were their guests in Sailfish Point, in Stuart, Florida, where they have a great condominium in what might be one of the finest gated communities anywhere, surrounded by a golf course, directly on the ocean, and with its own marina!

When Muriel sold the acreage to Herb and Julia, the house they built became Fifty-five Cornwell Beach Road, and they moved in at the beginning of 1980. Although the house was extraordinary and the views magnificent, somehow the house did not work for them, and in 1984 they asked Muriel to put it up for sale, and she sold it for them.

The buyers and our new neighbors were Agnes and Andy Bodony. They had come to this country from Hungary as very young people, and working hard and being intelligent, their story was a typical American fairy tale. They moved into the house in August 1984 and lived there for fifteen years until December 1999. We got on very well together, and it was great to have them as neighbors. When they decided to move on, they, of course, asked Muriel to list the house; and she sold it again.

Our new neighbors were Annette and Marty Lorber, who immediately moved in and asked Muriel to sell their house in Great Neck as they were impressed with how she had presented herself in selling the house to them. Annette had three daughters, each one more beautiful than the other, and Marty had a married daughter and grandchild and a single son who lived with them and was a salesman in Marty's firm that imported slippers from the Far East. We were very close to them and were invited to every family function, including weddings, birthdays, and all barbeques. Unfortunately, Marty became gravely ill and passed away a few years after living next to us, and Annette continues to live in that wonderful, beautiful house.

She is a beautiful lady both inside and out. She is fine and elegant, with always a good word for everyone. She is a delight to be with, and Muriel and I cherish our friendship with her.

Building on Momentum:
The Mid-1960s

The textile business of Futterman Maya continued well, and we always looked for other opportunities. In 1965 I took a trip to London, Frankfurt, and Zurich, specifically to meet with prospects for a die-cutting business. I knew nothing about this business except the opportunity to sell it, and I was met in Europe by the owner of the business here as well as our agent from El Salvador, Pedro Schmid, who is originally from Switzerland and also an entrepreneur. Despite several interesting conversations with prospective investors, nothing came of this effort; but I did want to mention the wide range of opportunities that existed then, and probably still do in this world, if you only keep an open mind and are willing to work very hard and be honest at all times.

One of our friendly competitors Jerry Rubin, who was in business with another friend Morty LaPayover, often met me while we were traveling in West Africa, and we would spend the evenings together.

Jerry hated traveling, but the firm he worked for saw the success that I was having, especially at Fisher Fabrics, and sent him out with samples to most of the places that I had visited. One of his favorite stories was that he arrived in the Belgian Congo, Leopoldville, which was truly the end of the world at that time, and the very first customer he met asked Jerry if he knew or had heard of Alvin Futterman. He never dreamed he was going to meet someone who spoke fluent English in Leopoldville and certainly not someone who was going to ask about me. We were not truly competitors, as most of what Jerry sold, men's suiting fabrics, were totally different from the shirtings and ladies' dress fabrics that I was offering.

Our way of selling was also totally different, so we could sell to the same customer usually without competing with each other. If I met Jerry on a trip, he would try to rearrange his trip so that he could spend the evenings with me. He hated being alone and somehow wound up being alone while I was always kept busy by customers and friends. But it was pleasant for me as well, seeing him and having someone to meet in the evenings, especially in places like West Africa.

As I have mentioned, Frank Maya (my partner) was a very handsome young man with a personality to match and got us introduced to great connections with mills and large converters. He would get the connection and then usually call me in to finish the deal, as my strength was the business itself. Probably the best connection that Frank obtained for us was with Klopman Mills, which was a part of Burlington Mills, the largest textile business in the United States of America and probably the world. Klopman had just come out with a line of 80 percent Dacron polyester and 20 percent cotton men's shirtings and ladies' blouse fabrics. It was light in weight, completely washable, and unshrinkable (and did not require ironing because of its high percentage of Dacron). This became, for us, the most important fabric we ever sold; but at that time it had just been introduced, and not too much quantity was available to us. However, we had this exclusive connection, and once the fabric became popular and production increased, it was a miracle fabric for us as well.

Early in 1965 Jerry approached me with an interesting proposition while we were on a trip together in West Africa. He told me he was doing fantastic business in a large country there (it had to be Nigeria) with a certain fabric, and he suggested that he would give me all the names of customers wanting these goods if I would give him the assurance that I would buy the fabric from him. He was making a large profit, so he was able to sell it to us at a price that enabled us to also make a nice profit and compete with him, but he wanted my word that I would always buy this particular fabric for that market from him. I thought it was a good deal and discussed this matter fully with Frank, and he also agreed that it was a no-brainer. Jerry would give us the customers' names and a profit with which we were satisfied; sell us the fabric; and between his firm and ours, we could cover and control the entire market, which was a huge market. He, of course, could not sell to every single customer; but if we were selling to those he could not, for reasons of competition, no one could complain.

The market was, of course, Nigeria, and most of the customers were in the capital city of Lagos. As I was traveling to that area, I did the original sales of the fabric; and the numbers were very good, and of course, very profitable. Frank took the next trip there, and we had a wonderful year, between Jerry and Morty's firm and ours. We, of course, continued to do our other business in other markets in other fabrics.

At the end of that year, Frank told me that he felt we should be converting that fabric ourselves, even though I had given Jerry my word that we would never do that. He said we could make all the profit and there was no reason to give it to anyone else. I pointed out quite passionately that I had given my word to someone who trusted me, and I could not go back on it merely to make a larger profit, and he had agreed to that originally. People would lose faith in what I said, and eventually, not only would I suffer, but I felt it would affect our business as well. He insisted that he was going ahead with this idea of doing it ourselves despite my warning that it would break up our business, as I could not allow our business to go back on my word. He insisted he was proceeding, and I regretfully told them that I could no longer remain his partner if he truly was going to do this. For some reason—and I am sure he knew it was wrong—he probably had gone too far and could not or would not go back and withdraw his insistence on doing it all himself "for the benefit of our business." It was a very sad and unfortunate impasse.

Our business was very profitable, but we broke up and went our separate ways. I sincerely wished him well, but I knew he could not do well if my word, or I should say "our" word, did not have to be kept. After speaking to Frank almost every day for six years, I do not think we spoke half a dozen times after we split. There was no anger, just a big difference of opinion on one of the basic rules of life: you have to be honest. Frank was an honest and honorable person. I do not know why he changed on something so important. Frank went to church every week and often attended mass during the week, at lunchtime, at a nearby church in the garment and textile districts. He was devoted to his family, his wife, and five children; and yet a few years later, I heard that he separated from them and was living with another woman. It was so unlike him to change like this, and yet he did, as if he were a totally different person. I have learned that we cannot understand everything that someone else does; and we simply have to accept that we, or they, are different, even when it makes absolutely no sense. It was like he turned himself inside out and became someone else.

He was not successful in his new business, which was the same as our old business, only broken in half; and I sincerely believed we would both do well, although we would have to work a little harder. It didn't work out that way, and I think that greed and an inflated ego caused him to crack and change his personality so completely. Most of our important suppliers, forced to make a choice, decided to go along with me. I did not want to break up the business, but I could not continue by breaking my word to a friend, even though I felt a lot closer to my partner Frank. When Jerry heard of our split, he immediately asked me to join him and his partner, but knowing how difficult it is sometimes with *one* partner, surely two partners would be even more troublesome.

So I was back where I was before Frank joined me, although now we had an actual staff of people who all stayed with me to help run the business, and I hired a salesman to travel in Latin America and the Caribbean islands while I pursued the other areas and other businesses.

Before all this happened with Frank, I had taken Richard, who was then ten years old, on a trip with me early in August to Maracaibo and Caracas in Venezuela; and then to Paramaribo, Dutch Guyana (Surinam); Georgetown in British Guyana; and Trinidad, getting home just before Labor Day so that he could go back to school. Richard absolutely loved the trip and going out to dinner every night. I took him with me to visit the customers, and while I worked with them, someone in their office usually kept him occupied either giving him work to do or taking him on short trips or to a local museum. Richard remembers that trip vividly today, just as I do, and it was good company having him along.

Government Encounters

After parting ways with Frank Maya, I had two very interesting interviews with different branches of the U.S. government. After returning home from one of my trips, I received a phone call from the FBI. The agent came in as scheduled to my office, and I soon learned that they thought of the possibility that I might be Alexander Futerma, who at that time was wanted for several international financial crimes but could not be found. It was not too much of a stretch from his name to mine, and they wanted to check my passport accordingly. Any name similar to his was on the government's watch list. In those days, the watch list was not very long, but after 9/11 it is huge, containing, I am told, many thousands of names; and unfortunately, some innocent people have been stopped and arrested, questioned, and detained, because their name was the same as some suspected terrorist or even very close to it. Obviously, Alvin was not Alexander (although I was named after my grandfather Alexander).

A few months later I came back from lunch one day, and Maria, my secretary, informed me that someone had called, leaving a name and telephone number and stating that he was with the CIA. Of course, no one at the CIA, I thought, would leave a message like that, and it was probably a friend of mine just playing around. Naturally, I called that friend back, even though he had left the name of Hans Stern, but I did not recognize the voice on the other end. "OK, I give up. Which crazy friend is this?" I asked. The voice insisted that it was Hans Stern from the CIA. I still did not believe it, but doubt was beginning to creep into my mind. I told him that I did not think the CIA would leave such a message, and his reply was that it was the only way he could get people to call him back. He came in the next day to speak to me, and as I waited for him, I still thought it might be a practical joke. It was not.

He told me that they had noticed from my arrivals that I made regular trips to East Africa, and they were interested in information regarding Tanzania. He asked if I would be willing to be interviewed after my return from these trips. The United States was building a road from the interior, through Tanzania to the coast, and the Chinese government was building a railroad parallel to the road. I told them that I could not believe that the CIA believed that I, a textile salesman, could give them more information than the many agents that they must have had, especially with all the workers that were building the road. I told them I just sold textiles, never got information of any kind that I thought was worth repeating; and besides, I did not like the CIA, and I did not like the president Lyndon Johnson and his policies.

He told me his wife also didn't like the president, and besides, the CIA only gathered information; so anything I could add to their

244

reports would be appreciated. The conversation continued, with him being serious and me incredulous. I thought I was funny when I told him that if I got caught spying, I could not swallow a pill as even my aspirins had to be mashed. He repeated that the CIA only gathers the information, and I agreed to be interviewed by some agent upon my return from trips to Tanzania. Muriel and I went to a dinner party that night, at a neighbor's house in Sands Point, and I repeated word for word this ridiculous meeting that I had had that afternoon with the CIA. Everyone there, about a dozen people, all thought it was ridiculous and hilarious.

About a week later I received a call from Hans Stern telling me that our conversations in the future should not be repeated. I then learned that one of the guests at that same party was a graduate of the naval academy at Annapolis, Maryland, and surely must have reported my apparently disrespectful story. I have told this story many times, to great laughter, but always after making sure as to which school everyone had attended.

On one of the interviews, I had informed the CIA that the Chinese government was nine months late in their textile deliveries and that half the country of China was opposed to its strict regulations. Both pieces of information, I am sure, were readily available without using me as a spy. Six months later, Muriel informed me, via telephone as I was overseas, that *Time* magazine had a feature story that quoted "unimpeachable" sources that stated that Chinese factories were nine months late in their deliveries and that half the country was opposed to the government. Hey, that was very clearly my interview, and I was the "unimpeachable source"!

In 1966, back in business alone, I traveled to Australia once more and was very pleased to meet Doug Willy's wife, Lois, whom he had just married, after being introduced to each other by mutual friends. It was too lonely for him to live alone, and she was such a lovely lady that I was very happy for my friend, as he certainly deserved all the happiness he could get.

Melbourne and Sydney often have temperatures of over one hundred degrees during their summer, in January, and the time difference is fourteen hours ahead.

Business in Australia was good, and as usual it was very nice seeing my friends. I met a lovely female African American singer performing at a jazz club in Melbourne. Her name was Barbara Virgil, and her brother, Ossie Virgil, was a major league baseball player. She knew no one in Australia as her agent had booked her into the club from California. As fellow Americans we became friendly, and I introduced her to some of my friends there who helped her get around. She came up to Sydney a few days before I left, and I was happy to introduce her to Sammy Lee, who signed her up for an engagement at his club, having heard of her success in Melbourne.

I flew from Sydney to Singapore, which was a ten-hour trip. Jerry met me there, and he was starting to enjoy our trips together. He was not very sophisticated, and there was not an acquaintance I had, either overseas or in the United States, who could understand how I could spend as much time as I did with him. We were totally different people, with different interests, but he was so anxious to learn and change that it was interesting to see him develop. We were not competitors, as I mentioned; so there was no problem, businesswise, being there at the same time. He had different agents and usually different customers. His business reputation was not the best, but in time he also changed that. He admired me very much and now truly enjoyed traveling.

In Singapore I was working with an agent, Sobraj Ramchandani, who was one of the most kindhearted people I have ever met but one of the most exasperating to be with; and he wanted to be with me every moment, taking me to lunch, to dinner, and wherever else I wanted to go. I sometimes thought he was with me every minute to make sure another agent would not "steal" me. I had met him through Frank Maya, but Sobraj stayed with me after Frank and I split. It was difficult explaining to him that I needed to be alone sometimes, as I am sure I was hurting his feelings, but he never changed throughout the years; and he remained a very old-fashioned, kind gentleman. Rather than use the telephone to call a customer to make sure he was in, he would send his office boy to look in the store to confirm that the client would be there. He was my agent there for all the time that I did business in Singapore, and despite all my misgivings, I can only think of him very fondly. I am sure that his diet consisted of only Indian food when I was not around, but for me, he would try everything. He was honest, and he was good, and Singapore was always a very important market.

From Singapore I flew to Hong Kong, which was now like a stop on the subway for me. Jerry was not with me in Hong Kong, and I went back to my own routine of walking for hours both in Kowloon and the island of Hong Kong. Every night after dinner, I would take off on one of my walks and was fascinated by everything. As

I said before, if I could only eat one type of cooking for the rest of my life, it would be Chinese, from every region of the country. My experience, in my memories of everything that happened to me, in business and in the social company of my Chinese friends was always pleasurable and rewarding.

In 1967 I went back to the Far East in April, and via Japan I flew to Taiwan to meet some people who were doing business in South Africa through Nissy Shapiro; and, of course, the Chinese hospitality continued nonstop, as usual. It was just too much food and drink, but when you are the guest of Chinese people, there are no limits.

I visited various clothing factories, and the hope and expectation was that I would be able to sell some of these products in the United States as Nissy was doing in Cape Town. I did not but only because it was a totally different business, and I couldn't take on at that time these extra activities, although I thought I might before seeing everything that was involved. I had visited at least a dozen and a half factories and was very impressed with all their products and prices. As I traveled throughout Taiwan, I was able to see the countryside and the people working up to their knees in water, in the rice paddies. It was a shock to see young children working in the factories and being told that their hearing would be lost at an early age from the constant noise and pounding of the machinery, especially in the textile mills. We had the same industry here, but these were *children*.

From Taiwan I flew to Hong Kong where my favorite hotel in the world had opened. It was called the Mandarin, and when you stayed there, you knew you were enjoying luxury. They had men on every floor who took care of the rooms and would straighten out everything, even if you left for two or three minutes to pick up something in the lobby. When you returned, there was always a pot of tea or anything else that you wanted to drink or eat. These men almost anticipated your wishes and were at your door in ten seconds after you pressed the button to call them. Muriel had been there with me in 1960 for our tenth anniversary; and now, only seven years later, businesses, buildings, and population had at least doubled.

Our great friends in Hong Kong, along with our customers, were Wally and Shirley Williamson. They were originally from Scotland and became prisoners of war of the Japanese during World War II while Hong Kong was occupied by Japan. It was not a pleasant time for people, particularly of British descent; and while Wally was treated rather roughly, he still had a wonderful disposition. Shirley and her family were treated a little bit better, and she too was such a happy, friendly person. They later visited us in New York and stayed with us in Sands Point; but unfortunately, the day after they arrived, Muriel broke her hip on our tennis court, just hitting the ball with Richard when she fell, and, of course, was immediately taken to the hospital.

Unfortunately, Wally and Shirley left the next day, and we were unable to show them the hospitality that they had always given to us in Hong Kong. Wally was an important official at the Jockey Club, which was the centerpiece of Hong Kong society. The Jockey Club ran the racetrack, and the Chinese people are probably the biggest gamblers in the world, so being a member of the Jockey Club was really a sign of having arrived. Due to his position, I always was invited to a special box at the track and a fabulous lunch, which was served all day in the box. Every Saturday at the Happy Valley Racetrack is a big social event, and every one of any importance in Hong Kong is there. Being treated as I was, was very impressive to my Chinese customers, who all longed to be members of the Jockey Club; but the cost to belong was astronomical, and there were no openings for new members at that time, perhaps, I suspect, especially to Chinese members to this very British club.

The second half of 1967 was filled with every emotion possible. Early in August I left for a trip to West and East Africa. I was back in business alone, with all the responsibility on me again and the need to run the business while I was on the other side of the world trying to sell. The people working for me were very good and helpful, but despite the unpleasant and surprise ending with Frank, I knew I could never continue doing it all by myself.

Jerry Rubin, feeling a little responsible for the split in my business, besides wanting very much for me to be his partner, was constantly asking me to join their business, Dakota Fabrics. I wasn't quite ready to do this, and I especially did not want to take on two new and very different partners. It was necessary to make several stops for refueling, as they still had not started using jet planes, and the whole trip seemed long and unending. On this particular trip, our first stop was Dakar in Senegal. We would then fly on to Roberts Field in Monrovia, Liberia; and my destination this time was Accra, Ghana, the next stop where I anticipated doing some nice business with a new agent. The agent was very well connected with the government, and he also owned a chain of thirty-nine gas stations and an engineering business that was staffed by more than a dozen engineers from Hungary. He was very successful, and it was, of course, due to his political connections and the tribe of which he was a part of: the same one of as then-president Nkrumah. He was also a village chief, and when we would come home after working, there were always at least ten people from his village who were waiting in his front yard to have him work out their problems and adjudicate any disputes among people from his village. It was an extremely interesting experience in a society that I had never witnessed before and the power that the chief wielded, even though we were a hundred miles from the actual village.

I was only there for a few days, and business was very good, as expected, due in great part to his influence and the fact that many of the customers had originally come from his village. On one of the evenings that I was there, he invited me home to dinner, and though I was not feeling so great and not looking forward to whatever he was going to serve, I, of course, accepted the invitation and a promise from him that only plain food would be served as my stomach was not perfect. He said he understood, but he did want to have me eat at his home. After solving whatever problems existed that evening and with all transactions carried out with those who had been waiting for him, we went inside to what looked like a mansion to me to eat. Unfortunately, that morning his wife had gone back to the village to take care of some personal matters, so it was just me and Kwame who were eating. The dining room was huge; and the large banquet table was set for twenty-four people, with beautiful china, crystal, and silverware. There were three forks on the left, three knives and three spoons on the right, and up above the serving plate was another fork and spoon for dessert. I had a small amount of a French white wine, and then the "plain" dinner was served. The main course was a chicken in peanut sauce. Peanuts—and, of course, peanut sauce—was a staple in West Africa and was served with practically every dish.

I hate peanuts, but of course, I could not tell that to my host, who was trying to make me as comfortable as possible. I started to begin eating by picking up a knife and fork only to discover this was not possible as the cutlery was all sewn in place! There were actually threads holding down the knives, forks, and spoons. Kwame explained to me that the reason this was done was that the servants could not remember the order of the settings so that if people used the cutlery it would never wind up in the proper English setting in which it belonged. So while the table was set magnificently, we ate in the fashion of the people in the village: with our fingers. It was quite another experience, and I can remember it vividly forty years later.

Accra was a typical West African city: dirty, dusty, and quite primitive. Hordes of people constantly in the streets, with seemingly nothing to do, just milling about. Despite all the inconveniences, I always felt comfortable in Africa, especially with the people, and never felt endangered in any way.

Lagos, Nigeria, was another of the West African cities, only dustier, dirtier, and even more crowded than the others. I recently read in a magazine article that the population of Lagos was now about fifteen million people but only one million when I was first there! It was supposed to be my next stop, and I still had the arrangement with Jerry and his partner Morty to sell their fabrics as well as mine, especially to the customers who were usually neighbors to *their* customers, and I was especially looking forward to a very successful trip. The particular fabric that Jerry and Morty were doing so well with, a sixty-inch wide pants summer-weight plain fabric, would ordinarily not be allowed to be imported into Nigeria as the local mills were producing a similar fabric. However, by putting on a small cheap embroidered border, the merchandise came in under a different heading and was much cheaper than the local product. Once received, the embroidery could be removed easily, and then the customer had the desired plain fabric.

However, there was a civil war that had just started going on in Nigeria, and Lagos had been bombed, and the airport was closed. I faxed our agent there for his advice. Buxani & Company was a family business consisting of four brothers, all originally from Bombay, India, and extremely nice people. Much of the big businesses belonged to Indians as they were forbidden from having small retail stores (which were reserved for local Nigerians only), but their capital was very welcome for larger industries that employed Nigerian workers.

Of course, I could not get into Nigeria, and he suggested that I either wait in Accra for a few days or visit another country in West Africa in the meantime. With business so good in Ghana, I stayed two extra days and then flew to Abidjan, Ivory Coast, which was going to be my stop after I left Lagos. The language spoken in the Ivory Coast, besides the native patois, was French, and the country was actually considered part of France. The French way of living loving, eating, and dressing was all a part of Abidjan, which was a beautiful city, modeled after Paris.

In the least expected area, West Africa, I felt like I was in Europe, in one of the most fantastic hotels anywhere. It was the Hotel Ivoire, right in the center of Abidjan, and it was unlike any hotel I had yet seen. There were five swimming pools, six restaurants, all chic, either French or a mixture of French and African. The hotel had its own movie theater, ten bowling lanes, and several cocktail lounges. I am not exaggerating when I say that I saw crocodiles from my balcony, in the lagoon, and people water-skiing not too far away.

I was in Abidjan to see just one account; and since I had come there before going to Lagos, he was not expecting me, and I could not find him. I spent the weekend in Abidjan, speaking only French and enjoying every minute of being there. In most of the West African countries, the merchants were Indian, Lebanese, or Syrian; but apparently they were not allowed to open businesses in French colonies as the French usually kept all the good things for themselves, and Abidjan was surely a treasure trove.

On Monday I saw my customer, did my business, and made myself a promise that I would come back and find many other customers. It was certainly a great place to visit. The airport had opened in Lagos, and flights were now landing, and I took the first available plane I could to get there. I remember the experience at the airport was simply awful, and I had to extend a fair-sized bribe to the officials to even let me in, though I had a valid visa. Then the ride into town by taxi was somewhat frightening, with soldiers along the roadside, carrying automatic rifles. The agent, Sunder Buxani, the youngest of the four brothers, had gone to the airport twice that morning; but since all flights were delayed, with all the confusion of the war, they were not even giving out times of arrival for the incoming flights, which is why I was in a taxi in the first place. We were stopped several times by soldiers to examine my luggage each time, with a bribe at every stop. Eventually, I got to my hotel, the Federal Palace. It was the kind of a hotel, large and grand, that you could imagine intrigue behind every door. Due to all the uncertainties, business was not very good, almost nonexistent.

The Ibos, who were often called the Jews of Africa due to the fact that they were the businessmen of Nigeria, had all closed up and gone home to the east or had been murdered. The Ibos were the natives from the breakaway rebel, eastern state. The Buxanis and I agreed that it was best to leave Nigeria and wait until most of the major problems were solved before coming back.

In Lagos, you had to have your passport and airplane ticket with you at all times for most soldiers' inspections. Soldiers carrying machine guns were everywhere, and when I said earlier that I never felt endangered in Africa, that did not include this particular trip to Lagos. I remember that I had to fly back to Accra to catch the Pan American flight to East Africa as Pan Am was no longer landing in Lagos due to the war. Flights all over Africa were delayed and changed, creating quite a mess. It was like flying from Chicago to Los Angeles to catch a flight to New York. The flight from Lagos to Accra was in a small two-engine plane, and since we could not fly too high, you could see that this part of Africa and its tribes is still a land of little villages connected by dirt roads. Because of the conditions that existed at that time in Lagos, it was a very frustrating visit, although going to Lagos is always frustrating.

The Pan Am plane flew from Accra to Kampala, Uganda; and my agent there, Mr. Doshi, was a brother-in-law of my agent in Nairobi, Kenya. Muriel had been with me to East Africa on my previous trip, and all the customers, as usual, were very impressed with her and the fact that she was with me on a business trip. We became very friendly with a couple our age, Mr. and Mrs. Jaffer, who was also a very good customer of mine. They had the nicest store in town, and I always made them my first stop whenever I landed in Kampala. Almost all the customers in Uganda and Kenya were Indian.

From Kampala I flew to Nairobi, Kenya, and then Mombassa, on the Indian Ocean, which had lovely hotels all along the beach that were very popular with the Europeans. They were hotels that catered to specific countries. I remember one in which all the guests were German and all their meals, which were included in the hotel price, were, of course, only German. The people spent all their time at the hotel, which was right on the beach, and then flew home without ever seeing anything else in Africa, not even going on one of the fabulous safaris. It was like going to a hotel in the Catskills and never moving off the grounds, although there was an unlimited treasure of options. Germany had been active as a colonizer in East Africa; and there was a German presence in many places in East Africa, West Africa, and Southern Africa.

After leaving Kenya, I visited Dar es Salaam in Tanzania, which was also on the coast of the Indian Ocean, and had several tourist hotels there, the nicest of which was owned by Israelis. I stayed in a hotel in town called the Kilimanjaro, new and modern for East Africa, named after the very famous snowcapped mountain on the equator, which was not too far away. I always enjoyed going to East Africa, as it was not like West Africa, overcrowded but rather happier; and the people seemed more relaxed, plus the fact that it had this tremendous animal population along with the great beaches, with national parks in each country, and not only encouraged tourism, but is probably one of the best places in the world for tourists.

I arrived home at the end of August, not feeling that I had done the complete job; and, of course, with the war in Nigeria, it simply was not possible. I was going to have to return, especially to Nigeria, as soon as the difficulties were settled, as I had missed business in the most important market there. At the end of October, I left again for West Africa. By chance I met Jerry in Accra, and from there, I was going to Lagos and then back to Abidjan to see additional customers before flying home. I had been out a lot that year, but it was necessary to make this trip, as obviously Frank was also trying to build up his new business; and while he himself was not traveling, he was sending a salesman to these areas. As it turned out, the salesman was not very good at selling, and Frank was not the best at running a business. Jerry had asked me if I could change my trip a little, by going to Abidjan first then to Lagos, and he would be arriving in Lagos at the same time as me (if I made the change) and could help me with any questions I had regarding his fabrics, and we would at least have each other's company in that difficult place. I did make the change and went to Abidjan after finishing up in Accra and Monrovia.

In Abidjan I now had an agent, Bill Rogers, who was an American, who had fallen in love with the Ivory Coast after a visit as a tourist and settled there (very easy to understand!). It was November 8, 1967; and I had just arrived at the hotel in Abidjan, had lunch, unpacked, and was waiting for Bill to return as he had dropped me off since he had another appointment, which had been made before my sudden change of plans, which got me to Abidjan a couple of days early.

Bill showed up about two thirty and had a friend from the American embassy with him. They came to my room, and I immediately had the feeling that something was very wrong. He asked me to sit down, as he had some rather bad news for me. My mother had died the day before. No one from home could reach me as they did not know of my last-minute change in my schedule, which was going to be so short that I never thought it would make a difference. They tried reaching me in Lagos, where I was supposed to be, and then my brother Stanley, who had worked for the state department in Washington, suggested that they use the state department to try to locate me by contacting the offices of the United States of America in two or three other countries where I might be in West Africa. The appointment that Bill had, which he could not cancel, was with the very man from the state department who came with him into my room. During their lunch, this gentleman told him of the message he had received where he was trying to find out if an Alvin Futterman had arrived in the country, and he was going to check with immigration right after lunch. Bill told him that Alvin Futterman was the person that he was seeing after lunch, and that was why he, the gentleman from the state department, was with him to give me the news and see if there was anything the consulate could do.

I was immediately stricken with grief. I was very close to my mother, and it did not seem possible. She was only sixty-five years old, and I never thought for a moment that she could pass away so quickly. When I was home, we spoke almost every day, and there was nothing we did not talk about. I hadn't said good-bye, but there was nothing more to say to her than I had already said. Bill and the gentleman from the state department told me there was an Air France flight leaving for Paris that night, and I could make a connection to New

York in the morning, soon after arriving in Paris. They helped me pack (actually, they packed up everything for me), as I was simply stunned by the news and unable, at that moment, to function.

They made all the arrangements with the airline company, who were just terrific in handling the situation and making me as comfortable as possible at this terrible time. They got me to the airport on time; we flew to Orly Airport (outside of Paris) where there was a car that took me and my luggage to Charles de Gaulle airport, which handles flights to the United States of America, that was different from the one where planes landed from Africa. Both airports serviced Paris, like La Guardia and JFK here; and the airline, as well as the government officials at the airport, was simply great and understanding.

It was very difficult sitting on the plane from Africa for Paris and then JFK, thinking about so many different things but all, of course, about my mother. There was nothing that I had left unsaid, and in addition to speaking to me while I was home, we also corresponded while I traveled. On her tombstone it said that she inspired all of us, and I know that that is what she wanted to do. She wasn't very tall—in fact, she was short—but no giant ever had more love in their body than she did for her children. We all felt that love, and we all gave back our love.

The funeral had been delayed one day awaiting my arrival. My father had left the coffin open so that I could say good-bye to my mother and give her one last kiss. The sadness was huge, especially given the circumstances of me flying back from Africa, and my brother and sisters were equally stricken by the suddenness of her passing away. I had been met at the airport by Muriel and my father, but I cannot remember anything else about that day except for my kissing my mother good-bye. I do not remember going to the cemetery—which, of course, I did—or anything that happened after that moment. It was all, and still is, a blur. I have noticed during the years that once the body is actually interred in the ground there is a tremendous relief for the mourners, as that seems to bring everything to a final close. However, our loss was so great that momentary relief did not help or ease the pain. We sat shivah at my parents' house. My sisters, my brother, and I slept over every night with my father; and our spouses would go home and return the next day. It was an extremely sad time for everyone; but it gave us the chance to be together, reflect on our wonderful mother, and say our prayers for her every day.

The next week I went to a synagogue in Manhattan, which was on Sixth Avenue between Thirty-sixth and Thirty-seventh Streets, before going to my office. It was known as the Millinery Synagogue as it was founded and maintained by those in that industry. I would go into the city an hour earlier each day (at 7:30 a.m.) and sit in the very same pew next to the wall on the right-hand side every morning as I recited the prayers. I must have been in a complete fog and did everything purely by habit. It was not until the very end of this period, eleven months, that I noticed that right above me were two bronze plaques (among many others on the wall), although these happened to have the names of my own grandparents, my father's parents, Samuel and Ida Futterman. The plaques had been donated to the synagogue by my father and his brothers, all of whom at one time or another had been in the millinery business. I had no idea about this when I first went into that little synagogue. It was purely coincidental that I had picked this synagogue, which was near my office, to show my love and respect for my mother.

We now had another problem. Our son, Richard, was due to be bar mitzvahed on December 9. We spoke to the rabbi who informed us that we had to go ahead with our plans, as the Jewish religion required us to do. And so, through much sobbing and tears, Richard had his bar mitzvah and did us all proud on his important day of coming-of-age and joining the Jewish people as a full-grown participant. We had planned a party to reflect our own lives, and the caterer had set up half a dozen stations in the synagogue with food from each area of the world, including kosher Chinese. There was Russia, China, Italy, Latin America, Europe, and the United States, with decorations and flags from each country that I had obtained from the various consulates and returned to them afterward. We had a jazz quartet led by Sol Yaged, a well-known clarinetist that we had seen at different clubs in Manhattan, and enjoyed. It was a very happy time for everyone and still a sad time for everyone.

I had to go back to West Africa to complete my trip, and I decided to take my father with me when I did. Muriel was terrific in her support and understanding through all this period. We made arrangements to leave immediately after the New Year and flew to London on January 3, 1968, for one day where I had an appointment, and then on to Nairobi, Kenya. My father enjoyed being away, and it was very good for me to have him with me. During the day I worked, he took different tours or relaxed at the pool, and we were together every night for dinner. It was the kind of a trip that he had never been on, and especially being in Kenya, it was indeed a welcome respite for him and the chance to get himself back together again.

I was able to get him a reservation at the world-renowned Treetops Lodge, which was a rather small lodge built into a series of trees overlooking a natural salt rock lick to which all the animals came. There was every animal imaginable, and you could sit "in the treetops," observing them as they came to lick the salt and drink from the pond as dusk would approach. The lodge area was floodlit, so you could sit there as long as you wanted and clearly see the arrival of the different animals throughout the night. It was very exciting for him, and I was thrilled to have the opportunity of taking him there. Most of my customers in Nairobi were Indian, and they all loved the rich desserts, being vegetarian and not eating heavy main dishes, which could not have pleased my father more. He enjoyed it all immensely. We visited the Nairobi National Park, just outside of town, and saw lions, giraffes, zebra, buffalo, antelope, wildebeest, warthogs, and many other animals.

We also visited Mombasa and Dar es Salaam before going on to Kampala in Uganda, where we stayed at the Apollo Hotel. While I was working in Kampala, I arranged for my father to visit the Queen Elizabeth National Park, which was another wonderful experience for him to be driven through this beautiful nature reserve and seeing many hundreds of animals of all different kinds. He returned two nights later with his white hair completely red from the dust of the clay roads on which he traveled. It was quite a sight seeing my redheaded father. But after a long relaxing shower, he was once again my white-headed father. While on this trip, he visited Murchison Falls and saw alligators, hippos, elephants, baboons, buffalo, rhinoceros, many different antelope, leopard, and a huge variety of birds. He was not thrilled with the car rides to these places, over dirt roads, but was very happy with what he was doing and seeing.

After Uganda we flew together to Lagos, which, as usual, was a very difficult visit as you are just overwhelmed with all the unpleasant things that exist in this world and the poverty of Africa—starting with difficulties on arrival because I had a small amount of naira (Nigerian currency) with me from my previous trip there just a few months ago to being stopped five different times by armed soldiers on the way into town. He enjoyed meeting and being with the Buxanis, who were wonderful hosts and fun for him to be with. He enjoyed their food, especially the desserts. It was very good to see him with people as he came out of his sadness and began to show his own personality.

The next stop was Abidjan, and just as I experienced during my previous trip, he was also totally swept off his feet by the city, especially the Hotel Ivoire. After only the first day there, I remember him telling me that although he enjoyed everything that we had done up till now, I could have left him in Abidjan, done my trip, and then picked him up again three weeks later. I am sure he enjoyed every moment of the trip and every country we visited, but Abidjan can make you feel that way. I have not been back there since the early 1970s, so it is more than thirty-five years later as I write this; and I only hope that time has been good to Abidjan, as Abidjan was so good to us, my father, and me. The entire trip was wonderful and eventful, as not too many forty-year-old men get a chance to travel for three weeks with their father in Africa and get on so well together throughout that time.

My father was a kind man. He was very hardworking, and while he did not have the same drive as my mother (very few people did), he enjoyed the cruises she planned and all the other things they did together. He was quite lost without her, and although he lived with my sister Honey and her, husband, Hank for a while and also for a short time with Muriel and me, it was obvious to me that he could not stay unmarried for a long time. A little over a year and a half after my mother's death, he met a lady at a "singles" weekend at the Concord Hotel in the Catskills. Her name was Gilda; she was a widow for some years, and she was visiting some friends here. She was from London, England, and had a married daughter, Dolores, who had a lovely young daughter about fifteen years old; and they all lived in London. Dolores's husband, Geoffrey, was in the jewelry business, mostly designing; although he later bought his own store and was quite successful. Gilda was pleasant but not personable and may not have been the best choice after living with my dynamic mother for more than forty years. She was quiet and did not give my father the stimulation he had become accustomed to through the years. She probably felt a little strained in the company of his children, but I would like to believe that he missed my mother.

He was now a little older, and though he was completely mobile, he was very happy to retire to Florida and have a much easier life. They bought a small modest condominium in Homestead, Florida, and he seemed to be happy there. At the beginning of this new life, he came up to New York at least twice a year but in the later years found it difficult to travel. I made sure to see him at least every other month and sometimes would fly down just for the day and have lunch with them. Muriel and I developed a nice friendship with Dolores and Geoffrey and were entertained wonderfully whenever we visited London and tried to reciprocate when they came here. Purely by coincidence, during one of our visits to Barbados, they were also there, their daughter now married with two little boys with them, and we were able to get together on a couple of occasions.

My father lived a little more than twenty-one years after my mother's death. I was in South Africa in February 1989, and as always, I telephoned him regularly. It was about the tenth of February, and with a sad voice, he informed me that Gilda had just passed away that day. We were due to come back on February 20, and I asked him if he would like me to fly back immediately and help them with the funeral. He said it wasn't necessary and he was looking forward to seeing me when I got back. We left Africa on the nineteenth, and as we walked into our house on the twentieth, there were messages on the phone to call my sisters and brother. I immediately called and found out that they had all flown down to Florida the day before, as my father had had a massive heart attack. I did not even unpack, just picked up some fresh clothes, showered; and that very same night, three hours after arriving home from a twenty-four-hour flight, I was back on a plane to Florida. My father was still alive, and I was able to get into the hospital that night to see him. It seemed to me that he smiled at me; although he was wired up to all the monitors, I did manage to squeeze through and kiss his forehead. He passed away the next day on February 21, 1989. He was eighty-six years old and had a full life. I am sure that he thought of my mother often, after her death; and though it was contrary to Jewish law and customs since he had remarried, he requested that he be brought back and buried next to my mother. We all did exactly as he asked.

Trip around the World—late 1960s

About a month after I returned from my trip with my father, Muriel and I started talking about going away that summer on a trip around the world with Donna and Richard. We decided we would try to rent our house for the time we were gone, which would help pay for a good part of the trip, and we would also have another experience to remember for the rest of our lives. Among the many people who considered renting for that summer was Barbra Streisand, who was appearing on Broadway at that time. However, the house was too small for her and her entourage; and we were lucky to find a lovely family—the Novembers (yes, that was their name), a couple with two children about the same ages as ours—and they thoroughly enjoyed the time they spent at our house, with everything that it had to offer. When we returned, they thanked us profusely for allowing them to be the guests in our home, although they had paid us very well for the two months they were there.

We started our trip in Accra, Ghana, where I had a slight case of gout. I was treated in an African doctor's office with about twenty other people sitting around, waiting for the doctor's attention. He gave me a shot of a medication, Lasix, that I remember reading had been given to a racehorse that had won a disputed race. I was immediately fine again, and after doing some nice business, we flew to Lagos. It was as bad as ever, but with my family with me, it seemed to improve enormously. We were kept busy by the Buxani family; and everything was so much better with Muriel, Donna, and Richard along. Even business seemed easier. Our next stop was Nairobi, where I did business—good business—while the family enjoyed the local touring. We then hired a Mercedes sedan and driver and took off for a couple of weeks to the fabulous game parks of East Africa. We went to Ngorongoro Crater, created in prehistoric times by a volcanic eruption, and were able to see the migration of literally thousands of plains, game, zebra, antelope, wildebeest (gnu), and other animals that exist on the open plains, moving in unbelievably long lines, climbing in and out of the mile-wide crater as the seasons change from winter to summer. They would go into the crater for the protection from the cold as the winter started and then out again as the winter ended. We stayed at a safari lodge right on the lip of the crater with views from here to forever.

We traveled to Lake Manyara National Park, whose feature was lions sleeping on the huge branches of trees as we rode beneath them. We saw every animal, I think, that exists in Africa and rode very close to the slopes of Mount Kilimanjaro; we then continued driving southeast to the city of Mombasa, where we stayed at the Nyali Beach Hotel, right on the Indian Ocean; and as I resumed doing business, my family enjoyed a beach vacation. After this fabulous two weeks, we went back to Nairobi to return the car and driver. We then flew a little farther south to Dar es Salaam, of which

I have spoken previously. Experiencing all this, through the eyes of my children, was even better than the first exciting time. Business was good throughout the trip, and as we discussed each day, at dinner every night, we were able to relive every experience. From Dar es Salaam we flew to Uganda, and the magic of Africa simply continued. Everyone was loving it—and for good reason. As I said earlier, East Africa is one of the greatest places a person could visit. The animals, the people, the land—everything about that part of the world was enchanting. I could talk about that area, and especially that trip, for hours, but maybe I will leave that for another memoir on its own! From Kampala, Uganda, we went back to Nairobi from where we flew direct to the airport in Tel Aviv, Israel.

Tears filled all our eyes as we landed in the Jewish homeland, with all its signs, only in Hebrew. It was a very emotional moment landing there for the first time! We were about midway in our trip, and I felt it necessary for me to go back to the office in New York for a week while my family was in Israel touring throughout the country. This was not a sudden decision, as it was in our original plans; but it was very difficult leaving them, especially after that fabulous first month. However, it was important for me to spend a little time in the office, and this was a good opportunity to do it. When I got back to Israel a week later, they were able to show me the best of what they had seen, and we did other things that they had not done and were saving for me.

We visited Jerusalem together and prayed at the wall. Men and women were separated there, so Richard and I proceeded alone together to this holy wall. As was the custom, we left notes in crevices in the wall; mine was to my mother. Richard prayed wearing the tallit he had received on his bar mitzvah. It was a very moving time that we spent in Israel, and the memories will be with all of us forever.

From Israel we headed east, stopping off in Bombay. We traveled to New Delhi and took a car to Agra to see the magnificent Taj Mahal. Some things almost defy description, and India is one of them. The amount of people is unbelievable—the cows lumbering in the streets, the poverty, everything feeling as if it had never changed—and then you get to see one of the most beautiful, peaceful, and exceptional buildings ever built.

Luckily we had many flat tires on this trip to see the Taj Mahal because the last one occurred as we were leaving in the early evening to head back. This forced us to see this magnificent building at its greatest, under a full moon, as we waited for the tire to be fixed. We got back to our hotel in the middle of the night, but what an awe-inspiring visit that was. The hotels we stayed in and the restaurants we ate in were all the finest but not representative of the country that seemed so desperate, so very poor.

There may be a small growing middle class in India now, but the vast majority of the people in India are hopelessly poor. The caste system, which assigns a person to a certain station in life for his entire life, seems so unfair, and seeing with your own eyes these very people is something I can never forget.

We flew from Bombay to Bangkok, Thailand. Bangkok was also wonderful for us, as it is truly one of the most interesting places in the world, as I mentioned previously and will not repeat here. But we did it all.

From Bangkok we flew to Kuala Lumpur in Malaysia, where I have a wonderful friend, Kishu Jethanand, later titled by the government like an English lord: tan sri. He entertained us royally at his home, together with his family, and I will speak more of him later. His mother lived with him as his father had passed away, and she was enchanted with Donna whom she only wanted to introduce to her grandson, who luckily was in India at that time. Sobraj Ramchandani had originally introduced me to Kishu's father in Singapore, where he was probably the most well-known Indian shop owner, although his immense store was in Malaysia.

We then flew on to Singapore, which was always a good visit. It did not seem possible that we could have so many highlights in one trip, but Singapore, with its wonderful hotels and restaurants, is also something very special. We visited Tiger Balm Garden, a delightful park built by the owner and inventor of Tiger Balm, a delightful cream that helps every ache and pain and cures every illness. It is still sold all over the world with all these claims, and I have recently heard an advertisement for it over the radio here in New York. Singapore has changed tremendously since that visit of ours forty years ago, but I loved it then; and even if I didn't recognize it today, the memories are so strong that I am sure I would love it still.

Now it was time for Hong Kong. Hong Kong is, of course, the magic city of the world, and you can never say enough about it. We all loved it; enjoyed it; were thrilled by it; and did everything you can do in Hong Kong, including being on a private yacht in the South China Sea, having lunch of fresh fish that our host had purchased from Chinese fishermen from our boat, and then having it cooked by our friends' chefs on board minutes after they were caught. Before lunch we all jumped off the yacht and swam around in the sea, laughing like only immensely happy people could laugh! Oh, were we thrilled! We were one of three boats that tied together out in the water, and we all moved to the middle boat to have lunch together. Besides fresh fish, other food was supplied by the chief chef of the Hyatt President Hotel, a Swiss man who was also a guest of the Chinese boat owner, and the Williamsons, our friends, the hosts.

There was a small version of the United Nations at that lunch with people from every corner of the globe. We had dinner one night on board a floating restaurant in Aberdeen Harbor, and every minute in Hong Kong was followed by another exciting minute. Every night we walked through the streets of Kowloon and Hong Kong Island, as we had done during the day, and could not get enough of it. It was enchanting! No one wanted to leave.

However, it had to happen some time, and that time was drawing very near. Our trip was ending, and I know that each of us was thinking of that. Reluctantly, we left Hong Kong, and via Tokyo we flew to Los Angeles and on to Las Vegas for the Labor Day weekend. It was good to be home, but I am sure that each of us left a small piece of ourselves somewhere else in the world, be it in Africa or maybe somewhere in the Far East. It was a fabulous trip, and that is the word that I have always used in telling my story because most everything that has happened to me has been "fabulous" and "interesting" and "exciting" and every other special word to describe my wonderful life.

In Las Vegas, Richard could not go into any of the gambling casinos because of his age; and Donna was kind enough, as she always is, to stay out as well so that he would not feel bad. Muriel and I did not go into the casinos very often because of them, but we all had a marvelous time in Las Vegas over that weekend. We stayed at Caesars Palace, which was the place to be at that time, went to a show every night, and had great dinners as well as breakfasts and lunches together. It was a perfect place to end our trip around the world, from seeing everything that was so real and alive to now seeing a world that was totally *unreal* and not of our lives. However, we made the most of it that weekend. I think we all grew up a good deal during those two months, and the memories of that trip I know have stayed in my mind; and I'm sure in Muriel's, Donna's, and Richard's. Yes, the right word is "fabulous."

The Trip around the World Ends— back to Work!

We arrived home on Labor Day itself; and two days later Donna and Richard were back in school, Muriel was preparing to go back to work and her modeling business, and I was back in my office. Everyone was happy to see us, including Jerry Rubin, who was still determined for me to become his partner. Jerry and Morty made me a very generous offer. Since their business was worth much more than twice mine, it would normally be difficult to put them together unless I contributed a good deal of money to make up the difference or was willing to accept a much smaller percentage of the business than them. They offered to lend me that difference in money, without any interest, and I could pay it back from the profits of the new proposed company. We discussed the details over long dinners and had many meetings. I agreed to all their generous terms, and we set a date to do this on December 15, 1968. I do not think that Morty was as anxious as Jerry; but I don't think he had much of a choice, as Jerry was, by far, the more important part of the business. Jerry and I planned to take a buying trip to the Far East in January. The Japanese trading company Nissho Iwai had consented to pay for the trip if we bought through them!

First, though, I had to go back to East Africa; for I had met, when I was there with the family just months before, a Japanese gentleman living in Kampala, Yuichi Kashiwada, who was running a large garment manufacturing business on behalf of his Japanese company where he was a vice president, second in command, in partnership with the Ugandan government. I left in the middle of November; spent a week in Kenya; and after being in Uganda for three days, I received a frantic telephone call from Muriel, informing me that *her* mother had died suddenly, almost exactly one year after my own mother had passed away, also while I was in Africa.

I left Uganda immediately in a replay of the previous year and flew back to my saddened wife and children for the funeral. My mother-in-law, Evelyn, was a wonderful person. I never saw her angry or unkind to anyone—ever. She was always giving of herself and her money, even though she did not have much; but she gave her time to charities, working hard for them, and did very much for her grandchildren, Donna and Richard, who adored her. She had a good word for everyone, and everyone had good words for her. She was a very special person, truly loved and truly wonderful.

People in the Far East had never met a personality like Jerry Rubin, and they were truly enchanted by some of his actions, which were usually loud but not in any way obnoxious. He had no social graces but was a very quick learner, and as I said, he wanted to learn and change. Some of this may not sound true, but it all is.

I remember on the first trip to Osaka, Japan, we went down for breakfast the first morning, and he ordered scrambled eggs. The waitress did not understand what he wanted, and while he went through with the hand motions of breaking eggs over a frying pan, she understood and said "omelet." No, he said he did not like omelets, and I tried to explain to him that it would take until lunch to get scrambled eggs; so let her bring the omelet, and he could cut it up into small pieces, and it would almost look like scrambled eggs. He truly was surprised but enjoyed the "omelet" and swore me to secrecy that he had eaten one since everyone back home knew he would never eat an omelet.

This may all sound childish, but it wasn't. It was the mind-set of someone without much formal education, who was getting more from his partner than from business, or maybe he knew that before we started. He never resented this or any correcting on my part; it was a major overhaul. Together we were very successful in dealing with the Japanese, and it required a lot of dealing! Jerry was a great natural trader and knew how to handle people. I was more of the steadying influence and the one that the Japanese could appeal to. Together we were terrific!

Jerry could eat a lot, I could too but not as much, and Jerry could drink a lot, much more than I would ever dream. It did not affect him as he had these huge capabilities to do these things and enjoy himself immensely. He was fun. We were taken out and entertained almost every night, and the Japanese who love to drink but do not have the capacity to take in as much as they do often become drunk and fall asleep after singing American cowboy songs. Since they proposed toasts all night long, we worked out a system where Jerry would drink my drinks as well as his own. I still managed to drink too much on some rare occasions, but he was always there to look after me.

On weekends, we had our car and driver, who we would have take us on a drive into the country, out of the city into the surrounding areas. It was not nearly as good as being with Muriel, but Jerry was very interesting. Most of all, he did not lie or exaggerate with me, as those features seem to be an important part of his life and business. He spoke to me about everything: his innermost thoughts, his plans for us together, and his hopes for his children.

Dakota: Building a Future

My first two years with Dakota Fabrics had two very distinct features. As I said, it was very interesting traveling with Jerry as we plunged into new experiences and were creating a completely new and larger business. However, there was that constant pressure as Morty, sensing that he was being squeezed out, was becoming very unhappy; and he and Jerry started to argue quite regularly about everything. He also insisted on traveling and made a couple of selling trips to West Africa, which were moderately successful, but nothing compared to what Jerry did there. I always seemed to be left out of their disagreements, probably on purpose, and certainly it was my wish.

One day they had a very unpleasant argument, and this time, they decided it was best for everyone for Morty to leave the business. Jerry made a generous settlement with him, and I felt very uncomfortable about the situation, but I think it was inevitable once I became a partner with them. Morty was a very nice guy, but could not measure up as a partner with the type-A personality of Jerry and the knowledge I had of the business.

Their disagreements had become embarrassing for everyone in the business, and it was obvious for some time that a separation would have to take place. Although Morty had received a very nice settlement, he was very unhappy about leaving, as inevitable as it had become; but I don't think he blamed me at all but probably blamed himself for letting me come into the business, although whether I was there or not, they could not have lasted much longer than they did. Jerry graciously offered me half of Morty's half to be paid by me from future profits.

Jerry and I were traveling together, doing good things together, growing the business together, and Morty increasingly had felt left out. Our sales were very good, and I had a couple of trips in the Far East, after we had done our buying together, that were simply phenomenal. With the larger business, I had much more to offer and sell than ever before. We had retained our connection to Klopman Mills and were buying more and more, as much as we could, from them. All this success emboldened Jerry, not that he needed it, and encouraged him to buy out Morty. I was not totally innocent in this, as I benefitted greatly, but I did not take an active part in their disagreements that brought about the separation.

Morty's brother-in-law, Siggy, a survivor of the concentration camps in Europe, worked for the firm mainly in the warehouse but also did some traveling. He chose to stay with Dakota and continued traveling for us, in addition to Jerry and me, and we covered the world very well. One of my first trips for the new business was to

278

go back to South Africa, where I had not been for over five years, as South Africa had gone through some difficult economic times and was not doing very much importing of textiles from America during that time. But they were now ready to start buying again, and it was a good trip seeing that beautiful country again and seeing the people who were still very close friends of mine.

It was wonderful being together with them again, and while that trip was not great businesswise, it did start a new cycle of successful business in South Africa again. It seemed to me that business ran in six—or seven-year cycles. We could be very successful over that period of time in a market, and then the customers were looking for something different, and we either didn't recognize that or were doing business in some other markets more easily. Eventually, we would change our look and get back to selling in each market, but it did seem that something had to change after six or seven years. That same period of time, six to seven years, also took place in my business life. I worked for Lou Fisher for six years, and I was partnered with Frank Maya for six years. Fortunately, my personal life was not influenced by this business cycle; and as I reminisce and put my life on these pages, I am in the sixtieth year of a very happy marriage with my beautiful Muriel. It would be interesting to see what else in my life, or anyone else's life, has a six—or seven-year cycle, if it does.

After the departure of Morty, we continued on pace. Business was very good, and we moved into much larger space in the Freeport Industrial Park where we had a large warehouse, within our warehouse, that housed only fabrics that we had purchased overseas and were held "in bond." We did not pay duties to the U.S.

government on these fabrics since they were then reexported back out of the country and theoretically never entered the United States as they were in this completely enclosed, floor to ceiling (with an iron mesh wall), in an "in-bond warehouse."

We paid for the services of a full-time customs agent whose job was to keep records on everything in bond and to make sure that nothing was taken out of this special warehouse, that was not shipped to a pier for a steamer going overseas, or if it was sold in this country, we would have to make special application through this customs agent and pay the applicable duties to ship the merchandise within the borders of the United States.

This part of the warehouse was always under lock and key. None of us could enter unless the customs agent was there, as he kept the key. I had made a study of this operational concept and was responsible for putting it all together. It made a huge difference for our business, as we were the first individual company to have its own "in bond" or "bonded warehouse." There were, of course, other bonded warehouses, but these were owned by companies who performed a service for people with a need to do what we were doing for ourselves. Originally we had used such a public bonded warehouse and paid their fees.

Customers were, of course, very impressed to see this, and it all added to the importance of our business in the textile export field. While it was expensive to pay for your own U.S. customs agent, it was certainly worthwhile, as we had relatively easy access to the fabrics and, except for the formalities, were able to ship them quickly and efficiently, doing the work under our own roof. This bonded warehouse not only helped with impressing customers and making it possible for us to ship efficiently and eventually cheaper, but it also impressed the banks and other financial people who could easily see how our inventory was kept and had a very good idea as to its value. In fact, one of the companies that lent us money against the value of our inventory and our accounts receivable, which represented what customers owed us, felt that we were undervaluing our inventory and could accomplish much more by purchasing some other textile company that had lost money and, therefore, would have had a tax credit.

By combining a company with ours, we could correctly increase the valuation of our business without being responsible for additional taxes since we would be able to absorb the tax loss or a tax credit of the company we were absorbing. We were very lucky that soon afterward such a company was offered to us. The tax credit certainly had a value to someone in our position, and we were able to buy the company at a very favorable price. That company was Schlang & Company, and as part of the deal, we gave employment to the younger member of that firm who was a salesman but only sold in the United States. This was another asset for us, and we completed the transaction, which was a very profitable deal.

The true substantial value of our business was now public knowledge and impressed many people. David Schlang, known as Charlie, together with Vinnie Simonetti, an employee of Dakota, ran our domestic sales division; and while it never made very much money for us, it did hold its own and never lost anything, but it did increase our purchasing power. Jerry and I continued our trips to the Far East still paid for by Nissho Iwai, and our buying there increased substantially. In addition to all the fabrics from Japan, South Korea, and Taiwan, we also increased our buying in the United States; and Klopman was the most important supplier to us. We were receiving from this important division of Burlington Mills all the excess yardage that they produced and did not sell, in first quality.

These amounts were quite substantial for us, although in the big picture, they were probably relatively small amounts for the mill. Second and third qualities of these fabrics were sold to other jobbers. The mill was happy because all this excess production was being shipped overseas, so it did not interfere with their sales to the large manufacturers in this country. This was important to them because the mill was making good profits, and none of their unsold fabrics were showing up in the United States at reduced prices, even at the end of the season. To us and our customers, it did not matter, as whenever we received the fabrics, they were all new styles to us.

Gordon Joffe and South Africa

One of those new customers from South Africa was a young man who became the closest and dearest friend in my life: Gordon Joffe. Gordon Joffe was a rugged, good-looking guy (most women surely would say handsome), and extremely likable to both women and men, with a wonderful personality that won over people all over the world. All our friends here in the United States loved him, as did every one I ever met in South Africa, England, Germany, and the Far East who had met him. He truly was a winner. Sometimes people who have been blessed to that great extent get spoiled by the attention that is lavished on them and do not get all the benefits that they should. I knew Gordon for thirty years, and he was not spoiled by the attention and admiration that was heaped on him. He was successful in business, and in all of his relationships, and actually seemed to have an aura about him. He was truly a special person, and I don't doubt that he could have used his talents and good looks to even greater advantage; but he always seemed to be on an even keel, even to the point of being modest.

I was one of several investors in his business but even more so a very close friend. We confided in each other in the most personal way, and I am sure he told me many things that he never discussed with anyone else. The friendship and admiration went both ways, and we truly enjoyed each other's company immensely. We had many similar interests in sports and people and in business. One could not have imagined that we would become such great and intimate friends after our first meeting. Gordon worked for one of the finest shirt manufacturers in Cape Town, Monatic Shirt; and at a very young age, in his early twenties, he was the fabric buyer. He traveled overseas to Europe and the United States of America, buying the latest fashions for men from the various mills and converters. One of his suppliers was Klopman Mills, who also happened to be our largest and most important supplier as well, as we had the exclusive contract to receive all their excess production. The patterns were all stripes, and the fabric (80 percent Dacron polyester and 20 percent cotton) was completely washable and required no ironing and, of course, was very desirable. They would make about seventy to eighty different patterns, and each pattern had about twenty different color combinations. For their customers in the United States, they would produce about four hundred yards of every single combination for sampling purposes so that the customers could buy a small amount of yards and makeup garments and then present the shirt to their buyers to get the orders.

After a short period of time, Klopman, having received the orders, no longer needed the sample yardage as they were now going into production on large orders and would ship all that excess sample yardage (usually about three hundred yards per combination) to us. In effect, we had the fabric to sell before the shirt manufacturers in this country received their large orders. Since we were selling the fabric overseas only, it worked out well for everyone here in the United States.

Very few overseas manufacturers ever bought directly from the mills because of the long delivery time and the quantities required. An exception had been made for Gordon Joffe—I have no doubt because of his personality—which caused people to actually want to do things with him. He had placed an order with Klopman for later delivery, about two months previously, and would not get delivery for another four months, when the mill was into its production.

Then I showed up in Cape Town, South Africa, offering the same patterns and fabrics that he had bought, and my prices were even less; and I was also offering immediate delivery since we had the merchandise in our warehouse by this time. He could buy from me whatever small quantity per design that he wanted. Gordon was extremely upset, and after I left his office, he called Klopman Mills in New York to complain about the situation. The mill called my office to advise me of this the next day, and even though I was selling the fabric ten thousand miles away—and, of course, had every right to—I assured this young fellow Gordon that I would not sell any patterns that he had brought to anyone in South Africa.

Naturally, all his future purchases of these fabrics were made from me, and they became substantial. His anger dissipated when he realized he could put the situation to his advantage by buying from me and always being the first one in South Africa to see my samples. From being quite upset with me, he very quickly realized that I could be helpful and a good friend. He was very happy with the solution, and we went on to our great friendship.

When Gordon started his own shirt business two years later, I was with him through all his planning, together with his wife, Laura, a beautiful young lady. Gordon was twenty years younger than I, but I don't think that many friendships were closer. When he suddenly passed away in 2002 of a heart attack, it was a terrible loss from which, even today, I have still not completely recovered. I had a general power of attorney to sign any paper on his behalf, and he had the same power from me. Muriel felt the same way as I did concerning Gordon and Laura. Whenever he came to New York (twice a year), he stayed with us, and it was always a very happy occasion to be with him. When we first met, he was already very happily married to this beautiful young lady; and when they met Muriel, who was with me on a trip to Cape Town where they lived, it was a four-person mutual admiration group. We all loved one another and were very close.

Our business relationship increased every year, and it was with great encouragement from me that he decided to go into his own business. I had even offered him the choice of coming to New York, where I would back him if he wanted to start a shirt factory in the United States of America, but he wanted to stay in South Africa where life was very good and much easier. He called his business Polo Shirts, and I had a very small 3 percent interest in that business, though for the next twenty years, I never wore a shirt that had not been manufactured in his factory in South Africa. We were able to call the business Polo as Ralph Lauren had not registered the name in South Africa or even in England at that time. We also registered the name in London as well. We were later sued by Polo Ralph Lauren over the use of the name, but we won that case at the World Court in The Hague since we were the first to register the name in those countries and, therefore, entitled to use it. Polo Ralph Lauren was not allowed to sell shirts or any other clothes in South Africa since our company had the right to the name. Actually, in the United States, the name "polo" alone is considered a generic word that anyone can use. "Polo Ralph Lauren" is how their products are sold.

I was visiting South Africa two and sometimes three times a year, and in Cape Town, where I spent most of my time, I spent all my time with Gordon. We would also meet in Germany twice a year at the textile trade show, and then there were his two trips a year to the United States. I would see him at least on six different occasions every year, and our relationship got closer with the passage of time. We were together in Germany when he received the news from Laura that their marriage was in great trouble. Each one expressed to me very deep love for each other, but somehow something had happened that was so deeply personal that they could not get together again, and soon they divorced. Unfortunately, they could not work things out, although I know he tried; and he didn't want me to get involved, as he knew I would get them together, but he wanted it to be because *they* both wanted it.

We were very close to both of them, and Laura told both Muriel and me that she did not want to lose us as friends, despite the very closeness of the friendship between Gordon and me, and especially of our business relationship. However, it just couldn't happen; and slowly our friendship with Laura diminished, although two years later, when she had remarried and was pregnant, she was visiting

New York and came to our house and spent several hours with us, just reliving all the good times we had together.

Gordon remained a bachelor for about three years and then fell in love with a beautiful young college student, Mathilde Franco. Mathy had grown up in the Belgian Congo, and he was totally smitten by her and was determined to marry her despite the reluctance at first on her part, he being older and divorced. He lavished her with attention, and in the end, his perseverance won out. My friend deserved more than a spoiled young girl, but love does many strange things to us, sometimes making it impossible to see straight. Gordon and Mathy had three children, Michel, Daniela, and Marco. Mathy was thirteen years younger than Gordon, so considerably younger than Muriel and me.

Our friendship with Gordon never diminished, but unfortunately, after his death, Mathy was dishonest with us concerning certain mutual investments, making it very difficult to have an ongoing relationship with her; worst of all, it also made it too difficult to have the relationship we had had with the children throughout all the years as we were no longer speaking to their mother.

I was the master of ceremonies at the wedding of Gordon and Mathy, for which we especially flew to South Africa with Richard. On every one of our visits, we treated the children as our very own grandchildren, taking them out to dinner, buying gifts; and the loss of being with them, even today, is very great. Gordon had a $500,000 insurance policy here in the United States, which I looked after for him, that no one else was aware of. I, of course, told Mathy about it two days after the funeral. I lost a wonderful friend and also a part of our family.

Back to Business—without Morty

After Morty Lapayover left, the business continued to grow. My sales in East Africa and the Far East tripled from what they were just three years before. Our business in Nigeria continued also at a dizzying pace, and our purchases in the Far East also increased accordingly. It was truly beyond what we had imagined it could be. The only market that was no longer good for us was South Africa, where all my closest friends were. We would just have to wait for economic conditions to improve, and that was just a matter of time. I kept in touch with everyone there and made a quick trip to South Africa to keep in touch with everyone.

Gordon Browne and Nathan (Nissy) Shapiro were still our agents, but George James, the happy-go-lucky Englishman in Durban, was no longer in business; and I was able to appoint probably the best agent we ever had anywhere in the world, Barry Isaacs, in Durban. Barry was as knowledgeable and as hardworking as anyone I have ever met. He was extremely successful in South Africa; however, for his family's sake, due to the politics at the time in South Africa, he wanted to immigrate to the United States. After being my agent for four years, I sponsored him and his family by guaranteeing the U.S. government that I would be responsible for them, if it became necessary.

Barry and his family were overjoyed and have lived here successfully for more than thirty years. He originally came to work for me; but with my knowledge and complete blessing, he was appointed export manager at a very large textile converter, who had been a supplier to us, and he has been successful from the moment he entered this country. He is still associated with this same converter, and Barry has never forgotten what I did for them; and although we haven't seen them in several years, he periodically calls to say hello and always sends some sweets at the Jewish holidays. We hope to meet them for dinner in New York City before too much time has passed.

During this time, Donna was beginning her time at college in New York City. In the second half of her freshman year at Barnard College in New York, Donna decided that she was going to take time off from school and think about what she would like to do. She completed her freshman year, and for a while, she drove a taxi in New York City (!) and then sold umbrellas at Saks Fifth Avenue.

She was, of course, the best umbrella salesperson that they had, but I don't think it filled her with satisfaction. Her friends were all at school, mostly occupied studying, and she had little to do; and I am sure she realized that she should also be in school, but she just wasn't sure toward what end. In September of that year, I had planned on making a trip around the world, starting in the Far East and then proceeding via India to East Africa. It was going to be a six-week trip, and after discussing it with Muriel, I invited Donna to go along with me. I did not expect her to come, so her acceptance of my invitation was quite a surprise, although a very happy one. I felt it would be good for her to have the chance to clear her mind and think about the future while it would be good company for me.

We got along great, and the trip was fabulous, except for the very beginning when she had a stomach virus in Hong Kong after being there just two days. While I was working, she had gone for the day to the beach at Stanley, on the other side of Hong Kong Island, and must have eaten something that was obviously not good for her; and she wound up in bed for three days afterward. The Mandarin Hotel was extremely considerate and gave me a separate room on the same floor during the day where she could stay while I worked in our hotel room, as customers for the most part came to the hotel where they would not be disturbed, and there was always food and drink for them. Our room was at the end of the hall, so after I would finish with a customer, I would run down to her room to check on her and make sure she had everything she wanted. I would then run back to my room for the next customer. It was very hectic, but I was happy to have the chance to take care of my daughter.

After Hong Kong, the remainder of the trip was magic for both of us. Business as usual was good, and Donna kept herself busy all day walking the streets; checking out the little shops; and talking with anyone and everyone, which she does very well. She was in heaven, and I was very happy that she was there. We, of course, had dinner together every night, and she told me everything that had happened that day. Singapore and Malaysia were next on our itinerary, and she was thrilled with everything, and all our friends were thrilled with her. When we got to Bombay, I had no work there, so we toured the city together and were simply taken aback by the conditions there. The poverty, again, was overpowering and India so oppressive but so very interesting.

It was two weeks from the time we had left New York, and we flew on to where we both wanted to be: East Africa. Nairobi was, of course, fascinating; and we then went on to Kampala, from where Donna arranged a four-day trip to Murchison Falls and Queen Elizabeth National Park, from which she took some fabulous photos. I did not work on the weekends, so we took some short safari trips, which were great, memorable excursions. It was great being with her, and we got along extremely well. On one weekend safari, we sat in our safari Land Rover for about twenty minutes, only six feet away from two lions mating. On another weekend, Donna and I were sitting in the lounge of the safari lodge, having afternoon tea. There were two middle-aged ladies in the same room, and we struck up a conversation. In describing something that had happened, I used the expression "my daughter and I"; and immediately one of the ladies said to her companion, "See! I told you it was her father." The other woman had thought we were a couple despite the obvious difference in our ages. (Donna at the time was nineteen.)

We formed a great bond on that trip; and once again, traveling with your nineteen-year-old daughter for six weeks, on an exciting trip around the world, was not a blessing that many people were fortunate to have, as I did. When I say that I have had a great life, those six weeks must be close to the top of the list. Nothing will surpass the two summer-long trips that the four of us took together or even the many trips that Muriel and I took together, alone, but the one with Donna was very special.

I also had the opportunity of traveling and showing different parts of the world to Richard, including South America and the Far East, as the two of us traveled on business; and I had the special opportunity of seeing him mature, even as these individual trips progressed. I was very lucky being in a business where I had the opportunity of doing these things with my wife and my children, alone and together, and it has all added to the richness of my life. Donna and I went on to Tanzania, and the magic of that trip continued. We then flew back to Nairobi and on to London for a few days, where Donna was able to contact one of her closest friends from Sands Point, a young man who was there at the time; and we saw him one evening before flying back home.

During the 1970s our business in East Africa increased substantially, as my relationships there grew into a great bond of trust. In 1972 I took an order from the Japanese-Uganda garment factory for $1 million! It was probably the largest commercial export textile order taken up to that time. My relationship with Yuichi Kashiwada, the Japanese gentleman who was in charge of the factory, really grew into a wonderful friendship and a fabulous business relationship. I held up my part of the deal by making excellent shipments, and he had the power to place substantial orders, and he gave the bulk of them to me. Like everything else, the success was beyond imagination. At no time was I ever asked for a bribe or an extra commission from the buyer on any of the business that I did.

When Richard and Ellen were married, we sent an invitation to the wedding to Yuichi and his wife, and shockingly, they accepted. They flew in from Tokyo directly to New York on Friday night, and we entertained them for dinner in the city the next night, as they were exhausted on their arrival. The next evening we had a car pick them up at their hotel to drive them to Long Island for the ceremony and celebration. The car was delayed a little in traffic, and the wedding was held up for their arrival, which I felt was the least we could do after all their efforts.

We celebrated very happily that night, and the next day they flew back directly to Tokyo, Japan. It was quite a display of our friendship and his desire to be at Richard's wedding. His wife did not speak a word of English, but she made this grueling trip because it was obviously important for him to be there. I can never forget what he did, knowing how difficult it is to travel back and forth from Japan to New York for a weekend! Not everyone is willing to make that kind of a sacrifice for a friendship.

That same year, 1972, when he gave me that order, I had also traveled, for the first time, to South Vietnam. The war was still being waged, as it did not end until 1973, and my visit to Saigon was another unforgettable experience. There was no fighting going on in Saigon; but as I think about it now, I do not understand how commercial travelers, like me, were allowed to fly into an actual war zone. But I did, and I even did a small amount of business there. I remember being extremely upset, seeing for the first time American troops and their neatly pressed khakis, some of the officers carrying riding crops, like the British colonials used to, walking through the city. I knew it was wrong for the United States to be in Vietnam, as nothing would be resolved, but seeing American soldiers there was very upsetting to me. It did not take much intelligence to see how wrong it was.

In 1973 Cosata, the parastatal company owned by Tanzania but set up as a separate commercial business that handled the distribution (as well as the buying) of textiles in Tanzania, appointed me as the sole U.S. supplier of fabrics to that country. In exchange, I would have to make a trip throughout the country seeing all their distribution centers and offering my "expertise" and suggestions on whatever improvements I thought they could make. They gave me a car and a driver, and along with the man in charge of textiles, I set off on the most interesting trip throughout the country and visited most reasonable-sized towns and viewed their ways of selling the fabrics to local retail stores. We stayed at former plantation houses that were originally owned by Greek farmers, producing sisal or hemp to make rope, that were quite luxurious for their time and the place. There never were any hotels in those areas. Tanzania was a Socialist country, and everything went through the government. Though the customers originally gave me their orders, officially, they actually bought the merchandise through the government who placed the orders for them. In the smaller out-of-the-way towns, where no salesman would ever visit and the small shopkeepers could not afford to travel to the larger cities, the government distributed all sorts of merchandise to them. The word "parastatal," as I mentioned, signified that the company belonged to the government but was, in effect, a separation corporation, "Cosata," sort of like how the U.S. Postal Service is organized.

The man who ran that company (today he would be called the CEO) had been sent in by the United Nations and theoretically had been hired by the Tanzanian government, although the United Nations paid his salary and living expenses. He was from Iceland, and his name was Thor Thorstenson. He was about six feet four inches, very handsome, blond, and very imposing and impressive. Thor towered over the local people, and they literally "looked up" to him. He was scrupulously honest, never asked for anything for himself, hardworking, and obviously deserved this appointment. He was a young man of about forty who had brought his wife, his parents, and his son, also named Thor (which was also his father's name) to Tanzania for his five-year appointment. He was starting his third year there, and we had a great relationship between the two of us.

It was his idea to give me the exclusivity on textiles and for me to make the trip throughout the country. When I returned from my trip to the various distribution centers, he told me that they were giving ne an order for $7 million, all to be paid by a bank letter of credit; and since I had seen what they didn't have and knew what they should have, he wanted me to pick out the entire order, as he had seen the success they had had with my fabrics over the past two years of his stay there. I was totally shocked by this and thanked him and assured him that his confidence in me was not misplaced, and I would personally make sure that everyone would be very happy with our shipments. The $7 million was what the government had allocated for fabrics in this impoverished nation; unfortunately, but not totally surprising, before everything became official, the government ministers discovered that there wasn't enough food in the country, and regretfully, the order had to be cut to $3,800,000 with the balance going for corn and wheat. It was still the largest order that I, or anyone else in the export textile field in New York, had ever seen, and we were all thrilled. My hands actually ached from writing an order of that size, with all the details, and the very broad assortment that I wanted to make sure they received. I could not have been more certain that being fair and honest with my customers, large and small (some very small), was the only way for me to do business. They left everything up to me, including the prices, and I never took advantage; it was a long-lasting way of doing business, and for fifty years I was very happy and proud to go to work every day, knowing that people respected me and trusted me. You cannot imagine that feeling unless you experienced it.

Jerry could not believe it or anyone else who heard the amount and the conditions. Jerry wrote me a very touching letter of how proud he was to be my partner, and coming from him, it was something extra, as I didn't think he could express himself so sincerely.

Unfortunately, I think, within the next two years, my friend Thor met the stunning sister-in-law of Milton Obote, the recently deposed (by Idi Amin) president of Uganda, who was now living in exile in Dar es Salaam. She was six feet tall, ebony black, and very beautiful. Thor's appointment was for five years only, so I am not sure of the ending of this incredible story.

The following year, 1974, an order from UGIL, Ugandan Garments Industries Limited, was for $3 million. As I have said before, I never gave anything illegal in the form of money or gifts to any buyer, and their trust in me was very self-satisfying. I never wanted anything more than that.

Suddenly, in late 1975, Jerry Rubin told me that he would like me to buy him out of the business. I remember telling him that I did not have the money to do that, which he knew, and that obviously what he was saying was that he wanted to buy me out of the business.

We had never had an argument, business was good, and there was no apparent reason for what he wanted. I never asked him why. It really didn't matter if that was what he wanted; there was no point in trying to keep it together. He had been a terrific partner, and I felt we were equally responsible for the success of our business, even though my sales, especially in East Africa, had been so great. It was just a little over six years that we had been partners. The cycles of six—and seven-year phases of my life continued after that as well.

We called in the accountant, who had originally been the accountant of Jerry's company Dakota, whose name was Marty Bodian, and asked for current statements to be made up for our business. I called in my former accountant, Richard Feiman; he is still my accountant today, and except for the six-and-a-half-year interruption with Dakota, he has been my accountant for fifty years and a friend for fifty-seven years.

Jerry had been in charge of the finances since I had traveled so much more, so there really wasn't very much for me to challenge, which I now regretted. Accountants worked out the figures. Jerry and I worked out how the money would be paid to me, and after that famous six-and-a-half-year cycle, we were no longer partners.

I had never asked him for any reason as to why he wanted to end the partnership but couldn't help but think that it was a mistake on his part. In fact, he said to me that his wife, Maxine, had told him that he was making a huge mistake and losing a good friend and a wonderful partner with his decision, never realizing that she was next. She could not understand why he was doing this, but given enough time, everything becomes explainable. I have thought that perhaps Jerry was a little frightened by the fact that Richard was far superior to his sons in intelligence and personality and that he might overpower them in any future association, as we had always spoken of our sons taking over the business. There was nothing as deep as that, although as I have said before, Jerry liked to plan things ahead and never be surprised. I think it was all as simple as him wanting to change his life completely. He wanted to go into bankruptcy, which was ridiculous since we were quite fluid and had no money problems; but ever since that time we bought Schlang, he was intrigued by the fact that the creditors of that company only received 27 percent when that company was put into bankruptcy, and Jerry had obviously figured out a way to illegally put Dakota into bankruptcy and at least double his money.

He knew he could not do that with me as a partner, as I obviously wouldn't allow it, and therefore, I had to go. He wanted to divorce his wife and start again, and that could not happen while I was his partner, and Muriel and I both had this good relationship with his wife. Another reason for me to leave. His friend, best friend, Mac, died soon afterward; and Jerry did divorce Maxine and married Mac's widow, with whom he was having an affair. He obviously had put away a lot of money and felt comfortable in doing all this. Despite having a successful life, without explanation, he wanted to change that life; and he did.

One year after I left, Dakota applied for bankruptcy and offered the creditors 25 percent. They eventually settled for 40 percent as Jerry had been very successful in hiding the assets of the company, actually moving out a good part of the inventory, and the only one who could have gotten him in trouble was me. I knew what the company was worth. He paid me my share. It seems very strange to me that no one ever came to ask me a single question about the affairs of Dakota, as if it didn't matter, and let's get on to the next bankruptcy. After paying all the expenses attached to his scheme, Jerry had indeed doubled his money, although we could have done that together legitimately. I must bring out the best in people as witnessed first by Frank and now Jerry.

It had been a very interesting time and relationship, but I wasn't entirely sorry that it was over, as I was not always comfortable explaining my friendship and association with Jerry Rubin. No one had understood it, and looking back, I do not understand it. I do not think it was only for the money, as I really did feel that we had a good friendship and that he could actually change, and would; but obviously he could not, and he did not. *They* were right.

I decided to take off at least six months to decide what my next path was. I was not confused or hesitant, but I wanted to see how I felt about everything, and fortunately, I now had the money to take advantage of that luxury. I was not even hurt by Jerry's surprising actions, but a relaxing six months seemed very appealing. I was almost fifty years old and had always said, jokingly, that one should work until forty-five, then retire for fifteen to twenty years, and go back to work at sixty. But I was only joking. Muriel and I soon left on an extended trip around the world, with Richard joining us for the first month of it. One might think that with all the travelling I had been doing, just sitting on a beach would have been my choice, but traveling with Muriel was totally different; and I looked forward to the two of us, just the two of us, being together, morning, noon, and night.

I started working when I was thirteen years old. I stopped working when I was seventy-three. During those sixty years, I enjoyed every moment of my work, and I loved everything I did. I never thought for a moment of not going to work and looked forward to each day. Maybe it was the type of work that I was doing, meeting all different kinds of people in all different places in the world; but whatever it was, I liked going to work.

I had the opportunity of seeing the world and seeing it in different stages. I saw it before there were jet planes; before there were computers, even faxes; and before there were wireless phones. I remember the miracle of sitting in my friend Kishu Jethanand's car. I had originally done business with his father, and they owned the most successful textile store I have ever seen. It was in Kuala Lumpur, Malaysia, and it was in his car; and he was able to call Muriel, my wife, in New York. This does not sound like anything startling today, but back then, before anyone knew about a cell phone, it was truly a miracle, and I almost believe that I know how Edison felt when he first heard a voice over the telephone. The name of Kishu's store was Globe Silk Store, and it consisted of five large floors, each floor having fabrics of one price, and each floor a different price. The store was filled with textiles, which was all they sold; and his office on the fifth floor was like an Indian movie set, all in high-lacquered white and shiny gold. At first, I would fly into Kuala Lumpur in the morning, see Kishu, do business, have lunch with him, and maybe visit another customer or two before catching the last flight back to Singapore. After about two years, Kishu made sure that I never left Malaysia without an order for at least $100,000, even going back over the samples, if we hadn't yet reached that magical number. However, if he insisted for that order, I would have to stay overnight and have dinner with him in Kuala Lumpur. With all the huge numbers that are thrown about today, even by me when talking about East Africa, $100,000 may not seem like a lot of money; but for me and my business, it was huge. Kishu had a magnificent home—we used to call it the Malaysian Taj Mahal when he couldn't hear us—and it was always a treat to visit his home where he would have his whole family living with him. When his father passed away, it became his responsibility to take care of his three younger sisters, and they truly made me feel like a part of their family. We were able to reciprocate, in a small way, during a visit to the United States of America by Kishu, his wife, and his youngest son. We had a large party at our house in their honor, and they stayed overnight with us. Kishu was very pleased.

Travels with Muriel: A New Era in the 1970s

By 1973 both Donna and Richard were no longer living at home, and Muriel was able to travel with me on almost every trip I subsequently made. It was so much easier for both of us and also much more enjoyable. Half of the trips were to East Africa, where we'd never miss going on safari, and they were always spectacular trips; and at least once a year, usually twice, we would also go to the Far East to Singapore, Bangkok, Hong Kong, and Japan. Everyone seemed to be thrilled to see us and entertain us, and it was always overwhelming, no matter how many times we would visit a city.

In 1975 we had the very good fortune of visiting China. There was a trade fair in Canton—that city's name has now been changed to Quangzou, but they still serve Cantonese food—and although Americans were not allowed to travel to China, I was given special permission, probably due in large measure to the interviews with the CIA, and it made me the first U.S. businessman allowed to visit China for business reasons.

We traveled to China by railroad from Hong Kong, and like everything else in the Far East, it was fascinating. It was October 10, 10/10, the luckiest day on the Chinese calendar. We spent three days in China, not realizing that we would not be going back again. At the end of that year, after ending my partnership with Jerry, we traveled around the world, first to Papeete by jet plane, on to New Caledonia (a big disappointment), and then to Australia. Richard left us; and Muriel and I continued our trip to Singapore; Malaysia; Bangkok; Bombay (now Mumbai) where we connected with East African Airways to Kenya, Uganda, and Tanzania; before ending up in Johannesburg, Durban, Cape Town, and even Botswana, before coming home. We saw Mr. Kashiwada in Kampala, whose company, in partnership with the Ugandan government, were manufacturing for local consumption only. When he returned to Tokyo a couple of years later, he asked me to represent the Japanese company Yamato, who had a very expensive men's sportswear line, in the United States; and Richard was in charge of this business in New York, utilizing our warehouse.

After returning from our extensive trip, I decided that the business I knew best and enjoyed the most was the one that I would reestablish. But I also felt, as American fabrics became more expensive and fabrics from the Far East became more available and cheaper, that I would look for other opportunities, perhaps representing foreign companies in sales or purchases in the United States.

My trips continued to take us to Africa and the Far East and once in a while to the Caribbean. I also traveled to Brazil, seeking to represent a mill there, which produced 100 percent linen fabrics for sale in the United States, and almost received an order from Polo Ralph Lauren. Vincent Simonetti left Jerry to join me; and John Murray, who was in charge of the warehouse at Dakota, also left them to supervise our warehouse. One year later, David Schlang came to me asking if he could work out some deal, as he originally came to work for Dakota because I was there.

We had a real business again, and I rented a beautiful new building in Syosset Industrial Park, with offices and a large warehouse space. Among other trips that we took around that time were to Frankfurt, Germany, to attend the largest textile fair in the world.

I visited the Seychelles; and in 1978 I made a trip to Manaus, Brazil, to visit a customer, Juarez Gomez, whom Richard had originally met. Juarez lived in the beautiful coastal town of Fortaleza, in the northeastern part of Brazil, but had his factory in Manaus, as the Brazilian government gave many concessions and tax breaks to any company that established itself in difficult-to-reach areas in order to develop these places. The linen mill that I had visited was in a town called Sorocaba, outside Sao Paulo. Manaus, even in those years, was quite ancient as it was so difficult to get to the Amazon River; but of course, it was also very interesting and certainly added to my knowledge of the world and the way it originally was or at least after being settled and developed. Later that year we went back to Central America, which was now starting to change, not always for the better, although it was modernizing. The people were losing their civil rights, and life was becoming much more difficult for the working people. Uprisings, followed by restrictions, followed by uprisings, etc., became the norm in Guatemala, Honduras, Nicaragua, and El Salvador. A good part of the population of those countries, under extreme pressure, found their way to the shores of the United States and a better life for them and a future for their children.

At the end of the year, I made a trip to the Far East. I also spent a week in Indonesia, which certainly wasn't changing, just growing and growing—people, people, people. I never got comfortable in Indonesia, though I visited Jakarta and Surabaya. It never became a market for us but was extremely different. The world was changing in every part, in every way, and it seems to me that life in general was becoming more difficult. Of course, I was becoming older although I was just past fifty at that time.

At the beginning of 1980, we invited Murray and Sylvia Goldberg to accompany us to South Africa via Rio de Janeiro, where we spent three days before Christmas. Rio, one of the most beautiful cities in the world, is certainly something to see; and we had a great time touring and being on Copacabana Beach, with its famous bikini-clad beauties. We arrived in Cape Town on Christmas evening, where we were met by a very large contingent of friends and cars, which had to impress Murray and Sylvia, as it did us, even though it had become our usual arrival welcome. At 11:00 p.m. we all went out to dinner at La Perla, one of my favorite restaurants anywhere, overlooking the Atlantic Ocean.

We had rented an apartment in a converted building that I had originally stayed in twenty-five years previously, when it was a small hotel, the Clifton, named after the area in which it was located high above four small beaches and the icy, cold Atlantic Ocean. From the moment we arrived in Cape Town, it was one long never-ending party. January was the time to be in Cape Town, and all the Europeans knew this; so every apartment in every house, for miles around Cape Town, was fully occupied with people totally expecting to be entertained, and they were never disappointed. We had gotten used to the hospitality of our friends there, but I'm sure it must have felt like a whirlwind to Sylvia and Murray.

In addition to all the tourists, it was also vacation time for everyone in South Africa. Most businesses closed for about a month starting December 15, and Cape Town was one of the most desired destinations for local South Africans as well as Europeans of means. Every night there was another dinner party, and our friends were simply wonderful.

Friday nights, Shabbat, have always been a very important family night in South Africa. It has been very rare that I myself, together with Muriel when she was with me, did not go to a friend's home for Shabbat dinner. All the children, of all ages, even the anxious teenagers, knew that on Friday night they would be home for a great meal. After the final blessing, they were on their own and could then meet up with friends.

Our first Friday in Cape Town on that trip with the Goldbergs, we spent with Jeffrey and Shirley Fabian and their family and friends, and the next Friday we were at Mathy and Gordon Joffe's house, with their family and friends. It was very heartwarming to see the young boys reciting the prayers over wine and bread, with their fathers and mothers. Friday nights were very happy occasions. On days when we were not out touring the wine country, Cape Point, Table Mountain, and all the good things and places that the Cape area offers, we were on the beach, which was exactly forty-four steps down from the lobby of our building. The weather was ideal, and the holiday time in Cape Town was very festive with visitors from all over the world. Everyone was on holiday, so why not have a great time?

Jill and Henry von Embden had a twenty-person singing group, very famous in South Africa, who performed on their spacious front lawn after we had enjoyed a very luxurious dinner. Henry owned the largest mail-order business in Cape Town and was originally from Belgium. Jill, an absolute beauty, was a native-born South African, whose father was one of the most well-known bookmakers (quite legal there) in Cape Town. I knew her father before I met Jill. He would always shout upon seeing me, "The Yank is back!" from his stand at the racecourse. Jill and Henry were among our closest friends and an absolute delight to be with.

The most spectacular dinner party was hosted by Irma and Raoul Bahrenblatt, a lovely couple, whom we had met a few years prior. They lived in an area called Bishops Court in a beautiful stately house. Desmond Tutu, the well-known African Anglican bishop of South Africa, had his home there, as one might expect from the name of the community, in one of the richest suburban areas of South Africa. It was on the other side of the mountain, with green woodlands and hills full of wild flowers, as opposed to our side, which looked out on the icy, cold Atlantic Ocean.

Raoul owned a clothing factory that manufactured pajamas, exclusively for Woolworths, the largest and best retail organization in all of Africa. Their quality was known to be the best, and the prices were also excellent, earning it the reputation of being the best place to shop. He also owned two movie theaters in the suburbs, one of which, strangely enough, was named "the Alvin." Irma was a beautiful lady, who also was extremely talented. She was an artist, a great cook, a fabulous designer, and an unbelievable hostess.

The dinner was in honor of our arrival in Cape Town. There were about twenty-four people for dinner, and each couple was given a menu, which had been hand-engraved by Irma in gold leaf. It was a sit-down meal, and the service was excellent. Of course, Irma supervised it all.

I do not remember all the dishes that were served, but I clearly remember the dessert, which was deep-fried ice cream balls! Followed by little boxes made of delicious chocolate from Belgium. It was a Chinese-themed dinner, with all the food invented and prepared by Irma herself.

You could not forget that night, and we spoke about it in detail for many years to come. Irma was probably the most talented person that we have ever met; but unfortunately, great artists can become moody and difficult at times, and Irma was no exception. We could never repay the ingenuity of her hospitality, but sometimes she just withdrew within herself, as she did on a visit to New York a little while later. I had picked them up at their hotel to bring them to our home for the weekend. We showed them their bedroom and did not see her again for the entire weekend, as she never came out of the room. Raoul tried to make all sorts of apologies, as he was clearly embarrassed, but I am sure this was not the first time this had happened; and our friendship, which should have been very long lasting, could not sustain whatever caused these unfortunate moments.

South African Friends: Reichmans and Gordon and Brett

The Goldbergs' stay in South Africa was for three weeks, and I was able to convince Sylvia that she had to go on a safari trip before going home, even though the plane was going to be a very small one, and she was not too comfortable even on the large ones. But Sylvia has always been a good sport, and she agreed to make the trip. It was, however, a little strange to see her sitting on the plane with a scarf draped over her face and doubled over her eyes. We all had a good laugh. We landed safely and were housed in a very stylish safari camp.

The large cabin was comfortable, though Spartan, and the food was certainly adequate. We did two four-hour safari drives each day, the first one at 5:30 a.m. and the second at 4:30 p.m., which are the best times to see the animals as they sought to move around, looking for food.

We were getting ready to leave to go back to Cape Town when the manager asked if we had seen the orphaned cheetahs. Since we had not, he arranged for a ranger, with his rifle, to take us over to the enclosure, a very large one covering at least fifty acres, where there were three cheetahs that had been orphaned as infants and were now being kept in this huge open enclosure that was surrounded by a formidable wire fence. The ranger drove us over in his Jeep and then got stuck in a rut just outside the gate of the enclosure. He informed us that he would have to go back to get help to pull the Jeep out, and in the meantime, he would lead us inside the gate where we should wait for his return. You could not be sure what other animals you could meet up with outside the enclosure. It did not sound like the best of ideas, but he was the ranger, and surely he knew. He led us in and then left, locking the gate behind him. We walked about twenty-five yards inside the area and then decided we would wait there. From rather far away, you could make out the form of an animal bounding toward us and then another and then another. They were "bounding." I cannot think of a better or different word.

But we soon realized that they knew we were there, and they were coming to welcome us as cheetahs would normally do. I honestly believed that we were going to be torn apart. Murray figured that I had been in Africa many times before and therefore must know what we were doing and what should be done. Muriel remembered from her Girl Scout days that if you did not show an animal fear, you would be okay. Sylvia, however, totally panicked and said she was getting out of there. By the time she had taken six steps toward the gate, which would have required twenty-five to reach it, the cheetahs had arrived.

We were not torn apart, we were not destroyed, and the ranger was right; the cheetahs were tame, and Muriel was obviously right because there she was, petting the one that was standing alongside of her. We have a framed photograph in our bedroom to prove the truth of this story, but it was one that I would have never expected to be taken, but Murray was quite calm since I obviously knew what to do as he took the photos.

Apparently, the cheetahs heard the engine of the Jeep; and since the Jeep brought them their meals, it was quite natural for them to assume that food was coming, even though they weren't hungry, thank goodness for that. I honestly believed that we were going to be torn apart.

At the dinner party at the Bahrenblatts, we also had the good fortune of meeting Alan and Di Reichman, from Johannesburg, who were spending an extended vacation in Cape Town over the holidays. Murray and Sylvia soon left to go home, and we spent an additional three weeks in South Africa. We met the Reichmans and their three children one evening at La Perla. After a brief greeting, Alan said that he would like to talk to me about the possibility of doing business together. We met the next day for lunch. Alan was in business with his father, Gus, who had founded the business, and another young man, Milton Levine, in Johannesburg.

The name of the business was Reichman's International and was somewhat like a bank and a factor, although it was known as a confirming house. They would confirm to overseas suppliers that they would pay for shipments made to their customers in South Africa just as soon as the shipment was made, and they then would give extended terms to the buyer, for which they naturally charged a commission and the interest. Alan had naturally asked about me from a number of people at the party, and obviously the reports had been very favorable, confirming once again for me how important your name and honesty counts.

He asked me if it would be possible for us to fly to Johannesburg at least for two days before leaving South Africa so that I could also meet with his other two partners, his father and Milton, and discuss the possibility of me running the New York office for them. I, of course, accepted the invitation and made arrangements to stop off in Johannesburg at the end of our trip in Cape Town before flying home. It was a two-hour flight, and Alan picked us up at the airport in Johannesburg. We had dinner that night with Alan and Di; his mother and father, Ba and Gus; and Milton and his wife, Tamara.

The next day we met at the office and rather quickly worked out a partnership agreement where I would run everything in New York, for the United States; and they would supply all the financing by establishing a bank account in the name of the new company, Reichman's International Shipping United States of America, with $3 million deposited. After expenses, the profits would be divided equally, as I was the president of this new corporation. I knew the business quite well, as I myself had often been paid by "confirming houses" for some of the shipments we made to South Africa. Some of those confirming houses were located in England, so at times it was cumbersome; and here we were, offering U.S. suppliers immediate payment from a well-funded company, and no one could resist that. It was a tremendous money earner and a lot easier than carrying samples halfway around the world, although I enjoyed that also. I had done very similar work to this myself, in addition to being on the receiving end, so it was an easy transition for me to make.

I continued in my textile business, of course, but now we had a second producing business. It was a long and very successful relationship, and it only ended when their company in South Africa was bought by a huge financial public corporation about ten years later. Alan and Di eventually moved to Sydney, Australia, following their two sons and daughters-in-law, who had gone there before them, and taking their teenage daughter with them. They remain today two of our closest and fondest friends, and we had a wonderful reunion with them in January 2009 in Palm Beach, Florida, as they returned from a cruise with their entire family, celebrating Alan's seventieth birthday. They too, like everyone else in our lives, were most generous hosts as we continued to visit South Africa regularly. For as long as they were there, we would spend weekends with them at their newly built weekend home on the Vaal River, a magnificent modern house, while also staying at their home in Johannesburg whenever we were there. Only once in a while do two couples all enjoy each other's company, but we have a unique relationship with Di and Alan and truly love every minute we have been together. We flew to Sydney for their daughter Lindy's wedding.

Another great benefit we received from our association was that we got to fly on the Concorde, the commercial supersonic jet that now no longer flies. Only two airlines ever had the Concorde, British Airways and Air France, and the flights were only from London or Paris to either New York or Washington DC. There were a few other routes added, but it was very expensive to operate, and even with full planeloads and an extremely high price for the ticket, it was not workable for the airlines; and eventually, the Concorde had to be abandoned. I don't think that there were ever more than twelve airplanes built, but it was a very glamorous and exciting plane. It flew at the speed of sound, about 1,200 miles per hour, and the flight time from London to New York was three hours and twenty minutes. After takeoff and the caviar, pate, and French champagne were served, it was almost time to get ready for landing. Flying from London to New York, you actually arrived at an earlier time than the hour that you left! If you left London at 10:30 a.m., with the five-hour difference in time and the three-hour twenty-minute flight, you would land in New York before 9:00 a.m.! Incredible to think of it.

We used the Concorde to ship our documents, both to London, where the Reichmans also had an office, and also to South Africa via London. The Concorde had a unique setup where a passenger could take up to ten pieces of luggage with him, paying, of course, for the extra eight pieces. Those ten pieces could be filled with documents and other papers from various companies. However, a passenger was required; and the shipping company that was handling all these different documents, including ours, offered a free trip to us if we went along as the courier. We would board the plane, the same as any other paying passenger; and when we got to London, we would turn over the baggage receipts to a representative of the company who would handle all the necessary paperwork, and we could go on our way to do whatever we wanted. When we were coming home, we did just the reverse. Muriel and I could not travel on the same plane, but the shipping company and the airline were very accommodating and allowed Muriel and me to take one plane after the other. The Concorde carried one hundred passengers, twenty-five rows of four seats separated by a center aisle. The plane was rather narrow, but the seat was certainly comfortable, and the time of the flight was excellent. I probably flew on the Concorde on at least eight different occasions, and every flight was full, or once or twice a passenger had bought two seats for themselves. Henry Kissinger, our former secretary of state, had two seats on one of those flights so that he could work more comfortably!

We flew to London on our way to other stops in Europe or even used it as the first leg on our flight to South Africa, connecting with an overnight flight from London, which we could not have caught on a conventional jet flight. It was a great experience, each time, and to have had the chance to fly on the Concorde was very special. I remember Richard spending the Thanksgiving Day weekend in London one year, and all that he took with him was a tuxedo and extra underwear and shirts, and it was all easily doable with the quick flights of the Concorde.

During that same trip at the beginning of 1980 with Murray and Sylvia, we had the wonderful good fortune of meeting Gordon Jones and Brett Gage, who had an apartment in the building where we were renting, just two floors below us; and they have become two of the most important people in our lives.

The apartment in which Gordon and Brett were living in Clifton was the lobby of the original hotel that had been redesigned into a luxury residence for them and the other fifteen owners of the apartments from the original hotel rooms. I had stayed at that hotel at the very beginning of my visits to South Africa but then preferred staying in town, which was much more convenient. Their particular apartment had a swimming pool, which was built into the original terrace of the hotel, with fantastic views of the beaches and the South Atlantic Ocean. The mountains came right down to the shore, and most of the homes in the area outside of Cape Town, going south toward Cape Point, were built into the side of the mountains, making the view of the homes and the view *from* the homes very spectacular. The building's renovation into condominiums had just been completed two weeks before our arrival.

We were introduced to Gordon and Brett one afternoon by Gordon Joffe. The Goldbergs left South Africa the next day; and practically every afternoon for the next two and a half weeks, which was the extent of our stay, Gordon would call me down for cocktails at 4:00 p.m., and then we'd walk down to the beach for a very brisk and cold swim. The Atlantic Ocean on the Clifton beaches is very often in the high fifty-degree range.

Our friendship with them simply flourished into the most important friendships of our lives. We all love one another, and that love is returned—always. Twenty-five years after we first met, Muriel and I flew to the island of Capri, another magical place, to be present at the celebration of Brett's fiftieth birthday. He had invited seventy guests from around the world, all friends; and Muriel and I were seated at his birthday dinner party, right next to Brett and Gordon, the two places of honor. I had received a transplanted kidney just one year before, but I was determined to be there with them, and they arranged to make everything as comfortable as possible for me. Capri is mostly a mountain, and it was practically impossible for me to do the walking that would be necessary; so they arranged for an electric cart to drive me to all of the special dinners and occasions, and a different party every night for a week, in different homes and restaurants throughout the island.

In 1981, the year after we met them, we rented the same apartment and again, as always, had a fabulous time in Cape Town in January. However, it was not available to rent after 1981, as the owner had moved down to Cape Town from Durban and was now occupying the apartment full time.

However, Gordon and Brett made their fabulous apartment, gratis, available to us for the following twenty years; and we luxuriously stayed there, with the exception of a few years where we rented a house on the west coast of Barbados, during January to February. However, the apartment of Gordon and Brett was magical and one of the most beautiful spots in the world, with four separate small white-sand beaches, the finest sand I have ever seen or felt, with immense boulders separating each beach, which were about three hundred feet wide and very deep. The apartment was magnificent; we had our own housekeeper, Pamela, our own car, and lived almost as well as our hosts. They had bought a house in Franschhoek, in the wine country La Rive, which they redid tastefully and luxuriously, which was absolutely lovely, and where they would move to while we were in the apartment in Clifton. Franschhoek was about an hour away, and we often were invited there for weekends. It is hard to imagine that these relatively new friends were so generous to us. A few years later, they were the developers of a fourteen-story building, which was only about five minutes away from Clifton, but they kept the penthouse apartment and sold the other floors mostly to friends, A few years after that, they purchased a new apartment in

New York on the fifty-fourth floor of the building next to Carnegie Hall; and I managed that apartment for them, seeing that it was rented, collecting the rent, paying the mortgage, and then selling it at what was then the highest price in the building when they decided they were not going to use it enough. I was thrilled to be able to help look after their interests here.

Gordon and Brett, Brett and Gordon. From the very beginning, they have been the most kind, the most caring, the most generous, the most giving, the most sharing; they have always been the *mostest of most*. Gordon, who is twelve to fifteen years older, came from a family that seemed to be financially very comfortable. He was educated in all the proper schools, and along the way, he learned to be the hardest-working guy I know, both mentally and physically. He was always a giving and sharing person. Many white boys, growing up in South Africa, had black friends, usually the child of someone who worked for their parents and probably lived on their property. Joseph was one of those boys and was a true friend of Gordon. Gordon got married to a beautiful young lady called Sugar; and together they have three beautiful children—Norman, Harold, and Victoria—now all happily married. This was no surprise as Gordon is a very accomplished, handsome man. Together with Sugar, the two of them made a very attractive couple and were probably the toast of Johannesburg society at that time. I can imagine the shock and despair that took place when he finally realized that he no longer could live that life while wanting to live a different one.

We have been together a lot of times during the twenty-eight years that I've known Gordon and have openly discussed the situation and his feelings. I am sure it was easier to talk to me about this situation since I have always been an understanding parent of our own gay daughter. My heart goes out to him when I think of him making that announcement to his wife, his children, and his very conservative parents, all of whom I have had the opportunity of meeting. He is so naturally warm and is loved by more people than anyone else I know.

Gordon is a true entrepreneur, has been in many businesses, and succeeded in all of them. He has been a car dealer and has been an official exporter of BMW spare parts, manufactured in South Africa. He has been the exclusive distributor, along with Brett, of the French beauty product Clarins, which Brett has marketed into a very important product in South Africa. He has been an investor in many businesses, and though gay in a very conservative country, he is well respected by everyone.

It seems like they have been together forever. We have known them for thirty years, and they were together several years before that. Gordon has always been close to his children, and they adore him and respect him and love him as everyone knows. Brett has, at the same time, been an important person in their lives, as they were quite young when Gordon and Brett met; and the children often called upon Brett to fix this water ski or that bicycle whenever we all got together on weekends. When we first met, Hack was about nine, Vicki about ten or eleven, and Norman about thirteen.

Brett's roots were also excellent, and the family was well-known in South Africa, so it is no surprise that Brett also had a fine and proper education. With his superior intelligence and extremely good looks, Brett did not lack for any opportunities, even though, as I mentioned before, it was a very conservative country, especially regarding sex; and gay people were certainly not acceptable to a large part of the South African population. They met and got together in the late seventies, and of all our friends, we probably are closest to them. We have been together with them in Capri, at the fabulous hotel Scalinatella, about twelve years ago, in addition to Brett's fiftieth birthday gala. Together they made a great couple and enrich everyone who knows them. I am sure that there are many throughout the world who feel about them as we do. They are wonderful hosts, and I am very happy that we met.

Gordon Jones's father was the sole distributor of John Deere tractors and all the other farm machinery that they manufactured for all of South Africa, which, of course, was and continues to be a wonderful asset in an agricultural country as South Africa. However, I believe that no matter where Gordon would have been born or started, he would have been the same successful person he is today. Stories about his extreme charitable nature abound. He has had a housekeeper, Pamela, working for him and Brett for more than twenty-five years, and I know that they paid in full for all the schooling of her daughter and bought an apartment for her in a very nice area. In fact, the daughter went to a Jewish day school, as that was the best in the area, and you can be sure that that was not too common for black African children. Gordon and Brett made sure to review the report cards of the several children they sponsored. Earlier, I mentioned his boyfriend Joseph, who came to work for Gordon after he married Sugar. Joseph and his wife had four children, two boys and two girls. As a middle-aged man, Joseph became very ill; and of course, Gordon took care of him financially, as well as spent time with him as he lay in a hospital. I say Gordon, but of course, Brett was equally giving in all these matters. Since Gordon knew Joseph from boyhood, I think of him as more of Gordon's friend, but Brett was very much a part of all of it.

One day, while visiting Joseph in the hospital, Gordon asked him if there was anything he could do for him. Joseph replied that he was worried about his children as his wife did not seem capable of taking care of them, if and when Joseph died. Gordon replied immediately that if they ever needed anything, he would act in the same way that Joseph would. Joseph passed away, and Gordon took over all the expenses of the family. The mother did leave and went back to her little village, as she was overwhelmed by it all. Gordon and Brett sent the children to private schools, among the best in the country; and one of the daughters, Indi, actually went to a finishing school in Switzerland and, together with her own talent, had the opportunity to really shine in South Africa. After Nelson Mandela was elected president, there were many important opportunities for her, and with her education, she went on to success. The two brothers, unfortunately, were not interested in school, but Gordon and Brett made sure that they went to a proper trade school to help prepare them for life. Although also given the opportunity, Indi's sister Pindi also decided to drop out and went to live with her grandmother in a very small village. Indi was always at the house on the Vaal River, whenever Gordon's children were there; and she was, and is, a friend of Gordon's daughter Vicky. It was such a pleasant surprise to see Indi in Capri, where they had flown her for Brett's birthday party. But why not? Gordon's other children were there with their spouses.

After meeting Brett and Gordon, our social lives in South Africa were tremendously enlarged. On one occasion, at lunch at the home of their friends John and Lola Newberry, in the Oceanside town of Hermanus, we met the ex-president De Klerk, who was responsible for releasing Nelson Mandela from prison, where he never should have been, and making it a certainty that Nelson Mandela, a great man, would replace De Klerk as the president of the country. De Klerk was a charming and obviously very intelligent man. As an interesting aside, Gordon Joffe manufactured the shirts that President Mandela wore, especially for him; and where patterns were involved, he did not use those patterns for anyone else.

We met Gordon and Brett on many business occasions outside of South Africa. We met them in London, and I spent some time with Gordon at the automobile show in Germany; and we traveled together to Torino, Italy, and tried to sell spare parts from the BMW factory in South Africa to Fiat, the giant Italian automobile manufacturer in Torino, where I had the most fantastic meal I have ever had. We had been taken out to lunch by the Fiat executives, with whom we had met, and I never saw a menu as this restaurant did not have any since they prepared whatever the customer wanted, although they certainly did make suggestions. Of course, it was quite elegant, and while you cannot experience the taste of an actual course that you have already eaten, I do remember it was one of the best meals ever. I was also introduced at that lunch to grappa, which is a very potent colorless Italian alcoholic beverage, and I experienced a high that I can still remember. What an afternoon.

One of the kindest and gentle men we met throughout our life was Luciano di Marchi, from Italy. Luciano was a friend of Gordon and Brett and spent a month each year as their guest in Cape Town. Like us, he saw them very often, but he also had his own set of friends with whom he socialized. Many times we shared our apartment with him, both in Clifton and at the Breakers, which was the fourteen-story building they had built.

Luciano owned an inn and a restaurant in a small mountain town, about forty minutes from Torino. Luciano was a handsome Italian, tall and thin, and was extremely popular in Cape Town, where he accompanied many of the beautiful single women who needed escorts. Luciano was gay and gallant and charming to be with. Everyone loved him, and I don't think there was a mean bone in his body. He often cooked for us at home, and he was a terrific chef. He owned a restaurant and inn in Italy, together with his brother, and it was always a happy time being with him. After many invitations, we decided one year to pay him a visit in Italy. He picked us up at the airport in Milan, stopped in Torino for truffles, and then we went on to his village and hotel. I spent an hour with Luciano at the restaurant, hearing him answer the phone and telling everyone that called that the restaurant was completely full that night and they could not accommodate any of the guests.

Of course, the restaurant was not full; but Luciano told me that if he were to accept all these reservations, he would have no time to spend with us as he would be involved with all the guests, and he wanted to spend all his time with us since we had made a special visit to see him. The inn was rather large and very old, located in the center of the village, across from the cathedral; and our room, the best in the hotel, was ancient but lovely. The dinner, of course, was magnificent; and Luciano was with us every moment as he wanted to be, and we were thrilled to have him with us. Luciano was another of those wonderful people we have been lucky to meet in our lives, and it was simply great seeing him in Capri at Brett's birthday party. The truffles he had bought were very expensive, and he spread it quite liberally over our food. Luciano was very special, and I look forward to the next time we meet.

The next day he drove us back to the airport, but it was certainly a night to remember.

At the time, I was in business with Gordon and Brett, selling BMW spare parts to BMW dealers in the United States of America at about one-fourth the cost of the parts from Germany. These legitimate spare parts were made in the BMW factories in South Africa. Of course, it was a successful business, but BMW USA objected in about a year's time and took over that business upon orders from Germany. Gordon had been successfully selling these spare parts to many other countries with the permission of the South African factory, but the United States of America was too large a market for them to allow us to operate in. We had a very large warehouse in Providence, Rhode Island, a partner there, and I visited there once a month.

In the late 1990s I met Gordon in Dubai, as he wanted to introduce me to a porcelain tile and bathroom fixture manufacturer, which was owned by one of the emirates, Ras al-Khaima, with whom he did business in one of his many other companies. The idea was for me to possibly represent them in the United States of America. Dubai is, of course, a miracle city built on the sand of the Middle East and wealthy beyond imagination because of the oil in Abu Dhabi. Dubai has also become the center for economic activity in the area; and huge hotels, buildings, and grandiose plans for businesses and real estate abound there, like nowhere else has ever been planned. Gordon spent two days with me there, making all the introductions, and then he left. I was entertained literally, royally, for the next three days and was ultimately given the exclusive rights to sell their products in America. Despite the fact that feelings about doing business in that area were uncomfortable for the buyers here, the prices were so advantageous that I was able to get some large companies, including Home Depot, to sample.

Something happened, of which I am still not sure, but the tile company in Ras al-Khaima sent me a check for $5,000 and thanked me for my efforts, but they decided they were going to work directly. Obviously, an order had been received, and they were at least gentlemanly enough to pay me that commission, but I was eliminated from any future business. I do not think this was the idea of the emirates, but rather something happened on this side. The thought of Gordon Jones traveling halfway around the world to introduce me to someone with whom I might be able to do business is a good indication of the type of friend he is. Dubai was spectacular, and its golf course was entirely floodlit as you could not play during the heat of the day, so the players were able to go out in the evening and nighttime on a course that had the same light as existed during the day. The sand was the main ingredient in the tile products, and there was plenty of that. The workers in the factory, one thousand of them, were all from the Philippines and were housed in a type of compound where each had a little room, and they received their meals in a huge dining room with very little else for them to do.

It was a little different for visitors, and I was taken to restaurants that were as beautiful as anything I have ever seen; and the food, of course, was excellent. Dr. Khater Massad was the managing director of RAK Ceramics and a true gentleman. It was a pleasure meeting him and almost doing business with him.

For the fifty-four years that I have been traveling to South Africa, there have been three important people that I met, all named Gordon. The first one was, of course, Gordon Robins-Browne about whom I have already spoken extensively. The second was Gordon Joffe, who introduced me to the third, Gordon Jones, and I have also spoken about both of these Gordons. But they all represented a very important part of my life, and so much of that life was spent with them that I am sure you will indulge me if I add other stories about them as they come to mind.

Gordon Joffe and Mathy were married on February 27, 1983. Muriel, Richard, and I flew to Cape Town for the wedding; and I delivered the speech that is usually given by the best man in this country. Mathy's brother, Robert, was the best man, but Gordon wanted me to be the speech maker. I did not know about this until we arrived, and I was very nervous about speaking to over three hundred people in a foreign country. My friends at our table were very helpful and kept refilling my glass with scotch whiskey to drink and loosen me up. They were right, and after my first words, I relaxed; and mixing in the few words of Afrikaans that I know, together with a great deal of Spanish, I did great and had everyone laughing a lot. The Spanish was used because Mathy's family, last name Franco, were Sephardic Jews; and they all spoke Ladino, which is basically Spanish and has been used by the Jews from Spain for centuries. Mathy had grown up in the Belgian Congo, before the family moved to Cape Town, and was a beautiful young lady. My speech was really a big success,

327

and I remember my closing line, which was "The true measure of a friendship is a friendship without measure." Whoever had not known me before the wedding but was there at the wedding certainly knew me afterward. Since I was pumped up with the scotch and my own excited feelings about being there and honored to give the speech, no one thought of me other than Gordon's American friend.

Mathy and Gordon had three children. Michel was the same age as our grandson, Evan; Danielle, a couple of years younger; and then Marco came into this world a few years after that. As I mentioned previously, both Muriel and I thought of these three children as our own grandchildren, and we treated them accordingly whenever we were in Cape Town. As a matter of fact, we even took Michel on safari with us on one occasion when Donna, Virginia, and Evan spent six months living in Cape Town (on a sabbatical for both Donna and Virginia); and we were there on our annual trip. Evan went to the Jewish school Herzliah during the time that they were in Cape Town, in the same grade as Michel. We were very close to Gordon and Mathy, and when I wasn't in South Africa, I spoke on the telephone to Gordon at least once a week.

It was a wonderful friendship; even though I was twenty years older, our interests were very similar. I know he counted on me for my experience and knowledge; and we enjoyed each other's company immensely, as well as our mutual interest in all sports (cricket as well as baseball), and I tried to take him to the different sports when he was visiting New York. Gordon died suddenly of a heart attack in early 2002, and the loss of his being there for me was a tremendous blow to me. The next year I also suffered a heart attack on our first visit to stay in Florida, in the town of Stuart where we had rented a lovely condo at one of the nicest places anywhere, Sailfish Point, in the same community as the Zacks. It was on the southern end of Hutchinson Island, which was just off the coast of Florida and surrounded by the beautiful Atlantic Ocean. They had to perform tests on me after the heart attack, injecting dye into me, which caused my kidneys to fail and forced me to go into dialysis. Gordon Joffe, of course, never knew this although about six years previously I had had a heart attack, which was very upsetting to him.

Some of the most pleasant evenings that we have spent anywhere have been at the home of Francine and Frank Greenblatt. Frank was a close personal friend of Gordon Joffe and was the same age as Gordon. Frank was a successful businessman, an owner of a textile mill that produced fabrics that were subsequently made into curtains and drapes. It was a business that he started himself and, through his hard work and winning personality, made it into a success. Like Gordon, Frank was also a rugby referee; and although a little overweight, it always amazed me that he could spend an entire game running up and down the field, keeping everyone in line, and controlling the game. They refereed high school and college games and were very much respected for their athletic ability and integrity. We would spend a fair amount of time with Frank and Francine during our visits to Cape Town; and although a very busy lady with three young children, a successful artist, a vivacious personality, she was able to put together marvelous dinners with some of the most interesting guests around. Francine painted a portrait of me, which is hanging in our apartment and portrays me exactly how I see myself. I was very happy with the results of this painting and always felt that she captured me perfectly.

Francine has had shows in South Africa, London, and New York; and in addition to being a wonderful portrait painter, she was even more known for exotic and sometimes erotic subjects. We were usually about twelve people for dinner; and the guests, in addition to some close friends, always included flamboyant, intelligent, and extremely entertaining guests from the art world of South Africa. There were great discussions, great humor, and great food. We grew close to their family, two sons and a daughter, and I think they enjoyed our company as well. Francine painted some huge pieces, many with sexual overtones, and their house was a veritable art gallery with every space available filled with her lush and vibrant interpretations of life.

There are some people about whom it is very easy to write, and the Greenblatts were certainly in that group. Tragically, Frank died suddenly of a heart attack just months before our mutual and wonderful friend Gordon Joffe passed away, and he was mourned by everyone. Due to my own inability to travel, which coincided with the passing away of both Gordon and Frank, I did not see Francine again for five years. In December 2007 Muriel and I made a trip to South Africa, along with our grandson Matthew, fulfilling a promise we had made to him to take him there and on a truly exciting safari.

I telephoned Francine on our arrival, and she, not knowing from where I was calling, immediately asked if there was any chance of our ever coming back to South Africa as so many people had missed us and had gotten used to us being there every year. When I told her that I was actually calling from Cape Town, she screamed in excitement and asked me to please, along with Muriel and Matthew, come to her wedding, which was taking place five days later. Her children were flying in for the wedding, and even at this auspicious time, all she could think of was making arrangements to get us to the ceremony and reception. She was now going to live six months in London and the other half year in Cape Town, pursuing her lifetime love affair with the arts.

The three of us went to that wedding, and it was fabulous for us to be there and renew so many of the friendships that we had had but which had lapsed in the previous five years. Francine was marrying a very successful and retired South African businessman, a former chairman of Woolworth's, John Rabb. I think that night in particular marked a great moment in our grandson's life, as he seemed able to show his own personality and mixed freely with people he had never met before. He was not in love with the food but made the best of everything, and we were very proud of him. That entire trip matured Matthew, and he came back to comments from almost everyone as to how much he had grown up in this short time. We really captured the moment when he became a young adult. The wedding was an Orthodox ceremony and performed strictly according to religious law, which was also a first for Matthew, and I know he loved being there.

Except for the years 1993, 1997, and 1999, during which time we rented a house in Barbados, in the West Indies, from the beginning or middle of January to the beginning or middle of February, we spent six weeks in South Africa, mainly on vacation during the months of January and February, the height of their summer season, from 1978 to 2001. I, of course, had been traveling to South Africa since 1954, mostly twice a year, sometimes at the beginning even three trips; so my total visits to South Africa were over sixty. It actually amounts to more than five years of my life, and obviously I enjoyed every minute of it, especially since 1978 when Muriel was able to accompany me and with both Donna and Richard finished with school and no longer living at home.

Barbados: Family Fun

In Barbados we rented a four-bedroom house right on the beach next to the world-famous Sandy Lane Hotel. When I say "next to the hotel," we were the home nearest to the hotel but still quite a walk on the beach before you reached the Sandy Lane. As you stepped off our patio in the back, you were on that beautiful beach. Along with the house came our own car, a full-time housekeeper, a cook, and a gardener.

The beach and the Caribbean Sea, one of the best in the world, were simply divine. Our family and friends visited us during our stay, and the bedrooms were all kept occupied throughout the time that we were there. The weather was always excellent, and we often visited the Sandy Lane Hotel for special dinners, as well as other hotels and many of the great restaurants that Barbados offers. Evan and Matthew, in particular, were enchanted by everything that the island had. Lauren, unfortunately, was too young to visit. We shopped for fish that had just been caught that day, and especially the flying fish, a specialty of Barbados, was everyone's favorite. Most evenings, when there were just adults in attendance, and when we ate in, we would visit the various hotels after dinner for a drink and music. Everyone looked forward to going to Barbados, and while we also missed South Africa on those occasions, Barbados was very special.

One occasion in Barbados really stands out in my mind. I was sitting alone on the beach one afternoon, reading a book, when out of the corner of my eye, I glimpsed a Barbadian man looking me over from every different angle of the compass. He would squat down, squinted at me from about twenty yards away, and then move to another corner to do the same thing. After finishing the four corners, he slowly ventured toward me.

"Is that you?"

"Yes, it is me."

"No, really, is that really you?"

"Of course, it is me." I had no idea what he was talking about, but I went along, knowing I would soon learn.

And it *was* me!

"Oh, man, if my girlfriend only knew I was here and it was you, she would go crazy! Can I bring her here to meet you?"

One of the most famous of all TV shows was the weekly *Dallas*. It was so successful that it quickly had a sequel even before it had finished its run. That sequel was *Knots Landing*. The star of the sequel was William Devane, who many people thought I looked like, and obviously my new friend thought so also; in fact, he was sure that he, William Devane, was me, Alvin Futterman.

Barbados had one TV station, and although *Knots Landing* had practically finished its run in the United States of America, it was only now showing in Barbados—years later. It was the number one show on the island, and it was not unusual for celebrities to be seen in Barbados, the premier destination in the West Indies during those times. I learned all this as our conversation continued.

"Of course, you can bring her. I would be very happy to meet her. However, I am sorry to tell you that I will not be allowed to sign anything or even pose for pictures as my contract does not permit me to do so."

"That's OK, man, just as long as she can see you. And it is great meeting you, Mr. Devane."

"Likewise."

I never met the lucky lady, and I don't know if she observed me from afar. She probably told her boyfriend he was crazy, though I know that he was thrilled, and so was I.

During the late 1960s and most of the 1970s, there was a huge economic slump in South Africa, and we made very few trips during that time through that area. However, in the late 1970s the economy improved, and our trips once again became regular. During the 1980s the Far East, mainly Hong Kong, Bangkok, Singapore, Malaysia, and sometimes Taiwan and Korea, also picked up economically; and the trips had to include those areas as well as East Africa, which meant Kenya, Tanzania, and Uganda, and also once or twice to Addis Ababa, Ethiopia. All in all, as I described it before, it was a very busy time; but the United States was slowly becoming an importing country and finding it very difficult to compete in textiles with the Far East, except for some very special lines, which we were lucky enough to have, such as Klopman Mills.

During that time, we also started doing business in Europe, which took us to London quite regularly, as well as to Dublin, Barcelona, Madrid, Rome, Amsterdam, and Paris, to either sell or to represent in the United States. From France we represented Boussac et Fils for all of Latin America. Boussac, to whom we were introduced by a former South African who now represented them in the United States, was a world-famous producer of fabrics for furniture as well as drapes and curtains.

At that time we also restarted doing business in the Caribbean, which was always a favorite place to visit. But our business was changing, and along with the exporting that we were doing, we started to represent companies from overseas who were buying in the United States and needed a representative here as well as some companies that wanted to sell in this country. We had earned a great reputation overseas and were well-known by a good deal of the business community around the world.

Central, Pennys, Tellermate, Yamato, and Harwill: The Last Ventures

The largest retail organization in Southeast Asia, Central Department Stores, in Bangkok, to whom we had sold shirting fabrics for their factory, asked us to represent them on their purchases in this country. They sold better-quality merchandise and bought many high-priced items in the United States. They purchased toys from Mattel, even some items that had been manufactured in Thailand but could only be bought through the United States—sheets and pillowcases from Cannon, jeans from Levi's, as well as many other items—and paid us a 6 percent commission to make these purchases and get everything together for large shipments to them and to reinvoice each item.

The chairman of the company Mr. Samrit Chirathivat had become a personal friend, as well as a customer, and it was a wonderful association. His parents had originally emigrated from China to

Thailand when he was an infant and their only child. His father married an additional two times and had twenty-six children in all. Except for one daughter, who is a doctor in Washington DC and the sister of my friend, the other twenty-four children lived in Bangkok, and all worked for Central in one of their various enterprises. And all *their* children, most of whom were educated in the United States, also worked in one form or another for the family company. The family name, which the parents adopted when they arrived from China, Chirathivat, was chosen as the father thought he would do better with a Thai name rather than his original Chinese name. They were one of the most successful families in all of Southeast Asia.

At the same time, we also represented the largest retail organization in Ireland. It was called Primark, and their department stores were named Penny's, although there was no relation to JCPenney's here in the United States.

I had met Arthur Ryan, the managing director of the Irish group, through my young friend Nissy Shapiro from Cape Town. He also represented Primark on their purchases in South Africa and Israel, as I did here in the United States. They also paid me a commission for all purchases made here; and just as Central Department Stores did, they made sure that all the financing of their purchases was here long before the bill had to be paid, so there was no outlay of money on my part.

I visited both these customers, on the opposite ends of the world, fairly regularly, with Muriel; and we were always entertained exceptionally well. In Bangkok we stayed at their forty-story luxury hotel and were taken out to dinner every night of the week.

In Ireland, one year, I remember Arthur Ryan arranging a car and driver to take us on a trip throughout Ireland, and we stayed for two nights in an old castle that had been completely refurbished and was unforgettable. Arthur's wife, Alma, was beautiful and had been one of the most popular recording stars in Ireland. She was lovely to be with, and the times we spent with them were also memorable.

Our most profitable venture was with the aforementioned Reichman's International Shipping, as we were a 50 percent partner rather than just the ones who received a commission.

Through our relationship to Penny's and Arthur Ryan, when they were asked to recommend somebody in the United States to sell a money counting machine that was manufactured in Wales, we were immediately mentioned. The inventor of the machine and president of the company called Tellermate was a gentleman named Edgar Biss. Edgar had a fascinating escape from the Nazis before World War II broke out. His family's plan was executed perfectly, and he was handed, this little boy, to his mother as she was boarding the ship to leave Europe for Great Britain. He was quite brilliant but not a very smart or good businessman. He had invented this machine that counted money, both bills and coins, by weighing them. Of course, there were different standards for each country's currency, but Edgar had worked all this out, and his machine was actually more exact than the ones in use. The machines in most of the banks flip the money and count the bills as they go through, though they can get stuck together, which the Tellermate resolved.

The United States government counts its money by weighing stacks of them, as the Tellermate does. In tests that I would perform when calling on banks and giving my demonstration, I was able to show that my machine was more accurate, even accounting for the dirt on the bills and coins, as we tested their models and mine. When Edgar offered me the exclusive sales agency for the United States, my hands were quite full with some of the other endeavors I have just mentioned, but I could not pass up this opportunity as it seemed to be a winner. And it was. We would buy the machines from Tellermate in Wales once we had an order, so there was no inventory to invest in; and although there was a suggested selling price, it allowed for a very reasonable profit and even special deals for quantity.

As the business grew, Edgar started to take certain areas in the country away from me, with which I was agreeable as it was obvious that I could not cover the entire United States. In the end, I kept the Northeast, the original thirteen colonies. However, after being quite successful, he decided that he would open his own business in the United States, even though he now had four exclusive distributors including us, and wanted to leave me with just New York City. Although we had done very well, and it was profitable, I could not accept those terms and refused to sign the new contract under those conditions. I had worked with Tellermate for four years, but Edgar was getting too controlling and too greedy. He wanted it all. At the beginning of our association, Muriel and I had traveled to Wales to visit the factory and spend some time in the area. We stayed at a very old hotel, which had originally been a small castle; but when Muriel got stuck in the room (because the doors were simply too old), Edgar and his wife suggested that we stay at their three hundred-year-old stone house, which turned out to be lovely. They were wonderful hosts, and we enjoyed all the time we were with them. While I would work during the day, going over logistics and future plans, Muriel was taken out touring through one of the most beautiful countrysides anywhere in this world.

Unfortunately, for everyone, this wonderful association ended with the unfair demands of Edgar Biss. The other three distributors were eventually forced out, and Edgar had the United States for his own company. I am told that that did not work out eventually, and I have not heard about the company since, though the product was really excellent. Through the original four distributors, tens of thousands were sold.

My great friend Yuichi Kashiwada, who was the managing director of UGIL in Kampala, Uganda, actually represented the Japanese part of that company. In Japan, the company was known as Yamato, and they produced a very expensive line of men's sportswear. They were represented in the United States by a Japanese company who they felt was not doing well enough for them, and they asked us as their representative. We took on that task; and Richard handled the sales, warehousing, and shipping of the items in this country. He sold it to some of the finest stores in America, including Barneys, Saks Fifth Avenue, Neiman Marcus, and all the others in that category, and was very successful with it.

Another venture, and one that I thought might be the best, was being the exclusive distributor in the United States for Harwill Industries. This was a South African company that had been founded by another of my close friends, Mr. Renier van Rooyen, and they produced innovative and very useful pharmaceutical products. Renier was originally a postman; and then, delivering mail to various companies, he came to the conclusion that he could run a retail organization, selling to the poor people, better than the stores to whom he was delivering mail. With a little money from his family and his wife's family, he started Pep Stores. These were originally small stores that sold mainly to the Afrikaner population, of which he was one, mainly items like blankets, school uniforms, plain clothing, and other household items. It was an instant success, and by the time I met Renier, he had one thousand large and small department stores and was growing. The stores by now carried almost everything that a department store has and sold at small profits, which enabled them to capture that entire market.

For those types of items he asked me to represent their interests in the United States and handle all his purchases here for him. Unfortunately, the nature of the business did not allow for too many purchases to be made in the United States of America, but it was a good business and added to our own reputation. He and I became very close. We spent a good deal of time with him; his wife, Alice; and their children. Despite the fact that Renier was an Afrikaner and expected to be very conservative and a staunch supporter of the Nationalist party, he most definitely was not and was a large contributor to the opposition's Progressive party. The Nationalist party consisted of some of the original advocates of apartheid, which my friend, Renier van Rooyen, found particularly distasteful. I heard conversations where he was told that many things could be done for him if he would only be supportive of the "Nats," but Renier was a man of great values and principles and was truly loved by all, white and black. His brother and sister, and their families, followed the party line and were very conservative. I am not sure what the final reason was; but he decided to sell the business, retire, and enjoy his homes in England, Portugal, and South Africa.

Previous to that, he and I spent a week at the very famous Golden Door, an expensive spa in California, where Muriel had given me a wonderful birthday present, a week there, the previous year. When I told him about this wonderful place, he flew over specifically to go away for a week with me, and we had a fabulous time. The Golden Door was quite a luxurious spa, although it was devoid of any frills but had everything it needed, very much like a Japanese spa. The week that we were there was only for men, and you were in a tracksuit or bathing suit all day and wore your Japanese bathrobe at dinner. We had exercise classes every hour on the hour, except for our meals, which were cooked by a gourmet chef and were designed to help you lose some weight while being absolutely healthy and delicious. We would take a three-mile hike before breakfast and then afterward go to an exercise class or play volleyball in the pool for that time period. The same schedule applied after lunch, and at night there were lectures on various subjects. Though it was quite expensive, I am sure that everybody felt it was well worth the cost. Most of the year, the spa was devoted to women, and many famous people attended throughout the year. I think there were only four weeks when couples were allowed, and it was run quite strictly and efficiently.

I was one of the first persons Renier notified of his retirement plans. I was in South Africa in February when he told me he was retiring at the end of March. There was going to be a huge black-tie party there, and he wanted me to come back for it. I flew back to Cape Town for that gala weekend for him, arriving Friday and leaving Monday! I was seated at the head table with Renier, Alice, the new owner of Pep Stores, his young beautiful wife, and some political leaders.

This was during the 1980s, and I spent a lot of time with Renier, both here and in South Africa. I did not believe that he could possibly retire completely as he was only sixty years old; and so it was no surprise, when three years after his retirement, he informed me that he was starting a new business: Harwill Industries.

The offer he proposed to me was more generous than anything I have ever heard of. He was a millionaire twenty times over, and he wanted me to be the exclusive distributor in the United States for their products, and he actually guaranteed in writing that I would not be responsible for any losses, were they to occur. Of course, neither of us thought there would be any losses, but the products did not sell either here in the United States or in Europe; and since they were mainly designed for those markets, the business failed but not before Renier made sure that I received the $200,000 that the business had lost here in expenses and sold the inventory at great losses. It was a very sad time for me as my friend lost a small fortune, and it turned out that his loss here in the United States was the smallest part of it as he lost all the money that he had built up in his original business. He was such a wonderful person. I have not spoken to him in a few years, and I was not able to contact him. When we were in South Africa in December 2007, no one knew where he was at that time; but I subsequently heard that he and his wonderful wife, Alice, had broken up; and he was living in a rented room, a very poor and broken person. I cannot seem to contact him, but I will! He was too important to me to just lose him like that.

The young doctor who had invented most of the genius pharmaceutical products that Harwill was selling, Dr. Marius van der Merve, has also found nothing but hard times, as some jinx seems to have settled over what was left of Harwill Industries. I managed to keep in touch with Marius and his wife, Anarika, who have entertained Muriel and me at their home in the Cape Town area. They lived originally in a small beach town, and Marius would dive for large lobsters when he knew we were coming and then cook them for us. It is one of the few sad memories that I have of South Africa, the demise of my friends Renier and Marius. We did manage to see Marius and Anarika when we visited Cape Town with our grandson Matthew in December 2007, but they seemed to have hardly anything to speak of, a young doctor and his beautiful wife. It was a very difficult time for me and Muriel as we left their home after lunch with them.

Another of the wonderful friends on that long list of good friends in South Africa was Henry van Embden and his wife, Jill, who had that wonderful party with the choir when we visited in 1980. Although we did not do any business together, we did spend a lot of time with each other. I remember one afternoon—Muriel was not with me on this trip—we were drinking five bottles of chenin blanc with Henry and Nissy, although I do not think that Nissy had more than one glass. We had finished a whole wheel of cheddar cheese with that wine, and I do not remember how I walked out of there.

Barry Isaacs was my agent in Durban when I sponsored him and his family to immigrate to the United States. Other people that I have also sponsored included Gary Salmo, the son of a good friend and customer, Len Salmo, of Star Shirt in Durban.

There was also the son of Francis Au, who was my longtime agent in Hong Kong, and while I did not sponsor him, there was another—a rather small frail, thin man from Mali—who came to New York and had my name that had been given to him by a customer to whom I had sold several years before. He did not speak English, only French and his tribal language. He came to my office, and it was quite obvious that he was ill. I took him back to his hotel, which was on Eighth Avenue and Forty-fifth Street. I arranged for the hotel to get him a doctor, who fortunately was able to treat him as I would not have known what to do since he knew no one else in the United States. I stayed with him until the doctor came and then arranged to get his medicine, and I remember feeling that I was really helping someone who needed me, maybe even saving his life. When he returned to Mali, where on a certain street corner they would have what would best be described as public stenographers or someone who can write a letter for you in the language that you want to be sent, he had one of these people write the most beautiful letter of thanks to me, with all the blessings that only God could bestow.

Another South African family that I sponsored was Mike Greenberg and his wife, Susan, and their three children. We had met Mike and Susan on a cruise through the Greek islands, and we both got off in Mykonos the night before the trip officially ended, as we found that island enchanting, and enjoyed each other's company. We spent three nights on Mykonos, and each one was better than the previous one. Our friendship was made there; and when they expressed a desire to come live in the United States, I was there for them, sponsored them, and gave Mike a job with our company. However, he was not comfortable or happy leaving his family to travel, and that was what our business did. He decided to open a retail store in Connecticut so that he would be able to spend all his time at home. I allowed Mike to sell the money counting machine in his area. My business was very good for our family and for other families as well.

All these other businesses were, in a business sense, much easier than the first one, buying textiles and then trying to sell them; but that original business was more exciting, and it was something that I had started and made a success. It also gave us the opportunity to try all these other ventures. During all the time after breaking up with Jerry, I always had a great staff of employees helping me. Without them I could never have accomplished what I did. The one that really stands out is Joanne Bonacorso; she was the partner that every businessman needs. She is now married to Richard Sequeno, and we still see them socially.

We have known Ronny and Susanne Fein for more than thirty-five years, but our wonderful friendship has truly blossomed over the last fifteen years. They are an extremely generous couple, not only in the conventional sense but also with their time and their emotions. They have always been there for us. Ronny was originally a woman's wear manufacturer, but when he realized it was no longer for him, he made a study of various fields and decided to become a breeder and developer of racehorses. In addition to their home in Sands Point, New York, they have a wonderful horse farm in Ocala, Florida, where we have spent some great time with them. On their honeymoon, they hitchhiked from Cairo, Egypt, down to Cape Town, South Africa. Incredible. They both have been on many big game safaris, and their homes are evidence of this with their many trophies adorning the walls. We spend a lot of time with them when we are both in New York, and it is always animated and very interesting. I usually have lunch with Ronny once a week, and there is never a dull moment in our conversations. They are real, true friends.

Dr. Chao: A New Lease on Life

One of the most important persons in my life, without question, is Dr. Stan Chao. He is responsible for the second part of my life that I am enjoying today. I met Dr. Chao on Tuesday, March 29, 2005; and on April 8, ten days later, he transplanted a kidney into my body that gave me a new life and the ability to enjoy it.

Early in December 2002, we arrived at Sailfish Point, on Hutchinson Island, just east of Stuart, Florida, to spend the next four months. On that very first day, after unpacking and having dinner, I began to feel very uncomfortable. Thinking and hoping that it was merely indigestion, I waited for the discomfort to go away, but it didn't; and at two o'clock in the morning we called 911, and I was taken to the hospital with a serious heart attack. They stabilized me, and I was started on the way to recovery.

Unfortunately, they had to check the damage that had been done and had to inject some dye into my system, which caused my kidneys to fail; and I was immediately put on dialysis, which was not a great surprise as my kidneys had indicated that this might be necessary. With dialysis, you are treated at a dialysis center by having your blood cleaned through a machine three times a week, four hours each time. It is totally debilitating, and there is a great toll that is paid for this life-saving technology, by you and everyone near and dear to you.

Dialysis is forever once you start unless you are very lucky and become one of the few to receive a transplanted kidney. I was on dialysis throughout that trip to Florida and then started again once we got home at a dialysis center near our condominium. It was very difficult being hooked up to a machine as your entire blood supply passed through it, and it was exhausting. I was now in the hands of the doctors and the dialysis machine. It is very hard to describe how difficult it was; but you try to think of all the good parts of your life and all the great people in it, your family, and you live for a miracle, if that can happen. I could conceivably have taken long trips, but it certainly was not recommended. I have a set of doctors in Stuart, Florida, and a different set in Port Washington, New York. Dr. Jeffrey Glickman was my nephrologist in Stuart; and during my appointment in March 2005, I asked him if I was being realistic in thinking that I could possibly be eligible for a transplant, given my age, my heart disease, and the general shortage of kidneys for transplant. He reassured me that I was definitely a possible candidate, even though four months before in New York, the hospital (Columbia Presbyterian), after a full day of tests and interviews, had told me that there would be at least a six to eight year wait; and by then I would be that much older and less likely to be a candidate.

Dr. Glickman said that he would register me into two programs in Florida. One of them was at a hospital in Orlando, and the other was at a hospital in the small beach town of New Smyrna Beach, just south of Daytona. He felt that I might have a better chance with the smaller hospital, and I should try to follow up with them. Once they received my application submitted by Dr. Glickman, they telephoned me to set up an appointment for an interview. I informed them that I was going home to New York in a little over two weeks, and the nurse who had called suggested that I come to see them before going North. This was a Friday, and she thought that it would be a good idea if I could come in the following Tuesday morning. I could not believe that this was taking place, and I tried to remain calm, remembering the time line given to me in New York of up to eight years' wait on a national waiting list. We were due to fly back home on April 9, Muriel's birthday, but decided to drive up to New Smyrna Beach about three hours away. Our appointment was for Tuesday, March 28, at 9:00 a.m.; so we drove up Monday afternoon and checked into a bed-and-breakfast just a block away from Bert Fish Hospital. We were at the hospital early the next morning and went through a series of interviews with the staff before meeting Dr. Stan Chao. He was a Chinese-American and had gone to school in Los Angeles at UCLA. He asked me why I wanted a transplant, and I told him that I had so many more things to do that I could not do on dialysis, and one of them was to take our grandson Matthew on safari in Africa. We had already taken Evan during his stay there.

We got along very well from our first meeting, but I did not fool myself into thinking that a new kidney would be available to me. There was a lot of information that the doctor wanted, and I was going to get it for him when I returned home. We drove back to Stuart and started preparing to leave for New York and sending our car home before us. Nine days later, sitting in our great apartment at Sailfish Point,

I received a call. It was Dr. Stan Chao himself; and he asked me if I could be at the hospital in New Smyrna Beach by that evening, Thursday, April 7, at 8:00 p.m. I calmly said yes as he informed me that he expected to have a kidney flown in that evening, which, to all indications, looked like it could be a good match for me.

This was incredible. This was the miracle that you live for, and the miracle was mine. I was going to get my life back. I was going to be able to do all those other things I wanted to do and never dared to dream that they were possible any longer. We drove through one of the worst rainstorms that I have ever been in but managed to follow the rear lights of a large trailer truck in front of us that got us to New Smyrna Beach. Donna was at a conference in Atlanta, and Muriel reached her there, and she made all the arrangements necessary to get herself to New Smyrna Beach that night. It would have been impossible for Richard to arrive on time. We got to the hospital early, about 7:00 p.m.; they prepped me for the operation, the kidney arrived, and then the hospital had to postpone for a few hours my kidney transplant as someone had a broken arm that they were treating.

The doctor was, of course, furious, but we waited; and soon after midnight, Dr. Stan Chao began the transplant operation on April 8. I remember thinking what a wonderful birthday present he was giving us for Muriel's birthday on April 9. The transplant was a perfect success, and the doctor, my savior, was simply wonderful. Over the next few days, he would come to visit me, not only to examine me and see how I was doing but to also sit down and talk about life and family. I might be a little prejudiced, but he is one of the finest human beings I have ever met. Dr. Stan Chao was about fifty years old at the time and simply the most wonderful and compassionate person I have met. I have kept in touch with him ever since and speak to him regularly. It has never been explained to me how and why that kidney found its way to me. It came from a lady who was killed in an accident in Mississippi.

They do not ever give you the name of the donor, but I did write a letter to her family, although I am not sure that they ever received it since I never heard from them. (The hospital sent it for me.) My kidney transplant was the last successful one done at the hospital in New Smyrna Beach as the directors of the hospital suddenly and without notice decided to abandon the transplant program as they said it was too expensive for a small community hospital. Dr. Chao, who kept me informed of everything, was totally shocked by their actions, their unexplainable actions, and was never given any other reason for the closing down of the program. He is now living and working on the border between Idaho and the State of Washington, on the Snake River. He convinced his parents who were living in Denver, Colorado, to join him, his wife, and their three children; and he is thrilled that they are all living together. He is doing general surgery as he could not get back into transplant surgery after this tremendous letdown, and I remain his last successful kidney transplant.

He had wanted me to stay for two months after the operation so that he could look after me and my condition; but I explained to him that my grandson, who I could now take on safari to Africa because of Dr. Chao, was being bar-mitzvahed one month after my transplant, and he agreed that that too was very important for my recovery and let me go back to New York as long as he could speak to the doctor who was going to look after me. What a wonderful man he is, and how lucky of me to have met him. He let me live again.

So Many Travels!

From my first trip to Ireland in May 1950 to the last time we were in Italy in August 2007, we have visited Europe at least thirty-five times and have not left a stone unturned. From the Rock of Gibraltar off the southwest corner of Spain, the Blarney Stone in Ireland, Stonehenge in England, the ruins in Pompeii and the Roman Forum, the Acropolis in Greece, the coliseums in Rome and Ephesus in Western Turkey, the magnificent statues of David in Italy, Winged Victory at the Louvre, the Fountains of Trevi, to all the other breathtaking statuary throughout Italy, Spain, and France, Fontainebleau, and all the rocky beaches of the beautiful Mediterranean Sea, we left our fingerprints on all of it.

We saw every important museum, art gallery, garden, and place of interest that every tourist guidebook has ever mentioned. The Tate and the London Museum in London; the Prado in Madrid; the Louvre in Paris; the fabulous Vatican museums; the Uffizi Gallery, Hyde Park, the Tuillerie, and the Medici Gardens in Rome; and Tivoli Gardens in Copenhagen.

We ate at some of the most highly rated restaurants in the world—the Tour D'Argent in Paris, the Hotel Negresco in Nice, the original Alfredo's in Rome, the restaurants in the Savoy and Connaught Hotels in London, the Jockey Club in Madrid—but none were any more satisfying than the ham and cheese on a French bread in a small local bar in Paris off the Champs Elysees, except maybe that very special private restaurant in Torino where the executives of Fiat Motors took Gordon Jones and me and also introduced me to grappa.

We saw many shows at various theaters in the West End of London; we saw several at the Abbey Theater in Dublin, the Folies Bergere in Paris, the opera at La Scala in Milan, a concert in Verona, and a bullfight in Madrid. I don't think we ever went to sleep in Europe!

We stayed at some of the finest hotels in the world—the Connaught in London, the George V and the Bristol in Paris, the Carlton in Cannes, Excelsior in Rome, Danielli in Venice, Baur au Lac in Switzerland, Cala de Volpe in Sardinia, Villa D'este in Lake Como, Milano—and I cannot think of all of them! But we also stayed at many mid-level, small, and inexpensive ones. There were bed-and-breakfasts, pensions and pensiones, and the $11 per-night new hotel on the beach (a rocky one) in Mykonos where we spent one of the most exciting weekends of our life. (Of course, our introduction to completely nude beaches had nothing to do with it.)

I believe we have visited every church and cathedral in Western Europe, from Westminster Abbey to Notre Dame and everything in between, all the way to the awesome and striking St. Peters at the Vatican. I have been to the Vatican at least ten times, and each visit was different than the previous ones. I am totally captivated by everything that exists there. For me, it is the most interesting place in Europe.

Me, the Casinos, and the Mob

Gambling casinos were rather new for most Americans in the 1950s. Of course, there was Las Vegas and Reno and the whole state of Nevada and many illegal gambling places in the United States; but for the most part, you had to fly to Havana and later Puerto Rico for the glamorous and exciting casinos. Actually, gambling is probably the *second* oldest activity in the world, started by Eve in the Garden of Eden. When I first started traveling, one of the first bonuses for me was to enter a casino and stand next to celebrities, kings, Indian pashas, wealthy Arab leaders, and princes. I have gambled, luckily never too much, in almost every corner of the world and enjoyed every moment. I have placed bets at roulette tables, standing next to a former king of Egypt, King Farouk, in Estoril, Portugal. I have watched as Mario Moreno, better known as Cantinflas, the most famous Mexican actor and the star, along with David Niven of *Around the World in 80 Days*, lost tens of thousands of dollars in ten minutes in Havana, Cuba. I have gambled in Macau, a small Portuguese enclave off the coast of China and which today is part of China again. The Chinese are probably the most prolific gamblers in the world, and there were always mobs of people in Macau. I taught an Indian lady, who was wearing a sari, how to play craps at the international casino in Nairobi, Kenya. Some of the richest people in the world were at the casino in Monte Carlo when Muriel and I visited there. Our honeymoon was spent mostly at the casino of the Caribe Hilton in San Juan, Puerto Rico. I actually stayed at a gambling casino in London, England, while there on business. It cost less than a hotel, and the room was magnificent. Up until 1970, I am quite sure that I visited every casino in Las Vegas, although I am also quite sure that there are a hundred more that have opened since. I have gambled in Aruba, Antigua, Surinam (formerly Dutch Guiana), and in an opulent back-room casino in Rio de Janeiro. I have been in a casino in Swaziland, located in the middle of South Africa, full of a mob from that country where gambling in a casino is not legal; but of course, like every other location, betting on horse races is known as the sport of kings. On one of my very first trips, certainly my first to South Africa, we spent a weekend at the then-famous Polana Hotel, in Lourenco Marques, in what was then known as Portuguese East Africa. LM was another spot where South Africans could go to a luxurious gambling casino within relatively easy driving distance although unable to gamble in their own country. I love the whole gambling scene and fortunately have never been caught up in the frenzy that you often see in those locations. I have spent a couple of hours in some casinos, just watching the action without ever placing a bet. I think of myself as a gambler, but I know that I am not a part of that mob. And like most of the gamblers that I know and have seen and heard, I do not remember losing. For as many gambling casinos that I have visited throughout the world, I have been to ever more racetracks, and I have never left a racetrack without placing a bet. It is amazing how I cannot remember ever losing.

Although Bali has the reputation for magical beaches, some that are equally as beautiful exist along the coast of Malaysia. On one trip we decided to drive from Kuala Lumpur to Singapore. It usually was a one-hour plane trip, but after many visits to that area, friends convinced us that we should feast our eyes on the land and the coast.

Along the way is the city of Penang, known as the Pearl of the Orient, and it is a title that is well deserved. It is small but very charming, and when we were there, it retained all its delightful warmth and welcoming feeling. We stayed at a rather old but luxurious hotel with the most unique swimming pool, alongside the ocean, that I have ever seen. It was very large, long, and wide; and rather than stepping down into the pool, you actually walked in down a gradually sloping entrance as if you were walking from a beach into the ocean. It was absolutely beautiful, and the whole coastline of Malaysia was exciting and equal to the reputation of Bali and the great beaches of Indonesia.

It would probably be easier to list the countries I have not been to than to mention every one I have visited. However, so many names have changed that it would be confusing. However I'd choose to do it, I could list them by area or alphabetically.

For example, I have been to every island in the Caribbean and every country in South America. I have not been to any of the eastern European countries, nor too many of the ones in the Middle East, and I have missed quite a few in Southeast Asia but not too many in Africa. At the risk of being boring, I am listing every country and important city that I have had the opportunity of visiting, not just passing through, like an airport, but actually spending time and certainly at least one night there. It seems easier to go through a list in the world atlas and just list the names without too much comment about the places, which I believe I have already done (or maybe repeated myself a little).

I have been to Kabul in Afghanistan; Pago Pago in American Samoa; Luanda in Angola, which was Portuguese West Africa at the time; Anguilla in the Caribbean; the islands of Antigua and Barbuda; Buenos Aires in Argentina; Aruba, Bonaire, and Curacao, in what was called the Netherlands Antilles; Australia, where I stayed in Sydney, Melbourne, Brisbane, Perth, and Adelaide, as well as the capital Canberra and Hobart in Tasmania. In the Bahamas I visited Freeport Nassau and Grand Bahama Island, as well as stopped off in some of the other small islands in that group; Bahrain, a small monarchy in the Middle East; Barbados, where we spent much time vacationing and traveling throughout the island; Belize, formerly known as British Honduras; Bermuda; and the cities of La Paz, Sucre, Oruro, and Cochabamba in Bolivia; Brussels in Belgium; Bophuthatswana, a small state within the borders of South Africa; Gaborone in Botswana; and Ouagadougou in Burkina Faso, also known as Upper Volta, a tiny place in Africa where I stopped off with my father. That covers the places whose names begin with an *A* or a *B*.

I stayed in Douala in Cameroon, just below Nigeria on the west coast of Africa.

In Canada I have visited Montreal, Toronto, and Ottawa; the Cape Verdi Islands off the African coast; and the Cayman Islands in the

Caribbean; Colombo in what was called Ceylon but now know as Sri Lanka; N'Djamena, also known as Fort Lamy in the central African country of Chad; and Santiago, as well as Valpariso, in Chile.

I've visited China but only the city known as Canton now known as Guangzhou, the closest major city to Hong Kong; Ciskei, another small state within the borders of South Africa; and Bogota, Medellin, Cartagena, and Barranquilla in Colombia, South America. I've visited Brazzaville in the Congo, which was the French Congo at that time, as well as Leopoldville, Elizabethville, and Stanleyville now known respectively as Kinshasa, Lubumbashi, and I believe Mbandaka, which were the major cities of the Belgian Congo now known as the Democratic Republic of Congo (DRC), Zaire.

I have visited Aitutaki in the Cook Islands, in the Pacific Ocean, which belonged to New Zealand; San Jose, Costa Rica; and Havana, Pinar del Rio, Manzanillo, Camaguey, and Cardenas in wonderful Cuba; Nicosia on the island of Cyprus in the Mediterranean; Copenhagen in Denmark; the city and country known as Djibouti on the East Coast of Ethiopia; Dominica in the Caribbean; and Santo Domingo, Puerto Plata, and Santiago de los Caballeros, all in the Dominican Republic.

In Brazil, I have been to Rio de Janeiro, Sao Paulo, Sorocaba, Manaus, and Brasilia, all breathtaking cities. In Ecuador there was Guayaquil and Quito; Cairo in Egypt; San Jose, Limon, and Puntarenas in Costa Rica; San Salvador, San Miguel, and Santa Ana in El Salvador.

In the United Kingdom there was Bristol and Cardiff in Wales, and in England, London, Manchester, Liverpool, Birmingham, Leeds, and a bunch of small towns up the Thames that we visited on vacations; and Addis Ababa in Ethiopia, East Africa.

I spent a lot of time in all of East Africa. In Tanzania there was Moshi and Arusha in the foothills of Mount Kilimanjaro, always covered by snow though practically on the equator, as well as Dar es Salaam and more than a dozen villages that I had to visit as its sole American supplier. The island of Zanzibar, right off the coast; Kampala, Entebbe, and Jinja in beautiful Uganda; Kigali in Rwanda; Nairobi, Mombasa, Malindi, and Kisumu in Kenya; and all the fabulous game parks and lodges that we were able to visit throughout East Africa: Serengeti, Queen Elizabeth National Park, Ngorongoro Crater, Sabi Sands, Lake Manyara, Lake Victoria, and Victoria Falls.

Too many to mention or even remember all these fabulous places. Suva in the Fiji Islands. Paris, Moustier, Marseilles, Cannes, Nice, Lyon, and Limoges in France; Monaco; Cayenne in French Guiana; and Paramaribo in Dutch Guyana and Georgetown in British Guyana, all on the northeast coast of South America. Papeete, Tahiti, Moorea, and the rest of French Polynesia. Banjul in Gambia, West Africa, and Libreville in Gabon. Hamburg, Frankfurt, Stuttgart in Germany; Accra in Ghana; and Athens, Salonika, Piraeus, and all those wonderful Greek Islands, particularly Santorini, and especially Mykonos and the island of Rhodes.

Greenland, where I spent the night as they serviced the plane I was on. Grenada in the Caribbean, Guadalupe and Martinique, Guam and Wake Island in the vast expanse of the Pacific, Guatemala City and Antigua in Guatemala, Conakry in Guinea, and Bissau in Guinea-Bissau. Port-au-Prince, Aux Cayes, and Cap-Haitien in

Haiti; Honolulu, Hawaii; Amsterdam and the Hague in Holland; and Tegucigalpa, San Pedro Sula, Tela, and La Ceiba in Honduras.

Hong Kong, which deserves a paragraph by itself.

Reykjavik, Iceland, as well as Bombay (it is difficult to call it Mumbai), Delhi, New Delhi, Agra, Calcutta, and Bangalore Jaipur in the country of one billion people, India. Jakarta, Surabaya, and Medan in another difficult country, Indonesia. Dublin, Cork, and Galway in truly Green Ireland, and Belfast the quietest city I have ever been in, in Northern Ireland. There were no motorcars allowed because of fears of terrorism and car bombings, and this silence was unbelievable. You were searched at checkpoints before being allowed to enter the city. Jerusalem, Tel Aviv, Haifa, and Netanya, as well as the Dead Sea in Israel; Rome, Vatican City, Naples, Capri, Bologna, Genoa, Milan, Verona (with Paolo and Sandy Dibiase, two exceptional Italian friends), and the unforgettable Venice, Como, Lake Como and the incomparable Villa D'Este Hotel, and Positano are only a few of the enchanting cities of Italy; and there is Portofino where, when I am close to dying, please bring me here and just leave me. Abidjan in the Ivory Coast was outstanding. Kingston, Montego Bay, Ocho Rios, and Port Antonio in Jamaica, West Indies. Tokyo, Yokohama, Osaka, Kobe, Kyoto, Nagoya, and other villages in Japan.

Seoul and Taegu in South Korea; Kuwait, Beirut in Lebanon, Maseru in Lesotho; Monrovia, Liberia; Macau, a neighbor of Hong Kong; the large island of Madagascar off the coast of East Africa; Lilongwe in Malawi; Kuala Lumpur, Ipoh, Penang, Malacca, and Johore Bahru in Malaysia; Bamako in Mali, Nouakchott in Mauritania; and Port

Louis, Mauritius. Mexico City, Acapulco, Nuevo Laredo, Monterey, and Tijuana, which is just a small part of Mexico. Midway Island in the middle of the Pacific Ocean, Montserrat, Mustique, Rabat in Morocco, and Lorenco Marques (now Maputo) in Mozambique. Then it was Portuguese East Africa, Windhoek and Walvis Bay in Namibia; St. John's in Newfoundland; and Auckland, Wellington, and Christchurch in New Zealand.

Managua, Bluefields, Leon, and San Juan del Sur in Nicaragua; and Niamey in Niger; Lagos, Aba, Kano, and Port Harcourt in Nigeria; Oslo, Norway; Halifax, Nova Scotia; Karachi, Pakistan; Panama City and Colon in Panama; Asuncion in Paraguay; Lima and Arequipa in Peru; Manila and Quezon City in the Philippines; Lisbon and Oporto in Portugal; San Juan, Mayaguez, and Ponce in Puerto Rico; Harare in Zimbabwe (formerly Rhodesia); Gaborone in Botswana; Kigali in Rwanda; Basseterre in St. Christopher-Nevis; St. Lucia, St. Vincent, and the Grenadines all in the Caribbean; Sao Tome in West Africa; Dakar in Senegal; and the Seychelles, a subgroup of islands east of Africa.

There was Freetown in Sierra Leone and Mogadishu in Somalia. In Spain I have visited Madrid, Barcelona, Malaga, Seville, and Granada, as well as the fabulous Cala de Volpe Hotel in Sardinia owned by Aga Khan whose father, Ali Khan, was the quintessential playboy of his time. Singapore was always exciting as it continued to renew itself every year I visited. Khartoum in the Sudan and Mbabane in Swaziland.

In South Africa, where I spent a total of five years' time over all my trips there, I had the opportunity of visiting every corner of the country. I was in Johannesburg and Pretoria; Bophuthatswana and Swaziland Kimberly; and Bloemfontein, Durban, and Pietermaritzburg. I was in the Transkei and the Ciskei, Cape Town and East London, Port Elizabeth, Ladysmith and Oudshoorn, Paarl and Franschhoek, Hermanus and Umhlanga, and every stop in between. It was always spectacular.

I've spent time in Stockholm and Goteborg in Sweden as well as Malmo, which was just across a small body of water from Copenhagen, a short ferry ride. In Switzerland I have been in Zurich, Geneva, Lausanne, and St. Gallen; and in Taiwan, there was Taipei and Kaohsiung. Bangkok, Phuket, and Chiang Mai were great Thailand cities. Lome in Togo and Nuku'alofa in Tonga; Port-of-Spain as well as San Fernando in Trinidad; and small neighboring Tobago, Istanbul, and Izmir in Turkey. I have been in unbelievable Dubai, in Abu Dhabi, and in Ras al-Khaima in the emirates, Montevideo in Uruguay; Asuncion in Paraguay; Caracas, Maracaibo, Valencia, and La Guaira in Venezuela. I visited Saigon in South Vietnam to sell fabrics while that terrible war was raging. Charlotte Amalie in the U.S. Virgin Islands and Road Town in the British Virgin Islands, Apia in Western Samoa, Lusaka in Zambia, and Livingstone in that country, right at Victoria Falls across the bridge in Zimbabwe. The exciting Musi-O-Tunya (thunder that roars) Hotel where the constant source noise was the falls themselves, with a constant drizzle—the spray of those Victoria Falls.

Conclusion: What a Journey!

As I speak of all these places that I have visited, I am talking about times that happened fifty years ago; and I am sure that today, nothing resembles what I saw or did.

I never realized during all my travels how lucky I was to see and visit countries that were in their "original" state of being, so to speak. I often wished that the hotels were newer and more modern but now realize that today almost every location is the same with a big modern building, and you could be anywhere and not know the difference, even though it is, of course, much more comfortable today. However, traveling today is not comfortable. The airports are a total misery; the long lines are discouraging and tiring; the waiting and delays are intolerable; and the planes, no matter what you pay for your ticket, including business and first-class, are nowhere near as comfortable as they were when I first started to travel.

While I always knew that I was experiencing something that very few people had a chance to also see and do, I never knew how fortunate

I was to be a little less comfortable in a hotel room. I was able to enjoy the flavor, the smells and the feeling of what those different countries were. One of my biggest disappointments was to return to Tahiti and stay in a beautiful modern hotel with all the great amenities that they offer rather than in the cold-water bungalows on a black-sand beach, which identified Tahiti for what it was. It was no longer a Tahiti that I had originally met but could've been any beautiful island in the Caribbean with the same hotel.

They say that you can never go back and recapture the first love you have for something. My trip back to Tahiti was not the same as my first one there as the remake of *Mutiny on the Bounty* had been filmed in Tahiti, and MGM Movie Studios had built an entire village just inside the lagoon that we had landed in. They needed this village as homes for the filming crew, which numbered more than one hundred; and when the film was finished, this little village was left as a hotel. I did not know the entire story of what had happened, but I knew I would not be staying in that concrete box in town but in a rather new location. I arrived at night and was immediately taken with my samples and luggage to my room. One hour later the room started shaking like an earthquake but calmed down in less than five minutes as the plane was taking off. It was a rude awakening and the ending for me as to what was Tahiti. The landing strip that they had built was alongside the village, and that's where planes would land and take off from now on. The noise was tremendous, as well as the ground shaking, but progress is not always pretty.

Of course, the people were different, but they were a lot more different in 1955. The same feelings applied to almost every island or country I visited, whether it was Singapore or Hong Kong, Trinidad or Barbados, Rio or Sydney, Tokyo or Bangkok—nothing was the same twenty or thirty years later. Or possibly, everything was the same but not like these places used to be. Traveling was an excitement.

We did not have jet planes, but the ones that we did have were more comfortable. The most comfortable plane I have *ever* been on was Pan American's Stratocruiser. It was a Boeing 377, and it was fairly large. It had a fair-sized lounge *down* a circular staircase from the main cabin, and the main cabin had accommodations for sixty-four passengers, all in the luxury first-class, much more luxurious than first-class today. The seats were far more comfortable than anything I have had lately, and on the very long flights, they had berths, where the current overhead luggage racks are, sleeping berths above and the seats folded back very close to flat. That was in 1954!

If you liked, you could have dinner in the lounge or at your seat, and the service was unmatched. Steadily airplane service has gone down to almost nonexistent. At that time, there was only one class of passenger: first-class. You arrived at the airport, were welcomed in, taken to the airline's lounge, and boarded the plane, which was always close. It is hard to imagine how pleasant and enjoyable it was to travel, especially to someone who travels today. The conditions we accept today are awful by comparison. You were able to relax on an airplane, even though the traveling was only half as fast as today; and once you arrived, the customs and immigration did not examine you as if you were a possible terrorist but rather as a welcome guest in their country (except for Panama and Nigeria).

The food on board was excellent, freshly cooked; and even though we did not have TV screens, we did have movies, and you had the opportunity to be with your fellow passengers at a bar on board the plane or in the lounge. Every destination was an adventure, and not knowing what was coming made the accommodations certainly very acceptable and enjoyable. I loved every trip I made, including the time spent on the plane. Today, taking into account that I am older and maybe need a little bit more attention, the airports, the flying, the customs, and immigration are simply unpleasant. I knew it then, for different reasons, that I was on a trip of a lifetime; and I know it now, from the experiences, that it is simply not the same and not nearly as enjoyable.

In Bonaire, I slept in a hammock; in Aruba, I slept at a rather crude motel-type residence; in Africa, I slept in huts; in Tonga, on a mat on the floor (there was a large open-air room, no walls, but it did have a roof); and in Nicaragua and Georgetown, British Guyana, there were old run-down hotels, messy, that brought tears to your eyes; but thinking of it today, it was an honor and unforgettable adventure to be in every one of those places, and all the others, before the new modern boxes of hotels that made every destination the same. Yes, I did wish for those modern boxes at that time but realize how lucky I was, as I was with everything, that I had the chance to live and be in every part of the world the way it was originally.

Hong Kong and Singapore were villages. There were no skylines, but today Taiwan has the highest building in the world, and Dubai, a rather small emirate in the Middle East, will soon have the largest and tallest building. I am thrilled to think that I had the opportunity to see all this, and to live all of it, because it no longer exists in most parts of the world, the way it did fifty years ago. It is exciting for me to think that I had these full experiences in my wonderful life.

The world changes all the time, but it is wonderful to think back and be thankful for all the opportunities that were given to me to enjoy and remember.

I had gone to college and graduated with a BA degree in romance languages; but if you did not have a profession like doctor, lawyer, or accountant, you had to do whatever it took, like traveling alone, to be able to accomplish something in the business world. I knew that, Muriel knew that, and since we had started our married life without any money but thrilled to have each other, we were both willing to sacrifice; and I don't ever want to minimize that sacrifice.

As I write about all my adventures, I never forget how much of a huge sacrifice it was for her and me to be apart as much as we were. Muriel had the additional job of keeping things together at home and seeing that the children were happy, which she did better than anyone could have done, which gave me the peace of mind to make me a better businessman and a more successful one since she did all the things that allowed me to concentrate on business and develop a reputation that was the cornerstone of our success.

Wherever I traveled, I always met wonderful people, almost all of whom became very good friends. I cherish their friendship, and they were a very important part of my life as they filled in the time from what was otherwise a very lonely time when I was away from my family.

Traveling was an excitement and an adventure for sure yet was at the same time very boring. I missed Muriel, Donna, and Richard every moment of every day; but these friends enabled me to keep going, although I was always thousands of miles away from where I had left my heart. It is very hard to describe the loneliness every night and every moment during the day that was left empty and allowed my mind to think, and it was always about my family and the sacrifices we were all making.

You never know when you are doing something if it is the right thing to do, and sometimes you're not even sure after the fact; but Muriel and I had decided that we would be able to handle being apart even for long periods of time, and in exchange, we had our deep and real love to keep us going. The traveling I did gave us many comforts in exchange for the loneliness, but not knowing what the alternative would have brought, you never know if you did the correct thing. It was all very difficult. My travels certainly were adventurous and exciting and always extremely interesting, but at the same time it was very difficult and extremely lonely, feeling helpless when there was so much to do at home with my wife and two children.

As I have mentioned many times before, in addition to the adventures, it was friends and good friends that made life bearable. All this is evident in the letters I wrote every day to Muriel and the children. I was crabby and always complaining, not only about my aches and pains, real and imagined, but also when the mail was delayed, through no fault of anyone, but just accenting the pains of loneliness and missing everyone.

I started working when I was thirteen years old. I stopped working when I was seventy-three. During those sixty years, I enjoyed every moment of my work, and I loved everything I did. I never thought for a moment of not going to work and looked forward to each day. Maybe it was the type of work that I was doing, meeting all different kinds of people in all different places in the world; but whatever it was, I liked going to work. I had the opportunity of seeing the world and seeing it in different stages.

It was all part of that wonderful life. We saw places and things that would not have been possible without that original business. We ate foods and stayed in exotic hotels and even countries that we would have never seen without that little business I started. I had a family that shared my excitement for adventure, and we were able to check off almost every place and item on that list that people make up for things they would like to do in their lifetime, and we could not have done any of that without that business.

I look back often; and sometimes I am somewhat embarrassed by all the riches that I have had the opportunity of seeing, doing, and living with. I could not have dreamed up the fullness of my life, and especially the wonderful and fabulous friends that we have met during our travels, and still enjoy today almost every one of them. We have tried to share, in different ways, all this with our family, sisters, brothers, nieces, and nephews; and I hope they know that we would have loved to have had them all along with us throughout our wonderful journey.

What a life! I wouldn't change a minute!

CPSIA information can be obtained at www.ICGtesting.com
Printed in the USA
BVOW07s1417181113

336617BV00002B/394/P